Ethiopianism and Afro-Americans
in Southern Africa, 1883–1916

Ethiopianism and Afro-Americans in Southern Africa, 1883–1916

J. MUTERO CHIRENJE

LOUISIANA STATE UNIVERSITY PRESS
Baton Rouge and London

Copyright © 1987 by Louisiana State University Press
All rights reserved
Manufactured in the United States of America

Designer: Laura Roubique Gleason
Typeface: Trump Mediaeval
Typesetter: CSA Press
Printer: Thomson-Shore, Inc.
Binder: John H. Dekker and Sons

10   9   8   7   6   5   4   3   2   1

Library of Congress Cataloging-in-Publication Data

Chirenje, J. Mutero, 1935–
Ethiopianism and Afro-Americans in southern Africa, 1883–1916.

Bibliography: p.
Includes index.
    1. Ethiopian movement (South Africa)   2. African Methodist Episcopal
Church—Missions—Africa, Southern.   3. Africa, Southern—Church history.
I. Title.
BR1450.C45   1987   276.8'08   87-3199
ISBN 0-8071-1319-0

To Jemima, Musariri, and Natasha Matiemeka

Contents

Acknowledgments   xi

Abbreviations   xiii

Introduction   1

1 / Missionary Activities and the African Response,
        1792–1892   7

2 / The Seeds of Ferment and Birth of the "Ethiopian"
        Church   25

3 / The American Connection and Responses to
        Ethiopianism   50

4 / Growth of the AME Church, the Witch Hunt, and Its
        Aftermath   84

5 / From Tuskegee to Fort Hare   118

6 / Ethiopianism in Action Again   144

7 / A Consummation of Sorts   163

Appendixes: Excerpts from Contemporary Publications   171

Bibliography   199

Index   225

Illustrations

Map of Southern Africa 6

following page III

The Alabama Cake-Walkers

John L. Dube

Chief Kgama III

Thomas C. Katiya as an undergraduate

Reverend Katiya in 1954

Reverend Livingstone N. Mzimba in 1954

Simbini Mamba Nkomo in 1917

John Tengo Jabavu

Acknowledgments

I would like to take this opportunity to express my gratitude to several scholars, librarians, and archivists who assisted me when this study was undertaken. At Harvard, members of the Inter-Library Loan Department of Widener Library as well as of Baker Library at the Business School always rendered cheerful service. Archivists in the Houghton Library were equally helpful.

To this list must be added librarians in the Manuscript Division, Library of Congress, Washington, D.C.; Congregational Library of Boston and the Boston University School of Theology Library; the Missionary Research Library, Union Theological Seminary, New York City; African Methodist Episcopal Church Library, New York City; the Hartford Seminary Foundation Library, Hartford, Conn.; Schomburg Collection, New York City Public Library; Wilberforce University Archives, Carnegie Library, Xenia, Ohio; Oberlin College Archives, Oberlin, Ohio; Fisk University Library, Nashville; Dorothy Porter, Curator Emeritus of the Moorland-Spingarn Research Collection, Howard University, Washington, D.C.; Eleanor L. Rice, assistant registrar, Hampton Institute, Hampton, Va.; archivists at Lincoln University, Lincoln University, Pa.; H. R. Bronson, president, Lincoln University; and librarians of the Interdenominational Theological Center, Atlanta, Ga. In London, individuals at the Public Record Office, the Wesleyan Methodist Missionary Society Archives, the London Missionary Society Archives, and the Royal Commonwealth Society Library were most helpful. In Edinburgh, assistance at the Free Church of Scotland Archives, the National Library of Scotland, and at New College Library, University of Edinburgh, was generously offered. I also thank archivists of the Botswana National Archives, Gaborone; National Archives of Zimbabwe, Harare; South African Library, Cape Town; Killie Campbell Collection, University of Natal Library, Durban; and University of Cape Town Libraries.

Finally, I would like to express my gratitude to the Faculty of Arts and Sciences, Harvard University, for providing me with funds that enabled me to consult archives in Britain, Africa, and the USA; to the University of Zimbabwe, for awarding me a grant to visit South African archives; to Josephus Roosevelt Coan, of the Interdenominational Theological Center in Atlanta, for his willingness to share his knowledge of sources on AME church history; to Josephine Wright, a former colleague of mine at Harvard, for drawing my attention to sources on the Virginia Jubilee Singers; and to Martin L. Kilson, of Harvard University, who suggested that a paper I had written on church independency in southern Africa could be expanded into a book. To R. Hunt Davis, of the University of Florida at Gainesville, who read the manuscript and made some valuable suggestions, I offer my thanks. However, I alone am responsible for any shortcomings in this book.

Abbreviations

ABCFM	American Board of Commissioners for Foreign Missions (Zulu Mission)
AME	African Methodist Episcopal
ANC	African National Congress
BNA	Botswana National Archives
CE	*Christian Express*, organ of the Free Church of Scotland
JAH	*Journal of African History*
JRAI	*Journal of the Royal Anthropological Institute of Great Britain*
LMS	London Missionary Society
NAZ	National Archives of Zimbabwe
PEMS	Paris Evangelical Missionary Society
SANAC	*South African Native Affairs Commission: Minutes of Evidence*, 5 vols. (Cape Town, 1903–1905)
SANC	South African Native Congress
VOM	*Voice of Missions by Way of the Cross*, organ of the AME church
WMMS	Wesleyan Methodist Missionary Society, London

Ethiopianism and Afro-Americans
in Southern Africa, 1883–1916

Introduction

When it was first published in 1948, Bengt G. Sundkler's *Bantu Prophets in South Africa* filled an old gap in southern African social history. Hitherto, African church independency had been relegated to a few paragraphs in standard works on the history of southern Africa, or to even fewer articles mainly in church magazines in which the political import of church independency (or Ethiopianism) was highlighted. The religious aspects were largely overlooked. Yet Sundkler's work, though seminal in importance, did not treat adequately the influence of Afro-Americans on the rise of Ethiopianism. In this respect, Sundkler found himself trapped in the old historiography he was trying to break away from and seemed satisfied to mention "Negro" influences on the Ethiopian movement.

The present study is an attempt to shed more light on church independency by taking into account interaction between black Americans and Africans in southern Africa; it also keeps in focus the domineering presence of white missionaries and laymen alike in black life in southern Africa. But the book is not a study of white dominance or supremacy. This aspect of southern African history is covered in readily available comparative studies by George M. Fredrickson and John W. Cell.

Afro-American churchmen who went to South Africa in the 1890s arrived at a time when some African Christians were setting up churches of their own. This independent-church movement was called "Ethiopianism" because the secessionists' aim was to plant their church across the entire African continent. The secessionists used the terms *Ethiopianism* and *Ethiopia* in the Graeco-Roman and biblical sense, namely, that Africa was the land of black people (or people with "burnt faces"). In this sense, the reference was not confined to the Kingdom of Ethiopia alone but included all the then-known countries of Africa. In the Bible, Africa and the Africans are usually referred to as "Ethiopia" and "Ethiopians." Psalm 68:31, for example, contains the declaration that "Ethiopia shall soon stretch out her hands unto God." [1] The essence of these biblical references must have been known to Reverend Mangena Maake Mokone, who broke away from the Wesleyan Methodist church in the Transvaal in 1892 and formed his own church, the Ethiopian Church of South Africa. Mokone no doubt thought he was playing his part to enable Africa to "stretch out her hands unto God." In time, *Ethiopianism* became a generic term to describe a whole range of the black man's efforts to improve his religious, educational, and political status in society.

A few years after launching the Ethiopian Church of South Africa, Reverend Mokone took steps to affiliate his church with the African Methodist Episcopal church. And since little is known about this Afro-American church, a résumé of its genesis is in order.

The African Methodist Episcopal church (popularly known as the AME church) was founded in response to the more depressing aspects of the African diaspora. The Afro-American, having been shipped to the American continent as a slave, found his life so circumscribed as to make it difficult for him to enjoy meaningful religious experience. Nor did emancipation bring about total freedom. The perennial disabilities of the Afro-American were aptly summed up by W. E. B. Du Bois, who characterized him as "a sort of seventh son . . . one ever feels his two-ness, an American, a Negro; two souls, two thoughts, two unreconciled strivings; two warring ideals in one dark body, whose dogged strength alone keeps it from being torn asunder." This resilience, the ability to defy adverse conditions and survive, is an attribute the Afro-American deftly displayed before and after emancipation. Clearly, one manifestation of "dogged strength" was his founding free independent churches. The formation of the AME church was a sequel to a series of hostile acts by whites against Afro-American members of

1. Frank M. Snowden, Jr., *Blacks in Antiquity: Ethiopians in the Greco-Roman Experience* (Cambridge, Mass., 1970), Chap. 1; Frank M. Snowden, Jr., "Ethiopians and the Graeco-Roman World," in Martin L. Kilson and Robert I. Rotberg (eds.), *The African Diaspora: Interpretive Essays* (Cambridge, Mass., 1976), 11–36; George Shepperson, "The Afro-American Contribution to African Studies," *Journal of American Studies,* VIII (December, 1974), 249–68.

St. George's Church, a Methodist Episcopal church in Philadelphia. One of the motive forces was Richard Allen, himself a former slave who had purchased his freedom from a Delaware master in 1777 and had moved to Philadelphia in 1786. There he became a member of the predominantly white St. George's Church. By 1787, white church members had utterly alienated black congregants through frequent acts of discrimination. The breaking point came on a Sunday when black members were taunted and threatened with eviction from church, even though a prayer was in progress.[2]

In consequence, Allen and other blacks withdrew from St. George's. Some members of this incipient "Ethiopian" church thought of joining the Anglican church, but Allen prevailed on them to remain in the Methodist church. Allen's group purchased an old blacksmith's shop and had it converted into a place of worship, which they named Bethel. In July, 1794, Bishop Francis Asbury of the Methodist Episcopal church consecrated the new edifice; on September 12, 1796, Bethel Church was incorporated under the laws of the state of Pennsylvania.[3] Significantly, these blacks in the diaspora did not forget their African ancestry. The secessionists called their church "African" Methodist Episcopal because it was thought "appropriate for the descendants of Africans" to identify with their ancestral home.[4] The AME church subsequently went through a difficult period of gestation, during which time the white members of St. George's Church sought to control Richard Allen's group. The issue was resolved in 1816 when the Pennsylvania Supreme Court ruled that St. George's parishioners had no right to control the Allenites.[5] Having now acquired a measure of independence, the newly elected bishop of the AME church, Richard Allen, chose evangelism as one of the church's primary activities. In 1820, Reverend Daniel Coker, one of the founding members of the AME church, carried the banner of the church when he went to Sierra Leone under the auspices of the American Colonization Committee. The church took an even

2. W. E. B. Du Bois, *The Souls of Black Folk* (1903; Longmans edition, London, 1965), 2. See Daniel A. Payne, *History of the African Methodist Episcopal Church* (Nashville, 1891; rpr. New York, 1969), 483–92.

3. Carol V. R. George, *Segregated Sabbaths: Richard Allen and the Rise of Independent Black Churches* (New York, 1973), 66.

4. See testimony of Bishop Levi Jenkins Coppin, in *SANAC*, II, 229.

5. George, *Segregated Sabbaths*, 49–71.

more overt step to evangelize abroad when it sent an agent to Haiti in 1827.[6]

The difficulties that AME church members experienced while trying to gain independent status made them sensitive to racism everywhere, especially in South Africa. Significantly, Afro-American missionaries often stated that they sympathized with African church secessionists largely because they found much in South African Christianity that resembled the kind of practices that led to the birth of the AME church in America. This affinity tended to give black missionaries an edge over their white counterparts.

The other Afro-American church group that sent missionaries to southern Africa was the National Baptist Convention (also called Black Baptists). In 1894 the Reverend R. A. Jackson was its first agent to South Africa. Despite its earlier initiative to evangelize, the Baptist group does not seem to have been as effective as the AME church was. In 1897 the Baptists sponsored four South African students, including Monte Kama and Alfred Impeya, who enrolled at Eckstein Norton University in Kentucky and Shaw University in North Carolina, respectively; by 1898, the Baptists had converted 414 people and were supporting a student from Malawi called John Chilembwe.[7] The record of Baptists as missionaries, though modest, was not as feeble as Bishop Henry McNeal Turner's biased criticism in 1898 suggested. One of the Baptists who went to South Africa toward the end of the nineteenth century, Reverend Charles S. Morris, published perceptive if sometimes polemical articles on black life in South Africa. Nevertheless, the church's relative inactivity can be inferred from the fact that Baptists were hardly mentioned at all between 1903 and 1905, when the actions of the AME church and Afro-Americans generally in southern Africa were criticized by the South African Native Affairs Commission (SANAC).[8]

6. Llewelyn L. Berry, *A Century of Missions of the African Methodist Episcopal Church, 1840–1940* (New York, 1942), 41–46.

7. Lewis G. Jordan, *Up the Ladder in Foreign Missions* (Nashville, 1901), 21–23. For a fuller account of Chilembwe, see George Shepperson and Thomas Price, *Independent African* (Edinburgh, 1958).

8. See, for example, Charles S. Morris' account in *Report of the Ecumenical Conference on Foreign Missions, Held in Carnegie Hall and Neighbouring Churches, April 1st to May 1st* (New York, 1900), I, 471; "Bishop Turner Attacks Baptists," *VOM*, July 1, 1898. See also refutation of Turner's charges in P. S. L. Hutchins to

To the list of black churchmen who went to South Africa must be added the Afro-American laymen who worked as technicians and in other capacities in South African mines and industries as well as those who were visitors. One such was the eccentric sailor, Captain Harry Dean (a descendant of the famous Afro-American entrepreneur Paul Cuffe), who owned a boat and visited several chiefdoms in south-central Africa early in this century. Dean was critical of the white rulers of southern Africa and is more forthright in his diaries than in his book.[9] All these categories of blacks represent various aspects of what has generically been called the "back-to-Africa movement," undertaken by Africans of the diaspora.[10]

editor, July 13, 1898, in "About Rev. Jackson of Cape Town, South Africa, *ibid.*, August 1, 1898; "Foreign Mission Notes by Secretary Jordan, 8th July 1898," *ibid.*

9. Harry Dean, with Sterling North, *The Pedro Gorino: The Adventures of a Negro Sea Captain in Africa and on the Seven Seas in His Attempt to Found an Ethiopian Empire* (Boston, 1929). See also Harry Dean Diaries, esp. Notebooks 43, 53, 54 (in DuSable Museum of African-American History, Chicago).

10. The scope for research on this subject is dealt with by George Shepperson, "Introduction," in *The African Diaspora*, 1–10.

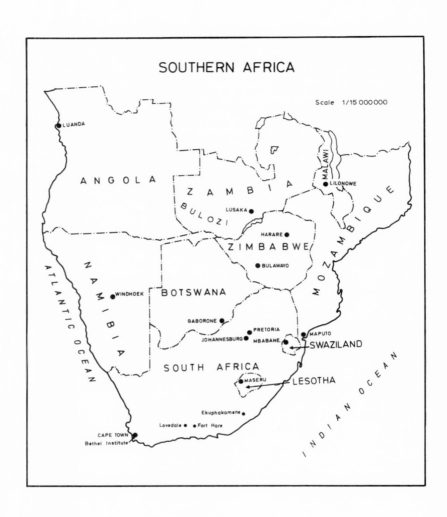

SOUTHERN AFRICA

Scale 1/15 000 000

LUANDA

ANGOLA

ZAMBIA

BULOZI

LUSAKA

MALAWI

LILONGWE

MOZAMBIQUE

HARARE

ZIMBABWE

BULAWAYO

NAMIBIA

WINDHOEK

BOTSWANA

GABORONE

PRETORIA

JOHANNESBURG

MBABANE

MAPUTO

SWAZILAND

SOUTH AFRICA

MASERU

LESOTHA

ATLANTIC OCEAN

INDIAN OCEAN

Ekuphakameni

Lovedale   Fort Hare

CAPE TOWN
Bethel Institute

1/Missionary Activities and the African Response, 1792–1892

The wave of dissent and schism, generally known as independency, that swept across Christian mission churches in southern Africa during the last quarter of the nineteenth century was by no means a historical aberration. The rise of independent African churches was in many respects rooted in the history of southern Africa and flowed from the tensions that had built up between blacks and whites since Jan van Riebeeck's settlement at Cape Town in 1652. Shortly after their arrival at the Cape, the whites proceeded to set up sociopolitical structures in order to make themselves the dominant group on the African subcontinent. This posture, which Africans resented and resisted in many guises, had by the nineteenth century become a permanent feature of life in southern Africa. In a word, South African society had by then been shaped.[1] Christian missionaries were very much a part of this evolving sociopolitical milieu.

Early Dutch contact with the San and the Khoikhoi influenced the settlers' attitude toward blacks. The majority of the newcomers tended to view in an unfavorable light any cultural practice they did not understand. They recorded their impressions of blacks at the Cape, and some wrote about the religious life of the indigenous population. Not surprisingly, the groups the early settlers commented upon were their nearest neighbors, the Khoikhoi, the San, and to some extent the Xhosa. While van Riebeeck attributed to the Khoikhoi a rather chaotic mode of life, some observers who took the trouble to try to understand saw merit in the Khoisan religion and cosmology. Significantly, some African neighbors of the Khoikhoi and the San had through generations of contact

1. See, for example, Richard Elphick and Hermann Giliomee (eds.), *The Shaping of South African Society, 1652–1820* (London, 1979); Monica Wilson and Leonard M. Thompson (eds.), *The Oxford History of South Africa* (Oxford, 1969), I, 157–232.

recognized Khoisan ingenuity in spiritual as well as secular spheres of human endeavor. An aphorism attributed to the Tswana is apt in this respect: "The Sarwa, with cunning, uncovered that which was concealed."[2] Europeans' recorded impressions became a little more subtle as more whites visited South Africa or went to live there as settlers. But the view that blacks were an inferior race persisted even among sympathetic missionaries.

In due course, Christian missionaries went to South Africa to evangelize the Khoikhoi and other African groups. Largely a response to the evangelical revival that swept across western Europe during the last half of the eighteenth century, missionary societies started the spread of Christianity in South Africa in earnest during the 1790s. They were not, however, the first to attempt to evangelize. In 1737, the Reverend George Schmidt opened the first mission station in South Africa among the Khoikhoi. The Reverend Schmidt was an agent of the Lutheran Moravian Protest Society, which was also called the United Brethren Society (Unitas Fratrum). His mission ran up against determined resistance: the Afrikaners were unwilling to let their Khoikhoi neighbors be proselytized by a group whose political orientation was suspect. To the Afrikaners, Christianity with its doctrine of the universal brotherhood of man seemed a disingenuous attempt to foment revolution. They surmised that the Khoikhoi and other African groups might well use it as a cue to revolt against white dominance. This generalization was not an altogether wild one, for practical experience had taught whites during the preceding century that the Khoikhoi and the San could wage wars of resistance and inflict staggering psychological and military damage on white society.[3] In consequence in 1742 the Dutch Reformed church at the Cape raised several objections to the Reverend Schmidt's ministry; a year later he left for the Netherlands and was not allowed to return. Despite

2. J. M. Orpen, "Glimpse into the Mythology of the Maluti Bushmen," *Cape Monthly Magazine*, IX (1874), 1–10; Theophilus Hahn, *Tsuni-Goam: The Supreme Being of the Khoikhoi* (London, 1881). The best account of the Khoikhoi is Richard Elphick, *Kraal and Castle: Khoikhoi and the Founding of White South Africa* (New Haven, 1978).

3. J. Du Plessis, *A History of Christian Missions in South Africa* (London, 1911), 50–60; Peter Hinchliff, *The Church in South Africa* (London, 1968), 8–12; Shula Marks, "Khoisan Resistance to the Dutch in the Seventeenth and Eighteenth Centuries," *JAH*, XIII (1972), 55–80; Elphick and Giliomee (eds.), *The Shaping of South African Society*, 12, 13–14, 16, 19.

this latent fear of the consequences of the Christian doctrine, however, the Afrikaners came to believe that God had sent them to South Africa, from which country they were to evangelize and "civilize" the entire continent. About this sense of calling there is also some ambivalence, which the Afrikaner has carried throughout his stay in southern Africa. One contradiction is that the mission has over the years become a never-ending assignment, placing the Afrikaner in a permanent position to minister to and rule over all Africa. In one attempt to fulfill this prophetic view, Afrikaners founded a South African–based missionary society that would spread the word of God in accordance with fundamentalist Calvinist interpretations.[4]

An opportunity came when in 1799 the London Missionary Society (LMS) independently sent Dr. John Van der Kemp to the Cape. The directors of the LMS gave Van der Kemp a letter to white Christians in South Africa, urging them to pursue missionary work in black communities. The letter said in part: "Arise then, brethren, we adjure you; unite for the attainment of these noble objects. The heathen who surround you call to you: 'Come over and help us'. You are situated in the vicinity of those parts which still lie wholly under the power of the prince of darkness and near those habitations of cruelty to which no ray of the Sun of Righteousness has yet penetrated. From feeble endeavours we have seen great issues arise." This message spurred members of the Dutch Reformed church to establish on April 22, 1799, a missionary society. It was called the South African Society for Promoting the Extension of Christ's Kingdom (Het Zuid Afikaanshe Genootschap ter bordering van de Uitbreiding Van Christus Koningrijk). The society was admonished to be subservient to the state: "The attention of the Directors of this Society is most earnestly drawn to the general duty of every Christian to render all submission and reverence to the temporal power for the Lord's sake, and carefully to refrain from anything which may be repugnant to the rules that have been promulgated in things civil and ecclesiastical." The society found a benefactor in the widow Moller, whose £1,250

---

4. J. S. Marais, *The Cape Coloured People, 1652–1937* (London, 1939), 134–35; Du Plessis, *Christian Missions*, 58; Hahn, *Tsuni-Goam*, 43; F. A. van Jaarsveld, *The Afrikaner's Interpretation of South African History* (Pretoria, 1964), 1–64; "The Natives and Their Missionaries," *CE*, February 1, 1908.

donation was used to purchase a meetinghouse. On March 15, 1804, Reverend J. P. Serrurier opened the house for public worship.[5]

In the meantime the Moravians had resumed their South African mission after a forty-nine-year hiatus. In 1792 the society sent Hendrik Marsveld, Daniel Schwinn, and Johann Christian Kuhnel, agents who settled among the Khoikhoi at Baviaans Kloof (later renamed Genadendal). The missionaries were elated to find at least one surviving convert of George Schmidt's, an old woman called Magdalena. They started a school that was attended by sixty-one pupils.[6]

In 1799, Van der Kemp of the LMS started a station at Bethel; in 1800, Reverend J. M. Kok (sponsored by the South African Society) and Reverend W. Edwards of the LMS traveled deeper into southern Africa than any missionary had and opened a station among the Tlhaping, a southern Tswana tribe. This station suffered because the missionaries not only built their residence far away from Chief Molehabangwe's capital, which minimized the agents' contact with the Tlhaping. As was also common, they spent considerable time hunting for ivory and selling their wares in Cape Town. This mixing of "God and Mammon" had as many drawbacks in southern Africa as it had in other parts of the world where missionaries dabbled in trade. The Tswana experience was tragic because Reverend Kok was killed by two Tswana servants in a quarrel about wages he had paid them for delivering ivory to Cape markets. His death had a demoralizing effect on Reverend Edwards, who quickly withdrew to the Cape, where he purchased some more slaves and land and engaged in farming. Reverend Robert Moffat, who joined the Tswana mission in 1820, made some fruitless attempts to bring Edwards back to mission work. In a book published in 1843, Moffat, who claimed to have known Edwards personally, had this to say about the pioneer missionary to Botswana: "He went to barter as far as the Bangwaketse, a powerful nation north of the Molopo River, and having amassed a handsome sum and long forsaken his God, he left the country, retired to the [Cape] Colony, purchased a farm and slaves, and is now or was some years since, a hoary-

5. Richard Lovett, *The History of the London Missionary Society* (London, 1899), I, 481–97; Du Plessis, *Christian Missions*, 92–93, 94–95; J. Du Plessis, "The Dutch Reformed Church and Its Mission," *CE*, December 1, 1909. See Appendix A.

6. Du Plessis, *Christian Missions*, 120–28; Lovett, *London Missionary Society*, I, 518–32.

headed infidel. I write what I know, having reasoned with him on the subject, when he treated my arguments with indignity and scorn."[7] Meanwhile, Reverend J. J. Kicherer was making some progress among the San (so-called Bushmen) at Blijde Vooruitzichts Fontein (*i.e.*, Fountain of Glad Prospect). Six months after his arrival there, he was obliged to go back to Cape Town to solicit funds with which to carry out mission work. He was partially successful, and he used the money to purchase 4 cows and 136 sheep. The livestock helped Kicherer attract San and Khoikhoi alike to settle on the mission station. By 1805, the Rotterdam Missionary Society had sent agents as far as Namaqualand. Between 1816 and 1859 a network of mission stations virtually covered southern Africa: the LMS founded Bethesda (1808), Zuurbraak (1811), Pacaltsdorp (1813), Theopolis (1814), Kaffraria (1816), Kuruman (1816), and Inyati (1859);[8] the Wesleyan Methodist Missionary Society founded Leliefontain (1816), Wesleyville (1823), Butterworth (1827), and Clarkebury (1830);[9] the Glasgow Missionary Society (Presbyterian) founded Chumie (1820) and Lovedale (1824).[10] The Paris Evangelical Missionary Society established their first station at Wagon-maker's Valley (Wellington) in the Cape in 1829 and moved to Basutoland in 1833; the Rhenish Missionary Society opened a station at Wupperthal in the Cape in 1829.[11]

North America gave an account of itself in the missionary movement and in some respects even inspired it. In 1784, Jonathan Edwards of Northampton, Massachusetts, wrote a pamphlet that is reported to have aroused considerable religious revivalism in England and America. It influenced William Carey, who took an active part in founding the Baptist Missionary Society. Missionary zeal was given more weight by the General Association of Mas-

7. Du Plessis, *Christian Missions*, 110–12; Du Plessis, "Dutch Reformed Church"; Robert Moffat, *Missionary Labours and Scenes in Southern Africa* (London, 1843; New York, 1850), 151. Until 1966, Botswana was called Bechuanaland, having been colonized by the British in 1885.

8. Du Plessis, *Christian Missions*, 112–18; Lovett, *London Missionary Society*, I, 582–608, 624–31.

9. Du Plessis, *Christian Missions*, 165–81; Basil Holt, *Joseph Williams and the Pioneer Mission to the South-Eastern Bantu* (Lovedale, South Africa, 1954).

10. Du Plessis, *Christian Missions*, 182–88; Robert A. W. Shepherd, *Lovedale, South Africa: The Story of a Century, 1841–1941* (Lovedale, South Africa, 1941), 1–22.

11. A. Jaques, "The Story of the French Mission in Basutoland," *CE*, March 1, 1902; Du Plessis, *Christian Missions*, 200–210.

sachusetts when in 1810 the group resolved to form the American Board of Commissioners for Foreign Missions "for the purpose of devising ways and means, and adopting and prosecuting measures for promoting the spread of the gospel in heathen lands." The society sent its first agents to South Africa in 1835, a particularly difficult time. Blacks, after incessant harassment by whites, were actively resisting the latter's encroachment on their institutions. On several occasions, the Boers and the Zulu fought on the highveld. In consequence, the ABCFM station at the Zulu capital Mosega was ill-fated: Boers ransacked it in 1837, the American missionaries barely escaping to the east coast. The Americans subsequently founded other stations in Zululand: Amanzimtoti (1837); Umvoti (1844); Ifumi (1847); Lindley (1847); Mapumulo (1849); Esidumbini (1850); and Umtwalume (1851).[12]

African communities generally extended a cordial welcome to missionaries; in this respect, chiefs and their subjects were only too willing to provide food and shelter for their European guests. One of the earliest missionaries to Botswana wrote in 1817: "On our arrival we went and visited King Mothibi in his house, found them all in the dark, a light being made, he and Queen Mahuto shook hands with us. Mr. Read then informed him through the interpreter that we were coming to live among them. He replied we must consider this land as our own and live and die among them."[13] Other missionary agents in southern Africa throughout the nineteenth century were also treated hospitably. This tended to enhance the initial efforts at evangelization.

Early missionaries to southern Africa found themselves having to champion the civil liberties of their black parishioners, because European settlers there believed in white supremacy, a notion they were resolved to preserve.[14] Among the early liberals (or philan-

12. See D. J. Kotze (ed.), *Letters of the American Missionaries, 1835-1838* (Cape Town, 1950), 1-20; Clifton J. Phillips, *Protestant America and the Pagan World: The First Half Century of the American Board of Commissioners for Foreign Missions, 1810-1860* (Cambridge, Mass., 1969), 206-32; ABCFM, Report for 1891, in American Zulu Mission, 1890-1899, Vol. I, Documents, Houghton Library, Harvard University. See Appendix B.

13. Rev. R. Hamilton to Foreign Secretary Hardcastle, May 15, 1817, in Box 7, Jacket D, Folder One, LMS Archives, School of Oriental and African Studies Library University of London; John Campbell, *A Journey to Lattakkoo in South Africa* (London, 1835), 49.

14. For theoretical and comparative perspectives, see George M. Fredrickson, *White Supremacy: A Comparative Study in American and South African History*

thropists, as they were called) to speak for African civil rights were Reverend James Read and John Philip, both agents of the LMS. Not surprisingly, their activities provoked the special wrath of white settlers who condemned them and missionary work as well, even though some white missionaries served as government agents. In this respect, the liberals achieved a measure of success in spite of the considerable opposition they faced from white government officials and laymen alike. The so-called Hottentot (*i.e.*, Khoikhoi) legislation of 1809 and Ordinance 50 of 1828, which improved the legal status of the Khoikhoi and presaged the emancipation of slaves at the Cape in 1833, were in the main the work of LMS agents. A student of race relations in South Africa has stated that the significance of the 1809 legislation is that Cape administrators went some way toward agreeing with missionaries' "desire to see the relations between colonial masters and Hottentot servants governed, not merely by the will of the master, but by the rule of law."[15] If the history of South Africa is a sad commentary on official measures that ought to have been enacted to perpetuate this legal norm, the record of missionary enterprise at the Cape has at least some redeeming features. Several agents spoke for African civil rights throughout the nineteenth century.

A special feature of European evangelism was that from the white missionary's place of residence, the mission center, the African evangelist carried it to the "bush" districts. During the pioneer stage, this individual acted as an interpreter and invariably as a guide to the white missionary's new place of labor. In this respect, accounts by missionaries depict the African evangelist as indispensable to mission work. Nevertheless, they often also criticized what they saw as the poor quality of the African evangelist's work. In due course, most missionaries came to believe, no doubt partly influenced by racist sentiments of the time, that auxiliaries were congenitally incapable of performing good work.[16] This in turn persuaded missionaries not to promote African

(Oxford, 1981); and John W. Cell, *The Highest Stage of White Supremacy: The Origins of Segregation in South Africa and the American South* (Cambridge, England, 1982).

15. Harry A. Gailey, "John Philip's Role in Hottentot Emancipation," *JAH*, III (1962), 419–33; W. M. MacMillan, *The Cape Colour Question: A Historical Survey* (London, 1927), 89–90; Marais, *The Cape Coloured People*, 155–62.

16. See, for example, J. Mutero Chirenje, *A History of Northern Botswana, 1850–1910* (Cranbury, N.J., 1977), Chap. 6.

evangelists to positions of responsibility. By so doing, missionaries were in fact sowing the seeds of discontent that grew in the form of Ethiopianism after 1880.

Some societies thought, especially after 1880, that the position could be improved by sending African men to train for mission work in metropolitan centers in Europe and America. Even before that time, a handful of blacks had been sent to Europe, but the results seem to have disillusioned their erstwhile mentors. One of the earliest experiments was carried out by the LMS. The circumstances were spelled out by Reverend John Campbell, who was twice in an LMS deputation to South Africa in the early nineteenth century: ''Various friends of the missionary cause having expressed regret, after my first visit to Africa, in 1812, that I had not brought home some Hottentot or Bushmen youth, to try what effect might be produced by a European education: on revisiting that country, in 1819, I resolved, if I could meet with a suitable Hottentot boy, whose parents were willing to entrust him to my care, I would certainly bring him to England.'' In the event, Campbell was able to persuade a Khoikhoi youth called Paul Dikkop to study in England, and both left South Africa in February, 1821. On arrival, Campbell arranged for Paul to attend Kingsland, a day school where he seems to have commended himself to the schoolmaster after his first year. His teacher reported:

> I am happy to bear testimony to the good behaviour of Paul and I think I may attest to his general improvement as his exertions and acquirements, during the short time he has been with us, have been quite equal to any European youth in the school. He manifests great ambition; in fact, it requires some management to keep his emulation within due bounds. He has generally been the first boy through all the classes he has passed. . . . He has passed through our first five classes in eleven months; which we reckon very fair improvement; few boys would be able to do more in that period.[17]

Nevertheless, fate conspired against Paul's fortunes. Illness overcame him and he died on September 14, 1824. His death dampened the attempt to promote a ''native agency'' by training future evangelists in England.

17. John Campbell, *Hottentot Children: With a Particular Account of Paul Dikkop, the Son of a Hottentot Chief, Who Died in England, September 14, 1824* (London, n.d.), 7, 41–42.

Not that missionaries gave up the idea of training Africans abroad, for in 1839 we find Reverend Moffat going back to Britain on furlough with a Tswana man called Mokotedi. When Mokotedi returned to Kuruman in 1842, he incensed Moffat and the missionary community at that station by what appeared to be untoward behavior: he no longer offered the humble deference to the missionaries that was expected of African employees. Mokotedi's mild assertion of human dignity, which he had come to take for granted during his stay in England, annoyed missionaries in Botswana; they in turn wrote adverse reports on his prospects for the mission field. The LMS foreign secretaries, subsequently wrote David Livingstone, in 1844, agreeing with their Bechuanaland District Committee (BDC) that Mokotedi not be appointed an evangelist: "We fear he will not do much good at the Kuruman Station. . . . When he left this country [England] we felt great interest in him and indulged the hope that he would prove a valuable labourer; and if, in any way, he has erred from the path of Christian consistency, we hope from a consideration of his youth and inexperience he will be treated with tenderness, and an effort made to restore him to his right position and bring him into some station of respectability and usefulness in connection with Missionary work."[18] By acceding to missionary bias against Mokotedi's becoming an evangelist, LMS directors had set a precedent. They unwittingly encouraged their missionaries to use arbitrary measures to bar Africans from responsible positions as, for example, ministers in the LMS mission in Botswana.

Four years after Mokotedi returned to Kuruman, another South African black went to Great Britain. This was Tiyo Soga, the son of a Xhosa headman. Tiyo attended Lovedale, a nonsectarian, multiracial school founded by the Free Church of Scotland in 1841 for sons of chiefs and missionaries. However, when war broke out between the Xhosa and whites in 1846, the school was closed. That same year Tiyo was taken to Scotland by Reverend Govan and was sent to school at Inchinnan and later the Glasgow Free Church Normal Seminary; Reverend John Henderson paid for Tiyo's education. Tiyo was baptized on May 7, 1848, and left for South Africa in October, arriving on January 31, 1849. He worked as a layman on

18. Arthur Tidman and J. J. Freeman (Foreign Secretaries) to David Livingstone, September 11, 1844, in David Livingstone, *Livingstone's Missionary Correspondence, 1814–1856,* ed. Isaac Schapera (London, 1961), 56–57, 81.

a United Presbyterian circuit for £25 a year. In June, 1851, Tiyo Soga left again for Scotland, this time with the financial assistance of the Niven family. In November he entered Glasgow University; he later moved to the United Presbyterian Theological Seminary in Edinburgh, where he qualified in theology in September, 1856. On December 10, 1856, he was ordained a minister. Tiyo married Janet Burnside on February 27, 1857, and returned to South Africa in July.[19]

In South Africa, Reverend Soga faced the old problems of racial discrimination. White parishes did not like him, as he wrote late in 1857 to an acquaintance in Scotland: "The prejudices here against colour, which I anticipated, gave way on my arrival in a most remarkable manner, so far as I am personally concerned. . . . I have found that only in Britain the Black man is admitted to be quite as capable of mental and moral improvement as the white man. In this colony, as in America, by a strange perversion of logic, some men seem to argue in this way in relation to the black man: 'Dark in face, therefore dark in mind.' "[20]

Tiyo Soga had the intellectual capacity to challenge much that he found wanting in the Free Church of Scotland's South African mission. However, his temperament and his unique position as the only ordained African minister restrained him. Rather than engage in open rebellion against the church that had educated him abroad, Soga confided his latent "Ethiopian" feelings to his diaries. Only once did he take issue with the unguarded comments of a white missionary: in 1865 he disputed Reverend John A. Chalmers' claim that the African race was heading for extinction.[21] But the point to note is that even a diffident Tiyo Soga was unhappy about his fellow white missionaries' attitudes toward Africans. The cumulative effect of this dissatisfaction among evangelists and ministers was to take the form of open revolt against Christian churches.

In the meantime, agents of various societies were plodding on

19. H. T. Cousins, *Tiyo Soga: The Model Kaffir Missionary* (London, 1897), 87ff.; John A. Chalmers, *Tiyo Soga: A Page of South African Mission Work* (Edinburgh, 1878), 1–45, 84–94; Shepherd, *Lovedale*, 112. See also Donovan Williams, *Umfundisi: A Biography of Tiyo Soga, 1829–1871* (Lovedale, South Africa, 1978).

20. Chalmers, *Tiyo Soga*, 147.

21. Williams, *Umfundisi*, 91; J. Mutero Chirenje, "From Paul Dikkop to Simbini Nkomo: Some Origins of Modern African Thought in Southern Africa" (Paper read at the November, 1982, convention of the African Studies Association, Washington D.C.).

with the business of teaching African communities the gospel of Christ and giving lessons in reading and writing. On many stations, missionaries discovered that chiefs were hampering progress. The initial enthusiasm was undermined by political considerations: most chiefs thought the presence of missionaries created a new factor that impinged upon their traditional prerogatives. In 1817, Reverend James Read reported that a Tswana chief was reluctant to let his subjects receive instruction: "He therefore hesitates giving his consent to his people receiving the word, by which many are kept back from coming to hear who otherwise are inclined and the children from the same reason keep from school. They believe that the very day they give their consent to receive the gospel, they that moment must give up their political authority." Not all African chiefs prohibited their subjects from attending mission schools, but the few who did so seemed to marvel more at the white man's technology than at his message of salvation. Reverend Samuel Broadbent, a Wesleyan missionary to the Rolong, reported that a chief was enthused by his dexterity in firing a gun: "He seemed as much delighted as he was astonished at it; and repeatedly tried to imitate the sound of the gunlock, and the report it made, and the sudden fall of the bird." [22]

If the missionaries made some progress in teaching Africans to read the Bible, they also sowed the seeds of Ethiopianism, for some converts found much in the Old Testament that negated the Gospels. Thus when Dr. David Livingstone demanded in 1848 that Chief Sechele of Botswana divorce four of his five wives before being baptized, Sechele complied reluctantly but impregnated one of them shortly after he was baptized. Livingstone suspended him from church membership. By 1854, Sechele, who had in the meantime been reading the Bible critically, was able to challenge Reverend Moffat to explain why the LMS required him to be a monogamist when the Old Testament showed that King Solomon had several wives. Needless to say, Moffat did not have a satisfactory answer. [23]

22. Rev. James Read to Hardcastle, March 15, 1817, in Box 7, Jacket C, Folder One, LMS Archives; Samuel Broadbent, *A Narrative of the First Introduction of Christianity Among the Barolong Tribe of Bechuanas, South Africa* (London, 1865), 58.

23. David Livingstone, *Livingstone's Private Journals*, ed. Isaac Schapera (London, 1960), 304; James Chapman, *Travels in the Interior of South Africa* (London, 1868), I, 100–101.

Between 1854 and 1892, the year he died, Sechele established a reputation for interpreting the Scriptures in light of Tswana experience. He came to adopt a pragmatism that enabled him to use Christian as well as African religious practices to enhance the well-being of his tribe. In addition, however, Sechele's equivocation was largely responsible for his long suspension, which the LMS lifted in 1889, barely three years before the chief's death.[24] Yet, viewed in the context of church schism in southern Africa, Sechele and other so-called backsliders, who irritated missionaries by clinging to African tradition despite their profession of Christianity, could be said to be forerunners of Ethiopianism. Church secessionists toward the end of the nineteenth century sought an authentic African church, one that blended Christianity with African customs and aspirations.

As the nineteenth century was coming to a close, however, there was no appreciable change in missionary policies. Their weakest point was their failure to promote an indigenous clergy. Paradoxically, some societies instructed their agents to train local men as clerics who could in due course replace white missionaries. When Reverend James Stewart, who toward the end of his missionary career was bewildered by the advent of Ethiopianism, was sent to Lovedale in 1866, a committee of the Free Church of Scotland gave the following instruction: "So soon as native congregations are formed, the care of them ought as speedily as possible, to be consigned to a Native pastorate . . . in time to be supported by natives themselves, while the Europeans should be free to press on to the regions beyond."[25] In the event, neither this directive nor black communities' pleas for self-determination in church government brought about any significant change. True, the Free Church of Scotland ordained about five ministers between 1875 and 1890; like other missionary societies, however, Free Church missionaries remained by and large indifferent to African aspirations.

Wesleyan Methodists were not faring any better. By 1880, they had ordained only one black minister. Thus the Kilner deputation to South Africa in 1880 urged the creation of a native ministry. Reverend John Kilner, who was impressed by the caliber of African

24. For an example of Sechele's interpretation, see J. J. Freeman, *A Tour of South Africa* (London, 1851), 281. For Sechele's reinstatement, see Howard Williams, Molepolole Report, 1889, in LMS Archives.
25. James Wells, *Stewart of Lovedale: The Life of James Stewart* (London, 1908).

evangelists, complained that blacks were being improperly kept out of the ministry: "There were many men who doubtless had a call to work who were kept back by a timid, if not at times, a jealous hand." Wesleyan agents in South Africa criticized Reverend Kilner's recommendation, maintaining that the time was not ripe to train local clergy.[26]

The American Zulu Mission was likewise dragging its feet, though the Boston-based directors were concerned about their agents' reluctance to create an indigenous clergy. So Dr. Judson Smith, the society's secretary, wrote about the need to promote a "native Pastorate," but the response was unenthusiastic. The reply of one agent, Reverend Holbrook of Mapumulo Station, was typical. He informed Dr. Smith in March, 1889, that missionaries were trying hard to build a native pastorate, but there were many obstacles. He submitted that black people despised their own color and so would not welcome an African minister; that officers of the church had no confidence in the financial stability of Zulu parishes; that experience had shown him that white ministers were more capable than were African ones. He concluded that blacks would never be able to discharge a minister's duties properly, even if they were given a chance to prove themselves. By October, 1889, Holbrook was advancing psychological reasons for stalling on the issue of a black clergy: "The objection to instituting a full native pastorate *at once* is that perhaps a half of those thus ordained lose their mental balance and so conduct themselves as to forfeit the respect of both the missionaries and the Christian natives alike."[27] Thus, missionaries, like colonial officers in Africa in the twentieth century, sounded the cry that the native was not ready to manage his own affairs.

In the event, the native had rude shocks in store for the white missionary, who was totally unprepared for Ethiopianism. (The same was true of the mid-twentieth-century African national-independence movements the church secessionists anticipated.)

26. Richard H. Davis, *Nineteenth Century African Education in the Cape Colony* (Ann Arbor, 1969), 229–30; John Kilner, A Summary Report by the Rev. John Kilner Deputation to the South African Mission Field, confidential, February 11, 1881 (MS in WWMS Archives, London), 11–15; C. C. Saunders, "Tile and the Thembu Church: Politics and Independency on the Cape Eastern Frontier in the Late Nineteenth Century," *JAH*, XI (1970) 555 n 10.

27. Rev. Holbrook to Dr. Judson Smith, March 9, October 29, 1889, both in American Zulu Mission, 1890—1899, Vol. I, Documents.

Nor were all the pioneers of church independency resolute men. They ranged from a Sotho evangelist at Hermon, Lesotho, who in 1872 led what appears to have been a short-lived revolt against the French missionaries there to Reverend James Mata Dwane, who resigned from the Wesleyan Methodist church in 1884 and then withdrew his letter of resignation. Dwane was born in about 1848 and belonged to the Amantinde tribe, but his father, Dwane Mcebuka, chose to live among the Amagqunukwebe, with whom Dwane became identified for the rest of his life. He was converted to Methodism by the missionary William Shaw and subsequently licensed to preach by Reverend Robert Lamplough at Healdtown, Cape, on May 14, 1867. He was appointed to serve on the Port Elizabeth circuit shortly after his ordination in 1881. The sensitive man he was, Reverend Dwane was soon incensed by discriminatory practices in the Wesleyan church; his protests were in vain. A sympathetic editor of an Afro-American paper wrote: "After his unsuccessful protests against what he considered to be class [discriminatory] legislation in the Church based on color line, he sent in his resignation to the president of the Wesleyan Church of South Africa, which remained unaccepted in the hands of the president for six months and was ultimately withdrawn. This was in 1884." [28]

Reverend Dwane's change of mind presaged his stormy career in the Ethiopian movement at the beginning of this century; the resignation also cost him the distinction of becoming the second African to try to start an independent African Christian church. That belonged to evangelist Nehemiah Tile in Thembuland in the Transkei. His withdrawal marked the first serious secession from the Wesleyan Methodist church. An evangelist among the Thembu in the 1870s, Tile earned a reputation as a competent preacher. He also wielded some influence with the Thembu chief Ngangelizwe, on one occasion persuading the chief to let Methodists open a new station in Thembuland. From 1879 to 1883, Tile served as a probationary minister, and during that time he quarreled with his white superior, Reverend Theophilus Chubb, over issues arising from racial discrimination. He had also in the meantime become

28. Henry McNeal Turner, "Vicar Bishop Dwane of South Africa Visits This Country [USA] by Special Orders," *VOM*, December, 1898; James Mata Dwane, "Historic Epistle. Rev. James M. Dwane, Superintendent of Our South African Work to the Bishops. His Personal Experience Told from Heathen Child to a Christian Divine," *ibid.*, December, 1897. For the Hermon incident, see Bengt G. Sundkler, *Bantu Prophets in South Africa* (Rev. ed., London, 1961), 38.

a close advisor of Chief Ngangelizwe. His involvement in the politics of Thembuland caused Wesleyan authorities some chagrin. The society accused him of stirring up hostility against the magistrates in Thembuland, addressing a political meeting on a Sunday, and contributing an ox at the circumcision of Dalindyebo, grandson of the Thembu chief. The church rebuked Tile for these misdemeanors, but the evangelist reacted by breaking with the Wesleyans during the second half of 1883.[29]

Tile was increasingly active in Thembu politics and, in so doing, enhanced the prestige of his own church. In August, 1883, Tile was instrumental in organizing a petition signed by Chief Ngangelizwe and his three sons, requesting the removal of all magistrates from his territory. Although his sons were said to have some misgivings, a report in June, 1884, was more forthright, proclaiming that Ngangelizwe and his brother ought to be supreme in Thembuland: "Here in Thembuland there are only two men—[N]gangelizwe the Lord of all, and Matanzima, the hand, speaker and eye for his brother Ngangelizwe. But nothing he can do in the land, unless he has received permission from his brother Ngangelizwe. Our antagonists say to remove magistrates is to remove civilization, justice, traders and to bring the smelling out [of traitors], murdering and war begun by petty disturbances."[30] On the contrary, the Thembu insisted, they wanted one magistrate for all Thembuland under Queen Victoria; they wanted unity, not sectionalism, and a Christian type of education. Tile's support for Thembu causes enhanced his church's standing, but his activities irked the British administrators. In November, 1884, a white official advised Ngangelizwe to "have nothing to do with Tile, he will do harm to your people." In January, 1885, Tile was arrested and jailed for allegedly inciting chiefs to resist lawful authority, but the charge was quashed by the attorney general.[31] Unfortunately, Tile's arrest came after the death of Ngangelizwe, with whom he had had a cordial relationship. His quarrels with the administrators seem to have adversely affected his relations with the new chief, Dalindyebo: after a spell of mutual understanding, tensions developed near the end of 1885 that lasted until 1889 when they

29. Saunders, "Tile and the Thembu Church," 556–57.
30. *Ibid.*, 557. See "Claims of the Thembus," *Cape Argus*, June 23, 1884; and "A Thembu Meeting," Grahamstown *Journal*, February 28, 1884.
31. Saunders, "Tile and the Thembu Church," 558.

reconciled. That renewal spurred people to join Tile's church, but then Tile died in December, 1891. Elsewhere in South Africa, however, Ethiopianism was by this time in ferment.

While American missionaries were justifying the lack of black ministers in their Zulu mission, they were in fact dealing with Ethiopian insurgency at Noodsberg, one of their oldest stations in Natal. The leader of the secessionist movement there was Mbiyana Ngidi. Converted by them in the early 1850s, he worked as an evangelist. American missionaries praised his work but were reluctant to ordain him. Although their reasons were spurious, it was not until 1878 that Mbiyana was ordained. By that time, however, he was already alienated because of the American Zulu Mission's practice of racial discrimination. He broke with the Americans to form the Zulu Mbiyana Congregational Church; two-thirds of church members at Noodsberg joined Mbiyana's church.[32]

Reverend Ngidi sustained his rebellion partly by having persuaded the local chief to support him; the chief in turn created favorable conditions for the growth of Mbiyana's following. For example, he summoned members of the American church to work on public projects while Mbiyana's followers were left free to organize themselves and to construct a church close to the American church. Reverend Ngidi launched his church formally in 1890. By that time, American missionaries in Natal were sufficiently disturbed to issue a joint statement: "Noodsberg has been sadly shaken by the repeated visits of uMbiyana, a renegade native pastor who would draw away 'even the elect.' " In 1891, they reported that missionary work at Noodsberg was "discouraging," but that the American church now had more members than did Mbiyana's.[33] An 1892 report complained that members of Mbiyana's church drank beer and accepted bridewealth (lobola) from sons-in-law; that the chief had asked the Natal government to remove an African preacher, Thomas Hawes, from his chiefdom; that Mbiyana's

32. Norman Etherington, *Preachers, Peasants and Politics in South East Africa, 1835–1880: African Communities in Natal, Pondoland and Zululand* (London, 1978), 158–62; Holbrook to Judson Smith, June 24, 1887, in American Zulu Mission, 1890–1899, Vol. I, Documents.

33. "Annual General Letter of the American Zulu Mission, 1890," in American Zulu Mission, 1890–1899, Vol. I, Documents; Etherington, *Preachers*, 158–62; American Zulu Mission, Report for 1891.

church was trying to replace a village headman with their own man.[34]

While Mbiyana's attempt, like that of his contemporary Tile in Thembuland, to get the support of the ruling elite was a shrewd political move, American missionaries saw it for what it was and lobbied government officials to undermine the Ethiopian's effectiveness. The ploy paid off, and the 1893 annual general letter said of Noodsberg: "Last year things looked very dark at this station and the breaking up of our work there, was threatened. The Government, at the instigation of the heathen chief, had ordered the removal of Thomas Hawes, our preacher. After a long correspondence the order was withdrawn, and the Government leased us a plot, for a glebe, for a period of 42 years, at a nominal rental. We are now independent of the Chief, and even of Government, in our operations there." Furthermore, Mbiyana's people had not completed their own church but were holding their services in a preacher's house. The letter also indicated that the Americans had prevailed upon the government not to appoint an Ethiopian headman in the Noodsberg area.[35]

In Thembuland, Tile was remembered for the several hymns he composed during his lifetime.[36] His church, a more potent testimony to the man's influence, was now headed by Reverend Jonas Goduka, a former Wesleyan minister. Between 1891 and 1893 the rapport displayed between the church and Chief Dalindyebo caused some concern to white government officials and laymen alike. They put pressure on the chief to dismantle a harmony they construed as potentially damaging to white hegemony. In March, 1893, the *Cape Mercury* carried a long article in which Tile's followers were portrayed as troublemakers who used dishonest means to recruit followers, a situation they prevented Dalindyebo from perceiving. The paper was elated to report that a group of Wesleyan blacks, led by newspaper editor, John Tengo Jabavu, was influencing the chief to turn against Tile's church. But the *Cape Mercury* also noted that the effort might come to nought, in view of Dalindyebo's display of independent thinking. The chief surprised white authorities when he refused, for example, to grant an An-

34. See Rev. H. D. Goodenough, "Report for Umvoti and Noodsberg Stations, 1892," in American Zulu Mission, 1890–1899, Vol. I, Documents.
35. "Annual General Letter of the Zulu Mission, 1893," *ibid.*
36. Saunders, "Tile and the Thembu Church," 561ff.

glican missionary permission to build a church in his chiefdom but instead allowed Tile's followers to open a new church. By July, 1893, the *Cape Times* could understandably devote an editorial to warning its readers against complacency in the face of Tile's church, which appeared to be "frought with serious consequences to this country," and stating that "it would be the height of folly to ignore [the Thembu church]." The church should not be viewed merely as a religious movement: "It is a patriotic movement, in that it seeks to enlist the sympathies and support of all natives *qua* natives; it is political in that one of the fundamental principles of the organization is to proceed much on the working lines of the Afrikander Bond, though of course with directly opposite aspirations, and it is ecclesiastical, and for this reason exercises a disturbing effect upon the Native mind."[37] The paper went on to lament that if the 200,000 Thembus and the Baca of Griqualand East should unite against whites, they could be a formidable force.

The *Cape Times* was perceptive enough to highlight both the religious and political aspects of Ethiopianism. Studies on independent church movements have not always stressed this dual nature. In the event, Dalindyebo broke with the Thembu church after being harassed and otherwise pressured by government officials; by 1895, he had turned away Tile's followers from his court and he himself rejoined the Wesleyan church.[38] But by the time Tile's church started breaking up, it had in fact set a precedent for church secession. There is evidence to suggest that its officers had even counseled would-be Ethiopians elsewhere in South Africa to agitate for self-determination in church government. The seeds of Ethiopianism had thus been sown and were ready to sprout.

37. "Tembuland Troublers," *Cape Mercury*, March 16, 1893; editorial, *Cape Times*, July 31, 1893; see also a report on Cape Colonial Parliament, House of Assembly debates, *ibid.*, July 29, 1893. The Afrikaner Bond was a quasi-cultural but largely political organization of Afrikaners, the descendants of Dutch and French settlers at the Cape. See T. R. H. Davenport, *The Afrikaner Bond: The History of a South African Political Party, 1880–1911* (Cape Town, 1966).

38. Saunders, "Tile and the Thembu Church," 563.

2/The Seeds of Ferment and Birth of the "Ethiopian" Church

The independent-church movement that Nehemiah Tile and Mbiyana Ngidi set in motion had in fact been embryonic during the second half of the nineteenth century. An indication of the nascent stage of Ethiopianism can be gained from a look at institutions that fostered a critical acumen in African communities. One such institution was the Western type of education that was introduced by Europeans as well as by American missionaries. To be sure, schooling was not unknown in African society; traditionally each tribe had its own system of initiating its youths into various responsible and productive positions within the tribe.[1] Western schools taught students to read and write a European and an African language, which skills they retained for the rest of their lives. The mission school also fostered pan-regionalism of a sort through its accepting students from all over southern Africa. During their stay at boarding schools, students who would otherwise have been confined to their respective chiefdoms could interact with peers from diverse ethnic backgrounds. In the process, some lasting friendships were formed. These seminal relationships were cemented when the youths graduated and invariably took up employment in industrial centers or went to schools away from their homes. This pan-regionalism, which in due course flowered into modern African nationalism, enabled church secessionists to spread their brand of Christianity across national boundaries without much difficulty.

1. See Wilson and Thompson (eds.) *The Oxford History of South Africa*, I, 260–68; Davis, *Nineteenth Century African Education*, 229ff.; Emil Holub, *Seven Years in South Africa: Travels, Researches and Hunting Adventures Between the Diamond Fields and the Zambezi*, trans. Ellen E. Frewer (London, 1881), I, 397–400; W. C. Willoughby, "Notes on the Initiation Ceremonies of the Becwana," *JRAI*,

Yet before 1900, only a handful of Protestant and Catholic schools had been established. Lovedale was one of the most famous of the Free Church of Scotland schools; Blythswood in the Transkei was another. The French Protestants had Morija in Lesotho; the Wesleyans had Healdtown in the Cape and Kilnerton in the Transvaal; the LMS had the Moffat institution at Kuruman in southern Botswana;[2] the Roman Catholics had Marrianhill in Natal; the American Zulu Mission had Adams College at Amanzimtoti in Natal. Zonnebloem, an Anglican school started at the Cape to provide a special education for sons of chiefs, was multiracial. That arrangement was not without embarrassment to a society fast becoming racially stratified: for example, Zonnebloem's headmaster reluctantly informed a government commission that African students at his school were doing better work than were their white classmates.[3] The blacks' performance must have irritated white supremacists as much as it reinforced the African students' self-esteem. By extension, this confidence was to spur some blacks into founding churches of their own.

Another factor that created awareness among the southern African elite was the African press. The newspapers had their beginning in leaflets published by missionaries primarily to inculcate Christian modes of living. In Tswana-speaking communities, the LMS had a church paper as early as the 1850s when *Molekudi ua Bechuana*, a monthly, circulated between 1856 and 1857. The LMS published two monthlies, *Mokaedi oa Bechuana* (1857-1859) and *Mahoko a Becwana* (1883-1898), and a weekly, *Koranta ea Becoana* (1901-1908). The Hermannsburg Missionary Society published *Moshupa Tsela*. The Paris Evangelical Missionary Society launched its Sotho-language newspaper, *Leselinyana La Lesotho*, in the 1870s.[4] The Free Church of Scotland published *Isigidimo SamaXosa*

XXXIX (1909), 228-31; Isaac Schapera, *A Handbook of Tswana Law and Custom* (1938; rpr. London, 1970), 104-17.

2. See Chirenje, *A History of Northern Botswana,* 159-200.

3. See evidence of Rev. William H. Pankhurst, in *SANAC,* II, 205.

4. Solomon T. Plaatje, *Sechuana Proverbs with Literal Translations and Their European Equivalents* (London, 1916), 4-5; Isaac Schapera, *The Tswana* (London, 1952), 18; Jaques, "The Story of the French Mission in Basutoland," *CE,* May 1, 1902. Significantly, the paper's name included *Lesotho,* not *Basutoland* (as aliens tended to corrupt that country's name). This suggests not that *Lesotho* is a creation of Sotho nationalists in the wake of independence in 1966, but that the name is of great antiquity.

(1870–1874) in Xhosa. The Free Church also had the *Kaffir Express*, first published in 1870. In 1876 its name was changed to the *Christian Express*.

These missionary papers did not altogether ignore news that had a bearing on the lives of their African readers. As Reverend John Brown, editor of *Mahoko a Becwana*, indicated in 1883, the paper covered several aspects of African life: "This periodical is not only for the news of God. It is also to tell news about this country and others. Anyone who wishes to tell other people the news of where he lives may send his report to the editor." One response warned the editor against confusing his readers: "For myself I say stick to one dialect in the printing; not the mixture which people use when writing by hand. Moreover, as book printing started in the Tlhaping area [at Kuruman] should not the dialect for printing be that very one in which books began?" *Mahoko* also featured several reports on mission work in Ngamiland by the Tswana evangelist Khukwi Mogodi. In one, an Mbukushu headman, Dibebe, was adept at making rain and for that reason wielded greater influence, at least in a religious sense, than did the Tawana chief Letsholathebe. The chief, Mogodi reported, was obliged to pay tribute to Dibebe in deference to his magical powers. In 1888, Mogodi contributed a story in which he said that several Christians had lapsed, and that a headman had tied a Sarwa (so-called Bushman) servant to a horse, which dragged her to death. Similar exposés tended to put the elite, especially the ruling class, on guard against what a missionary called being "pilloried" in the press.[5]

If some LMS missionaries imagined that *Mahoko* was championing the cause of their mission alone, they must have been rattled to have to publish a letter written by Chief Montshiwa of the Rolong. In 1893 the chief wrote to defend polygamy and the payment of bridewealth (*lobola* or *roora*), which the LMS had stigmatized since the beginning of its mission to Botswana. Montshiwa was himself a polygamist.[6]

5. J. D. Jones, "'Mahoko a Becwana'—The Second seTswana Newspaper," *Botswana Notes and Records*, IV (1972), 114, 119. See, for example, Chief Kgama III of the Ngwato, who in 1890 wrote to the LMS foreign secretary, refuting allegations published in *Mahoko a Becwana* that he had wrongfully punished a woman (Kgama to R. W. Thompson, April 11, 1890, in Box 47, Jacket C, Folder One, LMS Archives).

6. See Rev. Edwin Lloyd to R. Wardlaw Thompson, June 14, 1893, in Box 50, Jacket A, Folder Two, LMS Archives.

With typical pragmatism, Tswana Christians and traditionalists (so-called heathen) read *Mahoko* to acquaint themselves with
political developments in southern Africa and especially to keep
track of white filibusters' inroads into their territory. In January,
1893, *Mahoko* reported that Cecil John Rhodes intended to annex
Bechuanaland to chartered-company territory (Rhodesia). According to Reverend Edwin Lloyd of the LMS, the news upset the
Tswana elders: "I saw yesterday afternoon several leading men of
the town sitting as solemn as a congregation of owls
with . . . [*Mahoko*] in their midst."[7] This was the start of a campaign against annexation that was led by Chief Kgama III and two
other Tswana chiefs, who late in 1895 foiled Rhodes's plans. The
point to note is that Africans were increasingly becoming spokesmen for and architects of their own destiny, instead of being cowed
to silence by the white colonizers.

What was perhaps the most significant event among a series of
preludes to the Ethiopian movement was the launching in November, 1884, of *Imvo Zabantsundu*, an independent secular paper
owned and edited by a black South African. John Tengo Jabavu was
born in 1859 at Healdtown and later attended the famous Wesleyan
school there. In 1883, he passed the high school examinations
conducted by the University of the Cape (later, University of Cape
Town)—one of the first Africans to do so. He had in the meantime
apprenticed himself to a newspaper office in Lovedale.[8] *Imvo*,
published in Xhosa and English, was probably read throughout
southern Africa, if Jabavu's bold statements are a reliable guide. In
setting forth his editorial policy, he also offered an ingenuous
advertisement for his paper:

> The warm and hearty welcome that has met us on the very threshold
> of our career has given us great encouragement, and we take this, the
> earliest opportunity to convey to our friends our sincere and thorough
> appreciation of their good wishes. To the multitude of subscribers,
> whose names hail from the shores of Table Bay to those of Port Natal,
> and from Pretoria to Port Elizabeth—who have shown their confidence

7. Lloyd to Thompson, January, 1893, in Box 50, Jacket B, Folder One, *ibid.*
8. Davidson D. T. Jabavu, *The Life of John Tengo Jabavu, Editor of Imvo
Zabantsundu, 1884–1921* (Lovedale, South Africa, 1922); T. D. Mweli Skota (ed.), *The
African Yearly Register: Being an Illustrated National Biographical Dictionary
(Who's Who) of Black Folks in Africa* (Johannesburg, 1930), 23; Alexander Kerr, *Fort
Hare, 1915–48: The Evolution of an African College* (New York, 1968), 4ff. Davis,

in us by contributing their mite towards our support, we offer special thanks. We can only hope that our efforts—and we shall spare none—to prove worthy of this advance of confidence will be effective.

The editorial went on to suggest that *Imvo* would cater to the emerging mission-educated elite who had occupied an ambiguous position in the South African social milieu, being tossed "from pillar to post, despised by its former friends of the heathen state, and misunderstood by the representatives of civilization in this country," that is, white settlers and missionaries.[9] The paper did not, however, pander to overly elitist tastes. The articles generally dealt with subjects within the purview of the average literate South African black. In any case, the elite of the 1880s comprised only a few junior high and high school graduates; there were virtually no university graduates before 1900.

One of the first issues taken up by *Imvo* was the question of Lovedale's curriculum. The principal, Dr. James Stewart, had made a statement criticizing the inclusion of Latin and Greek, which he characterized as harmful: Africans who had studied those languages found them to be of no practical use and had in due course become frustrated. But some Africans were no longer prepared to have whites alone shape their curriculum. They debated the pros and cons of a classical education. A former Lovedale student, writing as "Lovedalian," took issue with Stewart for advocating the removal of the classics from the school curriculum, asserting that such a move would be tantamount to suppressing the truth and that Stewart's statement was substantively false ("suppressio veri et suggestio falsi"). John Knox Bokwe, another Lovedale graduate, impugned "Lovedalian" for being too severe in his criticism and for failing to interpret the principal's remarks correctly. Bokwe said Stewart should be understood as saying:

> The mass of the Native people of this country are still in gross ignorance which must speedily be overtaken. . . . Let us . . . give a practical and useful English education which will make them perfectly competent to meet all this life's demands at whatever station of life

---

Nineteenth Century African Education, 262–63, points out that the first African to matriculate was Simon P. Sihlali, who attended Lovedale and passed the examinations in 1880.

9. "The Launch," *Imvo Zabantsundu* (Native Opinion) (King Williamstown), November 3, 1884.

the man may be called to occupy. As some of the more ambitious of them will aspire to higher honours, after we shall have helped them thus far, and may wish for the luxuries of Classics, no doubt they will be willing to support themselves from their own resources, for the luxuries needed; and we shall be willing to show them the road to where such luxuries may be obtained and purchased, and how much they may cost.

Thus, for Bokwe, the study of the classics, though not harmful per se, was an exercise that could be undertaken later in life. The debate was joined by *Imvo* in an editorial that appeared on July 8, 1885. It stressed that "Lovedalian" and Reverend Bokwe had been largely shadowboxing, though the former was given credit for having pointed out that some former Lovedale students who studied classics had subsequently been gainfully employed in various parts of South Africa.[10]

Nevertheless, Lovedale and other mission schools were taken to task for their failure to provide black students with adequate facilities for studying the classics. The paper complained that the omission tended to give an unfair advantage to white students, as Latin and Greek were prerequisites for matriculation at the University of the Cape. Even multiracial schools tended to favor white students, a partiality that was again criticized: "As we said some time ago, it was the giving of Latin to European pupils in the same class and carefully weeding out the Natives that was occasioning this outcry from the Native pupils and their guardians. It is the drawing of the line at mere colour which exasperates the Native." In another editorial, *Imvo* maintained that reports that Lovedale blacks were better students than were their white classmates should be treated with caution, as "the test of a school course is the advantage it gives in real life." Further, African students were advised to correlate learning and practical situations, and not be content with acquiring only the theoretical aspects of a school education. "This is where the [white] scholar wins: he promptly adjusts his faculties to the work on hand, and constantly strives to do something original and yet within the limits of what is demanded by the times. This is the aim every Native must have who

10. John Knox Bokwe, "Classics for Natives," *ibid.*, July 1, 1885; "Native Education," editorial, *ibid.*, July 8, 1885. See also "Lovedalian's Reply," *ibid.*, July 22, 1885, in which Bokwe's intellect was impugned.

is to succeed in life."[11] It appears that *Imvo* was advancing a philosophy of education in which the success of an educational system was to be judged by the performance of its students in real life and not by examination results alone.

In 1889, *Imvo* broadened the debate, taking up the question of education for girls. The paper argued that the need to educate African women was so fundamental as to be self-evident. Other countries—Britain among them—had realized the necessity for equal access to education and were now stepping up efforts to provide schooling for women. "The part Native young women are called upon to play in our economical system is, in importance, second to none. All the domestic arrangements, for weal or for woe, hinge upon them. And great would be the happiness of households if native young women were up to the domestic ropes, while their ignorance in these matters, and incapacity to deal with them, has been, and will continue to be the curse and blight of many an otherwise promising home."[12]

Imvo spread its field of inquiry to living conditions in African communities. In 1888, Reverend Elijah Makiwane published a penetrating sociological study in which he dealt with wages and the cost of living in urban areas. He was critical of unsanitary quarters ("locations") in which blacks were housed; drinking habits of urban dwellers; and several hardships faced by newcomers. He described the demoralizing influence of town life, using Port Elizabeth to illustrate his findings: "A young man or young woman coming from the country, who is drawn into these dens of wickedness, is like a ship amidst rocks. His or her destination is certain, and so far as I am aware, municipal authorities do not think of dealing with this aspect of the condition of the location." He urged that municipal governments cooperate with ministers and African parents in combating the evils that beset urban communities, lest African parents prohibit their children's going to work in towns. If that should come about, white employers could suffer economically, because there was a shortage of labor.[13]

11. "Native Education," *Imvo*, July 8, 1885; "Native Students," editorial, *ibid.*, January 12, 1885. See also "Condition of Mission Schools," editorial, *ibid.*, September 22, 1886.

12. "The Lovedale Girls' School Report," editorial, *Imvo*, January 17, 1889.

13. Elijah Makiwane, "Natives in Towns," paper read before the United Missionary Conference, *ibid.*, July 19, 1888.

Jabavu's paper devoted space to an ever-increasing range of issues affecting the lives of black South Africans. In this respect, some of *Imvo*'s sharpest editorials dealt with political subjects, an area from which both whites and blacks rarely emerged unscathed. In 1886, Reverend Pambani Jeremiah Mzimba, a Free Church of Scotland cleric at Lovedale, provoked one of the liveliest debates of the 1880s when he advised Africans to eschew politics. Mzimba's thinking was that African participation in politics was likely to exhaust the patience of white missionaries, the only white group engaged in the all-important task of educating Africans. Mzimba maintained that he had come to this conclusion after reading a book by the Afro-American historian George Washington Williams, who he claimed had advised American blacks to improve their lot through education, not politics. "Let the experience of Africans in America give warning in time to Africans in Africa to let politics alone at present. Let us be content to be ruled by colonists. Let us only have to do with politics in order to encourage those white men who desire to give us schools and books."[14] The potential Ethiopian, who was to rebel against white clerical and secular authority twelve years later, had thus prescribed a remedy similar to what Booker T. Washington was teaching black Americans from his vantage point at Tuskegee Institute in Alabama. In another sense, Mzimba's advice against self-determination in politics seemed to indicate that church independency was also out of the question. What were the responses to his statement?

There was some rejoicing among Afrikaner nationalists and among white settlers generally. The Port Elizabeth *Telegraph*, a Cape Colony newspaper, reportedly welcomed Mzimba's advice and was quick with the assurance that it came "from a Kafir to Kafirs, spontaneous, undictated to, unsuggested." The *Cape Argus* said the statement ought to allay the fears of whites who imagined that blacks wanted to sit in the Cape Colony Parliament. The Afrikaner paper *De Zuid Afrikaan* expressed its "great regard" for Mzimba for engendering in blacks the feeling that the white man was *baas* (master).[15] Reverend Makiwane came to the defense of

14. Quoted in "The Advice of the Rev. P. J. Mzimba," editorial, *ibid.*, January 21, 1887. See also "Mr. Mzimba's Advice," editorial, *ibid.*, February 2, 1887; and George Washington Williams, *History of the Negro Race in America from 1619 to 1880* (2 vols.; Washington, D.C., 1883).

15. See "Mr. Mzimba's Advice," *Imvo*, February 2, 1887.

Mzimba, who, he said, had been misunderstood. Mzimba had not advocated withdrawal from all forms of political activity; he had all along encouraged Africans to register as voters. Makiwane observed: "All he meant to say . . . is that the time has not yet come when we ought to think of sending a native to Parliament." Makiwane added that what should be provided were conditions that would make Africans good citizens before they had direct parliamentary representation. In the meantime, blacks would be well advised to have liberal whites, such as advocate Rose Innes, represent them in the Cape legislature.[16]

Imvo dissented and accused Mzimba of overlooking "the fact that to deprive the South African Native of the franchise is to change his very nature" and of applying the Afro-American experience to a southern African situation that had little in common with it. The editorial, with a touch of humor, equated Mzimba and Don Quixote, for Mzimba found himself "tilting at windmills, applying, without examining the conditions of the two peoples, the case of the Negroes in America to natives" in South Africa.[17] Neither Reverend Mzimba nor Reverend Stewart seems to have bothered to reply to the letters and editorials that their respective statements provoked. In retrospect, however, that kind of debate had the cumulative effect of encouraging Africans to be their own spokesmen and masters on political and religious issues that affected African life.

By the 1880s, blacks were clamoring for higher education, and in Botswana, for example, missionaries introduced a two-tier system of education, one free and the other fee-paying, the latter offering more lessons in English.[18] *Imvo*, not surprisingly, offered some hints for improving its readers' command of the English language and for acquiring literary taste (based, of course, on *Imvo*'s own terms):

> When a Native young man begins to read English literature, he should take to easy and entertaining books such as Voyages and Travels, especially those written by persons who visited unknown lands for the first time. The Discovery of the New World by Columbus, Lord Anson's Voyage Round the World, Captain Cook's Voyages and John William's

---

16. Rev. Elijah Makiwane, "The Natives and Politics," *ibid.*, February 2, 1887.
17. See "The Advice of the Rev. P. J. Mzimba," *ibid.*, January 21, 1887.
18. See Chirenje, *A History of Northern Botswana,* Chap. 5.

Missionary Enterprise, are books of this class. The trash of so-called Adventures, written by literatteurs like Ballantine and Kingston should be shunned. They are mere dreams written by persons who never saw one of the countries they pretend to describe.

In the late 1880s, *Imvo* was urging its readers to learn from black Americans lessons of economic independence. Thus an 1889 editorial advised Africans to study the socioeconomic conditions of American blacks in order to appreciate the importance of acquiring an education and with it the ability to buy property:

> There are . . . reasons of a special kind why Kafir young men should learn from books the social problems of the Native races in other parts of the world. Here [South Africa], there is a hostile [Afrikaner] bond who seek to deprive the Natives of education and to cut them out of all hold on the soil. Experience elsewhere shows, that this means perpetual slavery not of the bondsman, now abolished, but the slavery of the nominal freeman, who as he cannot own a foot of ground must yield up to the landlord all the fruits of his labour in return for the merest pittance on which a human being can live.

This observation indicates that editor John Tengo Jabavu was familiar with the literature on emancipation in the United States and the attendant disillusionment that accompanied Reconstruction. Emancipation paradoxically made some "free" men more destitute than they had been during slavery, at least for the first few years of freedom. Yet the achievement of American blacks, limited though it was, inspired the black South African inasmuch as it provided a model of sorts to look up to.[19]

While this "American connection" was developing, an event occurred that greatly reinforced African faith in emulating Afro-Americans and substantially boosted black consciousness. In 1890 a company of American blacks staged a singing tour that took them to South African towns and some mission schools. The choir, variously called the Virginia Jubilee Singers, the McAdoo Minstrels, and the Virginia Concert Company, had ten members (four men and six women), five of whom were graduates of Hampton Institute in Virginia. The leader was Orpheus Myron McAdoo, a native of North Carolina who had graduated from Hampton in 1876

19. "Education Through Books," editorial, *Imvo*, August 29, September 5, 1889. For aspects of Afro-American life after emancipation, see John Hope Franklin, *From Slavery to Freedom: A History of Negro Americans* (New York, 1980), 227–67.

and subsequently joined a black "Quintette" that toured Europe, Australia, and New Zealand from 1886 to 1889. Upon his return, McAdoo formed his own company, the Virginia Jubilee Singers, ostensibly "to make money and endow Hampton," his alma mater. [20] The choir subsequently toured Britain and in May, 1890, went to South Africa. [21]

By 1890, McAdoo had become an accomplished performer. A contemporary newspaper described one of his shows in Australia: "Mr. O. McAdoo gave a bass solo, 'I am King o'er land and sea,' in which the capability of the vocalist thoroughly exceeded all expectations, the strength and mellowness of his rich, deep voice being used with splendid effect. In response to a vociferous recall, the singer gave a feeling rendition of that plaintive, yet beautifully pathetic, old plantation melody, 'Old Black Joe.' " The company's tour of South Africa lasted nineteen months, during which time both black and white South Africans were enchanted by the troupe. A white newspaper had this to say:

> While the Jubilee Singers were here the natives could not quite un-
> derstand what sort of people they were. Some of them hesitated to class
> them as Kafirs, as they seemed so smart and tidy in appearance, and
> moved about with all the ease and freedom among the white people
> that a high state of civilization and education alone can give. Occa-
> sionally, however, a Kafir would salute a "Singer" in his own language,
> and when he failed to get a reply he would look puzzled, exclaim
> *Kwoku*! and walk away wondering how his "brother" did not return
> the salute. The more of our natives who attended the Concerts were
> simply enraptured with the singing and some of them, I believe, would
> have pawned even their hat for the wherewithal to go to them. Their
> admiration of their American cousins must really have been very great,
> for on the day the troupe left the town one of the classic crowd was
> heard to say in the deep drawling style—"We shall never again hear
> such splendid singing until we go to Heaven." [22]

20. The choir's charitable aims are disputed by M. J. Sherman, in a letter to Miss Herron, May 10, 1912, in Eugene M. McAdoo file, Hampton Institute Archives, Hampton Va.

21. McAdoo to the editor, January 20, 1887, in "Letters from Hampton Grad-uates," *Southern Workman*, April, 1887, p. 41; "Items of Interest: McAdoo, Orpheus M. '76," in Hampton Institute Archives.

22. "Jubilee Singers' Concert," Castlemaine *Leader*, May 18, 1892; see Edward Osborn to Principal of Hampton, October 21, 1890, in *Southern Workman*, February, 1891; *Kaffrarian Watchman* excerpted in *Southern Workman*, January, 1891, p. 134. See also Eugene McAdoo to the editor, *Southern Workman*, January, 1894, p. 15.

The *Kaffrarian Watchman*'s observations are reinforced by an editorial in *Imvo*, which declared the choir's performance to be sui generis and assessed their impact on South Africa:

> As Africans we are, of course, proud of the achievement of those of our race. Their visit will do their countrymen here no end of good. Already it has suggested reflections to many who, without such a demonstration, would have remained skeptical as to the possibility, not to say probability, of the natives of this country being raised to anything above remaining as perpetual hewers of wood and drawers of water. The recognition of the latent abilities of the Natives, and of the fact that they may yet play a part peculiar to themselves in the human brotherhood, cannot fail to exert an influence for the mutual good of all the inhabitants of this country.

The paper surmised that Africans ("who escaped transportation to America") in South Africa would now study Afro-American history because of the interest aroused by the Jubilee Singers.[23]

McAdoo seems to have been a perceptive observer of South African life. One aspect he criticized was racial discrimination. Even though the white republics treated the Afro-American visitors as honorary whites, McAdoo had harsh things to say about the white rulers: "There is no country in the world where prejudice is so strong as here in Africa. The native today is treated as badly as ever the slave was treated in Georgia. Here in Africa the native laws are most unjust; such as any Christian people would be ashamed of. Do you credit a law in a civilized community compelling every man with a dark skin, even though he is a citizen of another country, to be in his house by 9 o'clock at night, or he is arrested? Before I could go into parts of Africa, I had to get out a passport and a special letter from the governors and Presidents of the Transvaal and Orange Free State, or we would all be arrested." McAdoo reported that Afro-American workers in South Africa were also discriminated against. By August, 1890, McAdoo had, in spite of some opposition from missionaries, arranged a seventy-dollar scholarship for an African student, Titus M. Bongiwe, to study at Hampton. But Bongiwe never reached Virginia: he died in England. His tragic death did not, however, deter other students. At least five African students wrote to the principal of Hampton, applying for places and financial support, but apparently no help was forth-

23. "The Jubilee Singers," editorial, *Imvo*, October 16, 1890.

coming. The editor of the *Southern Workman* pointed out that it was too expensive to pay for the passage and school fees of African students—even though some West African students had graduated from Hampton as early as the 1870s.[24]

While the Jubilee Singers were being accorded special status, to enable them to tour South Africa untrammeled by the segregation laws, a less prestigious and little-noticed group of Afro-Americans was feeling the pinch of white racism in the same country. Among these black Americans, some worked as technicians in the mines, some held other jobs, and some operated their own businesses. Although it is difficult to establish their exact number, they were part of the American expatriate group (mostly whites) that had lived in South Africa since the 1830s, when the first missionaries settled among the Zulu. By the mid-1890s, American nationals in South Africa were estimated to number between fifteen hundred and eighteen hundred.[25] Nevertheless, the few Afro-Americans were easily identified with black South Africans and subjected to the same legal humiliation, until such time as they could establish their citizenship, which too often came long after the indignity had been suffered.

A case in point was the January 15, 1893, assault of John Ross by one Boshoff, a state policeman serving the Delagoa Bay Railroad. Ross's case is indicative of the summary manner in which police officers could apprehend a suspect and mete out punishment on the spot. Following the assault, W. W. Van Ness, Jr., the United States consular agent in the Lydenburg District, wrote to Dr. J. W. Leyds, secretary of state of the South African Republic:

> I beg to call your attention to the fact that at 10 o'clock this morning, Boshoff, a policeman on the Delagoa Bay Railroad at the tunnel works, whipped a man by the name of John Ross, who is a colored citizen of

24. Orpheus M. McAdoo to General Armstrong [Principal of Hampton], n.d., in "A Letter from South Africa: Black Laws in the Orange Free State of Africa," *Southern Workman*, November, 1890, p. 120; letters of McAdoo, William W. Stofile, K. Charles Kumkani *et al.*, *ibid.*, February, 1891. For West African graduates of Hampton, see "Hampton in Africa," *ibid.*, June, 1897, pp. 120–21; and "Our Returned African Student," *ibid.*, January, 1891, p. 137. See Appendix C.

25. See J. C. Manion [American consular agent at Pretoria] to Acting State Secretary, January 15, 1896, in Record group 59, General Records of the Department of State, Microcopy T.191, Roll 18, United States Consular Despatches, National Archives; Clement T. Keto, "Black American Involvement in South Africa's Race Issue," *Issue* (1973), 6–11; and McAdoo, "A Letter from South Africa," 120.

the United States. The complaint was that he was impudent to one of the employees on the railroad works: the trial consisted in the policeman asking him if he was guilty of this impudence and when he answered to the affirmative, he was immediately tied and given 15 lashes. I might add that he was aggravated to . . . impudence.

The laws of the United States make no distinction in citizenship between white and colored and I hope thus you will kindly call your government's attention to this fact so that justice in the above-mentioned case may not suffer. As it was my duty I have reported this case to the government of the United States.

Hoping that you will give the matter your immediate attention.

According to Ross, his assailant was not justified in whipping him but may well have been irritated by the Afro-American's assertion of civil rights in a land where blacks were supposed to be subservient to whites. On September 16, 1893, Ross sued Secretary of State Leyds for damages: "I, John Ross, a citizen of the United States claim two thousand pounds (£2000) damages for the insult and degradation that I have been exposed to by having been publicly whipped at the Elands Valley Tunnel works on the Delagoa Bay Railroad by a policeman of the South African Republic, without any trial and without just cause or reason." [26]

Although Ross may have eventually been awarded damages, [27] Charles Williams, who succeeded Van Ness as consular agent in Johannesburg, reported in April, 1894, that Ross's case was pending. Williams, who freely referred to Africans in derogatory terms, informed the American consul in Cape Town about the continuing harassment of black Americans:

I have the honor to report to you that three colored American citizens called upon me today [April 14, 1894] respecting their privileges in the Transvaal: there being a law here as doubtless you are aware, that no niggers is allowed to promenade on the sidewalks of this town, under penalty of being fined or whipped. There is also another law that all nigers [sic] found in the streets after 9 p.m. without a pass from their employers, are liable to be imprisoned for the night and brought before the Landrost in the morning and fined. I frequently have complaints

26. W. W. Van Ness to Secretary of State, January 15, 1893, John Ross to Dr. J. W. Leyds, September 16, 1893, both in RG 59, Microcopy T.191, Roll 15.

27. Bishop Henry McNeal Turner, in a letter to the editor, April 16, 1898, quoted in "Bishop Turner Sees Pres[ident] Paul Kruger," VOM, June 1, 1898, suggests that President Cleveland forced the Boers to pay $25,000 because they beat some black American.

from our colored citizens as to the way they are treated in consequence of these laws.

Williams suggested that the status of Americans in South Africa could be improved if the United States signed a treaty of friendship with the white republics of southern Africa. These views were repeated by Consul Benedict in a letter to the assistant secretary of state in Washington, D.C., but Benedict advised that Americans ought to obey the laws of foreign countries in which they happened to be living.[28]

These incidents, which would certainly have made the headlines in Jabavu's paper, apparently did not reach the editor and were not reported in *Imvo*. So the happy memories that black South Africans had of the Jubilee Singers could linger long after the choir had left. To black South Africans, the Jubilee Singers remained a model to be emulated. It is therefore tempting to correlate the Afro-Americans' tour and the organization of an African choir that toured Britain and America soon after. This effort also had indigenous roots: in the 1880s, *Imvo* was advising its readers to develop "self-help" programs, and by 1890 its views on the need for a sound educational system had become proverbial. Early in the 1890s, Mr. Balmer, a white man, and an African businessman called Paul Xiniwe started a choir; the aim was to raise £10,000 with which to build technical schools in South Africa. Two members of the choir were Eleanor Xiniwe, a sister of Paul's, and Charlotte Manye, who was destined to introduce black South African church secessionists to the AME church of the United States. According to reports that appeared in *Imvo* and the *Christian Express*, the group was fairly successful in South Africa, but proved a failure in Britain. According to Paul Xiniwe, the reason was that the white managers were not Christians and British audiences during the Victorian era were unwilling to support a cause championed by heathen. Members of the choir, who were not properly clothed for the English winter, complained that the managers had not honored the agreement to pay them regularly. The management denied the charge but could not pay for the choir's passage back to South Africa. Charitable organizations provided the money. The choir returned to South Africa, and in February, 1893, the British colonial secre-

---

28. Charles W. Williams to Charles H. Benedict, April 14, 1894, Benedict to U.S. Assistant Secretary of State, April 23, 1894, both in RG 59, Microcopy T.191, Roll 15.

tary Lord Ripon warned South African blacks about the risk of undertaking uncertain tours. But the managers remained undaunted and, after dismissing Paul Xiniwe, who was leaking news of the unfortunate goings-on in Britain, reorganized the choir. Their singing tour of the United States began sometime in 1893 — after John L. Dube, who had gone to study at Oberlin College in Ohio in 1887, returned from the States early in 1893. His teaching appointment at the American Zulu Mission in Natal started in February, 1893. [29]

Early in 1893, Reverend Mzimba went to Scotland to attend the golden jubilee celebration of the Free Church of Scotland. Before he left Scotland, Mzimba raised about £1,500 ostensibly for improving church and school facilities at Lovedale. Assisting in the fund-raising activities were his Presbyterian hosts as well as Reverend John White, himself a Wesleyan missionary on furlough from the Transvaal. [30] That Reverend White was willing to lend his support to Mzimba, who was not a Wesleyan, may well have reinforced the latter's views on letting white liberals represent Africans in Parliament.

The Ethiopian spirit was nursed in a political climate in which whites were aggressively expanding their spheres of influence throughout the African subcontinent. In these new developments Christian missionaries took an active part, some of them actually receiving encouragement from their societies to support colonial schemes. For example, in 1885, LMS directors approved of Reverend John MacKenzie's role in the declaration of a British protectorate over Bechuanaland: they resolved that their agent's political acts were divinely inspired and would enhance the spread of Christianity. [31] Yet MacKenzie's role was resented by the Tswana, who complained that the LMS had been a party to a declaration that

29. Paul Xiniwe, "Affairs of the African Choir," *Imvo*, March 17, 1892; "Lord Ripon and the Native Choirs," *ibid.*, February 9, 1893; "Annual General Letter of the Zulu Mission, 1893," in American Zulu Mission, 1890–1899, Vol. I, Documents.

30. Rev. Mzimba to Dr. Smith, May 11, 13, 29, 1893, No. 7798; in Free Church of Scotland Archives, National Library of Scotland, Edinburgh. See "Rev. P. J. Mzimba in Scotland," *Scottish Weekly*, excerpted in *Imvo*, October 25, 1893.

31. See *LMS Chronicle*, March 10, 1885, pp. 119–20. See also John MacKenzie, *Austral Africa: Losing it or Gaining it* (London, 1886), I, 79; Anthony Sillery, *Founding a Protectorate* (London, 1965), 40; Anthony Sillery, *John MacKenzie of Bechuanaland, 1835–1899* (Cape Town, 1971), 38ff. However, some of Sillery's conclusions should be treated with caution.

resulted in the loss of some of their land and sovereignty.[32] At about the same time, *Imvo* was lashing out at the Cape Colony government whenever African rights were infringed, and African communities themselves were giving vent to their grievances. In 1887, residents of Oxdaal in the Cape petitioned Queen Victoria to continue to look after their interests, as a withdrawal of the British mandate could mean control by their old enemy the Afrikaners: "We therefore pray Your Most Gracious Majesty that the brave and generous English nation and the British Legislature will not abandon us to the tender mercy of those that are stronger than we are." Little did Oxdaal residents and other African groups realize how much the "official mind" of imperialism in London was in accord with their men on the spot in southern Africa: British rulers were happy to see their empire grow.[33]

The Wesleyan church was occasionally criticized by *Imvo* for supporting unpopular government measures.[34] The Wesleyan Society compounded its unpopularity by flirting with Cecil John Rhodes, a politician whose insensitivity to black aspirations was matched by his expansionist ambitions. In the early 1890s, Rhodes encouraged Wesleyan missionaries in the Transvaal to send agents to Mashonaland, a country then under chartered-company rule but that was to bear his name, and offered them free farms and an annual subsidy of £100. In 1890 a missionary wrote Rhodes, approving the Wesleyan venture to Mashonaland as if colonial expansion and evangelization were mutually interdependent phenomena. Reverend Owen Watkins said: "The Society shares with me, the conviction that the operations of the [Chartered] Company will not only open up new countries to the enterprise of white

32. For Tswana criticism of MacKenzie, see Chief Kgama's views in Edwin Lloyd to Thompson, August 20, 1909, quoted in Chirenje, *A History of Northern Botswana*, 159ff.

33. "Petition to Queen Victoria from 'the Native Inhabitants of the Location of Oxdaal,' July 1887," in Sheridan W. Johns III, *Protest and Hope, 1882–1934* (Stanford, Calif., 1972), 15–16. There is no agreement on the theory and practice of British imperialism in the nineteenth century. For perspectives on the subject, see Ronald Robinson and Jack Gallagher, *Africa and the Victorians' Official Mind of Imperialism* (London, 1961); W. Roger Louis (ed.), *Imperialism: The Robinson-Gallagher Controversy* (New York, 1978).

34. See, for example, "Again the Act," editorial, *Imvo*, April 23, 1895, in which Methodists were criticized for supporting the "Glen Grey Act." *Imvo* maintained that this act would, if implemented, uproot Africans and make them wanderers.

men, but will also tend to the civilization of the native races." Yet
the same society had watched with apparent impotence when,
between 1882 and 1885, Montshiwa and his Mafeking-centered
Rolong chiefdom succumbed to ruthless Afrikaner aggression.[35]
The close cooperation between Methodist missionaries and Rhodes
in furthering British colonial schemes was likely known to Reverend Mangena Maake Mokone, who was stationed at Kilnerton,
the Methodist school near Pretoria; he in fact worked in the same
district with Reverend Watkins. Mokone was one of perhaps four
African ministers ordained in the early 1880s. This seems to have
been a step Wesleyan missionaries, like Presbyterians and American Congregationalists in Natal, took reluctantly because white
opinion was generally against the ordination of black ministers.
Little wonder that when an African was ordained, he was merely
window dressing, denied some of the authority that went with his
office.

Reverend Mokone chose to register his disapproval of this state
of affairs in 1892 by resigning from the Wesleyan church rather than
continue to work under the humiliating conditions. According to
Reverend George Weavind, acting chairman and superintendent of
the church who worked in the same district with Mokone, the
latter had made up his mind to resign in 1891, but delayed his action
because Reverend Watkins was seriously ill. On October 24, 1892,
Mokone sent Weavind his letter of resignation, saying he wanted
to serve God "in his own way." Mokone left Kilnerton on November 1, 1892, and settled in Marabastad, an African suburb of
Pretoria. He again wrote Weavind, saying that he was starting an
independent mission to work among blacks.[36]

Before he left Kilnerton, Mokone issued a "Declaration of
Independence" in which he stated his grievances against the
Wesleyan church. He alleged that district meetings had been con-
ducted along racial lines, whites and blacks meeting separately, yet

35. Rutherford Harris (Secretary of British South Africa Company) to Rev. Owen
Watkins, undated, and January 8, 1890, Watkins to Mashall Hartley, December 17,
1890, and Watkins to Cecil John Rhodes, November 25, 1890, all in Transvaal Box
1881–1891, WMMS Archives, London. Montshiwa is reported to have complained
that he had trusted the English government and the Wesleyan Society and both
failed him. And Owen replied: "I told him I had nothing whatever to do with
politics" ("Report of a Visit to the Molopo Mission, December 17, 1882," in Watkins
to Kilner, January 13, 1883, *ibid.*).

36. See Weavind to Hartley, November 26, 1892, in Transvaal Box, 1891–1896, *ibid.*

blacks were compelled to have a white chairman and a white secretary. Mokone concluded: "This separation shows that we cannot be brothers." He complained that white ministers were paid more than were their black counterparts and were accorded fringe benefits that the latter were denied. He pointed out that his principalship of Kilnerton School was severely undermined by white colleagues who, having not consulted him, expelled African students with impunity. Mokone complained of the harsh treatment meted out to blacks by the *landrost*, a white government official. It was certainly a disillusioned cleric who asked: "If all this is so, where is justice? Where is brotherly love? Where is Christian sympathy?"[37] Mokone concluded his indictment by asserting that God would vindicate him.

In response, Reverend Weavind merely regretted Mokone's resignation, but sent him his certificate of ordination. And at Marabastad the incipient church was taking root. Reverend William Makanda, a Wesleyan minister who sympathized with Mokone's effort to found a new church, offered a tin shack that was used as a temporary church by Mokone and his followers.[38] In the aftermath of Mokone's secession, Weavind was obliged to write his London superiors:

> It is with much regret, that I have to report that the Rev. Mangena Mokone has resigned his place in this Ministry. It was a very great surprise to me, for our relations during the few months we have been together have been most cordial, and I had not the slightest intimation until I received his letter, that he contemplated taking any such step. His letter moreover was of the briefest and merely stated that he wished "to serve God in his own way." Subsequently, I had a friendly conversation with him, and then I found that he had resolved on taking this step so long ago as last year, and had actually written the letter, but destroyed it on learning that Mr. Watkins was very ill, as he did not wish, as he expressed it, to make him worse. He seems to be dissatisfied with his standing and treatment, and his grievances are of long standing. I urged him not to take so serious a step hastily, but to wait until the meeting of the District Synod when he should have the fullest opportunity of saying anything he wished to say, and assured him that the Brethren would not only listen to him, but if there were

37. See the appendix in Josephus Roosevelt Coan, "The Expansion of Missions of the African Methodist Episcopal Church in South Africa, 1896–1908" (Ph.D. dissertation, Hartford Seminary Foundation, 1961), 440.
38. *Ibid.*, 91

any real grounds for his dissatisfaction we should all be most anxious to remove them.[39]

Weavind's letter is typical in its underplaying the causes that led to Mokone's resignation and the impression it creates that Mokone could have found redress within the Wesleyan church. However, Weavind refrained from condemning Mokone's break with the Wesleyans, and that was not typical. It may well be that Weavind had not yet fully grasped the consequences of Mokone's secession.

Mokone spent the year propping up his fledgling church; in January, 1893, he recruited several officers: Reuben Dhlamini, Jantye Thompson, Joshua Mphela, Jantye Z. Tantsi, and Abraham Magqibesa, all of whom had been local preachers in the Wesleyan church.[40] Mokone had also in the meantime conceived of grand plans to send agents of his church as missionaries throughout Africa. This pan-African dream was reflected in the name he chose for his church. On November 5, 1893, he formally announced that it was to be known as the Ethiopian Church, a name that signified the intent to evangelize all Africa. Between 1893 and 1895 the Ethiopian Church added to its clerical ranks Reverend Jacobus Gilead Xaba, who had resigned from his Wesleyan post in the Orange Free State; Reverend James Mata Dwane, another Wesleyan who finally resigned in 1895; and Reverend Kanyane, who had broken with the Anglicans. Mokone was re-obligated to the Ethiopian Church in September, 1894, and Xaba, Tantsi, and Kanyane were obligated in January, 1895.[41]

In the meantime, what was destined to be an enduring American link with South Africa was gradually emerging. To be sure, the link had its roots in the days of the transatlantic slave trade, when Africans were shipped from West Africa as well as from south-central Africa.[42] A sizable number of Afro-Americans had in the intervening years entertained the hope of returning to their an-

39. Weavind to Hartley, November 16, 1892, in Transvaal Box, 1891–1896, WMMS.
40. Coan, "The Expansion of Missions," 92.
41. R. R. Wright *et al.* (eds.), *The Encyclopaedia of the African Methodist Episcopal Church* (Philadelphia, 1947), 318; Coan "The Expansion of Missions," 93–95.
42. This fact seems to be overlooked by many historians. Exceptions are: Mabel V. J. Haight, *European Powers and South-East Africa, 1796–1856* (London, 1967), 226–29; M. D. D. Newitt, *Portuguese Settlement on the Zambesi* (New York, 1973), 217–23; Colin Palmer, *Slaves of the White God: Blacks in Mexico, 1570–1650* (Cambridge, Mass., 1976), 21, 23.

cestral home. The sentiment was given more weight when emigration societies sent Afro-Americans to settle in Sierra Leone in 1787[43] and Liberia in 1821.

By the middle of the nineteenth century, there had developed a corps of articulate blacks who expressed divergent views on the issue of emigration to Africa. A complementary and less controversial topic was the black missionary enterprise by which Afro-Americans sought to evangelize Africa. In this respect, the initiative was taken by the AME church, which sent missionaries to Liberia in 1821. In 1860, Alexander Crummell, himself an Afro-American missionary to Liberia, urged his fellow countrymen to support the work: "As members of the Church of Christ, the sons of Africa in foreign lands are called upon to bear their part in the vast and sacred work of her evangelization. I might press this point on the grounds of piety, of compassion, or sympathy, but I choose a higher principle. For next to the grand ideas which pertain to the Infinite, His attributes and perfections, there is none loftier and grander than that of Duty."[44] Crummell also encouraged artisans and businessmen to emigrate to Africa but he made it quite clear that, in his thinking, missionaries were more important to Africa than were laymen. Crummell's emigration formula did not have the universal approval of blacks. Some opposed it on the grounds that the black man should fight for his rights in America and not imagine that there was a country where the good life was ready-made for him. Frederick Douglass, for one, was as much opposed to emigration to Africa as he was to migration of Negroes from the Deep South to the northern United States. In 1880, Douglass said: "I have thought the movement [to the North] unwise, and no remedy for the manifold evils from which coloured people suffer at the South. I have opposed it on many grounds; and largely on the ground that it is a wasteful and needless expenditure of time and money. 'Rolling stones gather no moss.' 'The men that made Rome worth going to see stayed there.' It is sometimes better to bear the

43. Johnson U. J. Asiegbu, *Slavery and the Politics of Liberation, 1787–1861* (New York, 1969), 4–7.

44. Walter L. Williams, *Black Americans and the Evangelization of Africa, 1877–1900* (Madison, 1982); Payne, *History of the African Methodist Episcopal Church*, 60–64; Berry, *A Century of Missions*, 41–46; Alexander Crummell, *The Relations and Duties of Free Coloured Men in America to Africa* (Hartford, Conn., 1861), 36. See also Hollis R. Lynch, *Edward Wilmot Blyden: Pan-Negro Patriot, 1832–1912* (London, 1967), for Afro-American sentiment on emigration.

ills we have than fly to others we know not of." Some opponents of emigration advanced the view that blacks ought not to embark on fresh battles in an African setting whose environment might prove hostile; that the Afro-American would enhance his manhood by demanding his rights on American soil.[45] In 1891, T. McCants Stewart, a black New York lawyer, criticized Bishop Henry Turner for his emigration schemes.

> For the past twenty years there has been much idle talk on this African question. I am in full sympathy with Bishop Turner so far as he has in view the advancement of Africa, but when he advocates migration there on the ground that our people cannot get along in this country, I must disagree with him. . . . The talk that we cannot get along here is pure nonsense. See the advance we have made during the past few years. When the bishop was a boy no one, except, of course, a little band of abolitionists, believed in the possibility of emancipation. . . . We can work out our destiny right here. . . . It is only a question of time.[46]

The conflicting views on the back-to-Africa sentiments are perhaps better illustrated by the following quotations from two poems. A Lincoln University student said in 1897:

> Who will go and feed the hungry?
> Who will make the sacrifice?
> Who will bear the name of Jesus?
> Who will listen to the cries?
> Oh, the harvest *now* is ready!
> Who will bear the harvest home?
> Who will heed the sound from heaven?
> "Africa's redemption's come."

Here the call was for blacks to go and minister in Africa. The author of a poem published anonymously in 1916 was clearly against

45. "Oration by the Hon. Frederick Douglass, on the Occasion of the Second Annual Exposition of the Coloured People of North Carolina, Delivered on Friday, October 1, 1880," *AMEZ Quarterly Review*, V (July, 1885), 174–75. See, for example, Rev. T. E. Knox, "The Negro is at Home Here," *Christian Recorder*, May 15, 1890; S. Henderson Smith, "Manhood Essential to the Negro's Elevation," *ibid.*, October 5, 1893 (available on microfilm, Interdenominational Theological Center, Atlanta, Ga.).

46. "African Colonization, Bishop Turner and T. McCants Stewart Disagree . . . ," *New York Age*, October 3, 1891. For similar views, see George Washington Williams, *The Negro as a Political Problem* (Boston, 1884), 34.

going back to Africa, pointing out, like Douglass before him, that working for improvements in the American South was better than going to Liberia.

> Although I'm trodden under foot,
> Here in America—
> And the right to life and liberty,
> From me you take away,
> Until my brethren in the South
> From chains are all set free—
> The Old Liberia
> Is not the place for me. [47]

Turner and his supporters were undaunted by critics of emigration and its twin, the Negro missionary movement. Turner's election as senior bishop in 1880 seems to have sharpened his messianic vision of improving the status of some blacks through emigration and saving Africa through Christ. Some blacks opposed Turner's schemes partly because the senior bishop was too often not persuasive but doctrinaire about the need for blacks to go to Africa. Yet Turner imagined that his detractors were deliberately misunderstanding him. In 1893 he complained: "I am abused as no other man in this nation, because I am an African Emigrationist, and while we are not here assembled to consider that question, nor do I mention it at the present time to impose it upon you, but if the present condition of things is to continue I had, not only rather see my people in the heart of Africa, but in ice-bound, ice-covered and ice-fettered Greenland." Turner thought his scheme of resettling blacks in Africa so reasonable as to defy opposition. He even suggested that the United States government finance the repatriation of about 500,000 to 1,000,000 blacks, arguing that Congress should have no qualms about the financial implications of the scheme, since it voted some money "for the protection of the fish in the sea and the seals that gambol in our waters." Turner typically maintained that any black who opposed the scheme was a "scullion." Turner's plan, which was issued more to ridicule than to persuade, had no effect on the U.S. government, which was

47. William D. Feaster, "Africa's Redemption has Come," in *Lincoln University Herald*, February, 1897, Lincoln University Archives, Lincoln University, Pa.; "Old Liberia Is not the place for me," *AME Church Review*, October, 1916.

indifferent to more skillfully presented emigration schemes in the 1890s. [48]

At various times, Turner's conception of the Afro-American commitment to go to Africa was cast in terms of mysticism, economic determinism, as well as a kind of pan-African humanism. On still other occasions, the exodus of blacks was supposed to vindicate the appalling contradictions in the transatlantic slave trade, chief among which was just how a loving God could have let slavery go on for so long without any apparent intervention. In 1894, Turner was reported to have told a Nashville audience:

> Neither the Southern man nor the Northern man was responsible for the Negro being on American soil, but that it was through the powerful workings of an all-wise God that the Black man came. He said it was God alone who brought him here to start him on a new career of usefulness, if he would embrace the possibilities awaiting him. It was not the desire on the part of man to enslave another fellow being, but when this country was first settled the settlers were in quest of labor and by God's providence the Negro came in answer to the call for labor. . . . He believed that contact with this powerful and dominating white race would fit the Negro for the redemption of Africa. Provided, he has self-reliance and sense enough to apply himself to the task but that he would never be a full man here in his present subordinate condition.

Turner had the support of most members of the AME Church's Council of Bishops, and, more important, J. James Cheeseman, president of the Republic of Liberia, agreed with him. In 1894, President Cheeseman informed Afro-Americans in a letter to the *Voice of Missions* that they were welcome to settle in his country and that Liberia offered vast opportunities for black settlers. Sierra Leone was reported to be equally accommodating to Afro-American settlers and missionaries. [49] These assurances had the effect of

48. "Speech of Bishop H. M. Turner Before the National Council of Coloured Men Which Met in Cincinnati, Ohio, November 28, 1893," *VOM*, December, 1893. See, for example, "Blyden and the Butler Bill," in Edwin S. Redkey, *Black Exodus: Nationalist and Back-to-Africa Movements, 1890–1910* (New Haven, 1969), 47–72. A well-planned scheme to get congressional approval failed in the U.S. Senate.

49. See "Bishop H. M. Turner, His Lecture on 'Whence Came the Negro?' " *VOM* May, 1894; "A Letter from President Cheeseman," *ibid.*, September, 1894. See, for example, "Letter from A. L. Brisbane, Brewerville, Liberia, February 12, 1893," *ibid.*, April, 1893; Casely Hayford, "Important Letter from Africa," [April 20, 1893], *ibid.*, October, 1893.

intensifying Turner's passion for emigration and the evangelization of Africa, opposition from some blacks notwithstanding.

Bishop Turner does not seem to have had definite intention to
plant Christianity in southern Africa. However, while he was
going to Sierra Leone in 1893 on board the steamship *Majestic*, he
met a white South African who suggested that the AME church
start some stations among black South Africans. The suggestion
fired Turner's imagination and he seriously thought of proceeding
to Cape Town. He had to shelve the idea because he lacked the
money to pay his fare.[50]

In America, the South African choir was again dogged by misfortune. Poor management caused the tour to fail and the group
disbanded in Cleveland, Ohio. However, some members, including Charlotte Manye, were rescued by Bishop William B. Derrick,
secretary of the Missionary Department of the AME church, who
arranged for them to study at Wilberforce University in Ohio, and
the costs would be borne by the church.[51] Charlotte enrolled in
January, 1895. In the event, the church's contact with her was
destined to strengthen the links between Afro-Americans and black
South Africans. These ties had hitherto been tenuous, confined
mainly to a handful of educated Africans who bothered to read the
Christian Express as well as Jabavu's *Imvo Zabantsundu* to find out
about the black experience in America. Now they were able to learn
more about America from their fellow countrymen. In due course,
returning graduates constituted the strongest link between Afro-
Americans and black South Africans.

50. See Henry McNeal Turner, "Enroute to Africa," *ibid.*, May, 1893.
51. Coan, "The Expansion of Missions," 101–102.

3/The American Connection and Responses to Ethiopianism

The Ethiopian movement underwent dramatic changes during the second half of the 1890s. During that time, Charlotte Manye initiated a process that led to Mokone's Ethiopian Church becoming part of the AME church; Bishop Turner visited South Africa and ordained more than fifty AME ministers, which was the bishop's way of Africanizing the Christian church in South Africa. And with discreet judgment that had not been typical of the former Georgia representative during Reconstruction, Turner dabbled in the politics of South Africa. At the same time, black and white responses to Ethiopianism reached a crescendo, and sociopolitical pressures exerted on African communities caused strong reactions even among diffident black churchmen. Reverend Mzimba, for example, was radicalized sufficiently to secede from the Free Church of Scotland. Reverend Dwane saw cause to break with the AME church and, in so doing, demonstrated that Ethiopianism was not as simple as some critics surmised. It was not just a revolt against white leaderships per se; a host of factors came into play in bringing about independent African churches. Before we consider in detail all these changes, let us examine the origins of the AME church in South Africa.

When Charlotte Manye enrolled in Wilberforce University in 1895, it was easily the leading center of learning of all AME church institutions. Founded in 1855 to train teachers for AME church schools, it was located on a fifty-five-acre tract near Tawawa Springs, north of Xenia, Ohio. Several new departments were added during the next forty years: theology and classics (1866), science (1867), and the normal department (1872). Payne Theological Seminary opened in 1891.[1]

1. See W. S. Scarborough, "Wilberforce University: Its Origin and Growth," *VOM*, May, 1909; and A .W. Donahey, "Wilberforce University," *ibid.*, August, 1914.

Wilberforce was under the spell of Turner's missionary zeal, its faculty and students contributing both ideas and cash to the missionary movement. The university's efforts complemented those of several groups that supported mission work, one of the most vigorous being the Women's Mite Missionary Society. Its Ohio branch encouraged adults and youths to contribute regularly to missionary causes. Not surprisingly, Charlotte became an active member of the society and addressed several meetings under its auspices. She seemed to appreciate the education she was getting. In one of her early essays written at Wilberforce, Charlotte said: "I wish there were more of our people here to enjoy the grand privileges at Wilberforce and then go back and teach our people so that our home may soon lose that awful name, 'the Dark continent,' and be properly called the continent of light."[2] By the beginning of this century, there were more South African students, sent to America by the AME church in the U.S., who were keeping the missionary spirit strong.

If Bishop Turner continued to dominate proponents of the Afro-American imperative to evangelize Africa, he seems to have overlooked the need to plant the AME church in southern Africa, even though he had been informed in 1893 that South Africa could be receptive to black missionaries. This observation was perceptive, for South African elites displayed a keen empathy with the black man's difficulties in those areas of the world dominated by whites. Their knowledge of Afro-American affairs seems to have deepened during the last quarter of the nineteenth century, and there is evidence to suggest that by 1895 the black elites in South Africa were thinking of the black experience in its global dimensions. When news of Frederick Douglass' death in February, 1895, reached South Africa, *Imvo* eulogized him as a leader of all black people.

> Among the more educated of our people in this land the name [Frederick Douglass] that heads this article is not only widely known, but held in the highest esteem. If, therefore, the news of the death of Frederick Douglass, the celebrated Afro-American orator, who died suddenly at Washington on the 20th [February], gives a rude shock to many even in South Africa, it is a matter for no surprise. He was a man of whom all of the African hues, both in America and Africa, had reason to be

2. Manye quoted in G. I. Shorter, "Women's Mite Missionary Society," *ibid.*, November, 1898.

proud, as well by reason of achievements on behalf of the race as for his august personality.[3]

The eulogy suggests that black elites in South Africa were aware of Afro-American sentiments about Africa. African awareness of black solidarity and the need to get support for the young Ethiopian Church were provided a boost by Charlotte Manye, who opportunely gave black South Africans the necessary link.

Early in 1895, Charlotte wrote to her sister in Johannesburg, Kate Manye, about her good fortune and also gave a brief history of the AME church.[4] In May, Reverend Mokone paid what turned out to be a fateful visit to his niece, Miss Manye, who showed him Charlotte's letter. The Ethiopian leader was sufficiently curious that he wrote Turner right away. Mokone acquainted him with the creation of the Ethiopian Church in South Africa, pointing out that "it is entirely managed by us Blacks of South Africa." Mokone asked for assistance in educating South African students at American colleges and for some advice on how to lead effectively the Ethiopian Church. Turner replied, encouraging Mokone to build up his church, and sent him a copy of *Voice of Missions*. In September, 1895, Mokone and Jacobus Gilead Xaba, secretary of the Ethiopian Church, both wrote, thanking Turner for his interest in their church and for sending them the *Voice*; they asked for subscription rates so they could get the paper regularly; they requested that Turner send them a copy of the AME church's polity to enable them to learn the rules governing membership in that church. A month later, Reverend Xaba again wrote Turner, saying how much South Africans appreciated his interest in them and how informative the *Voice* was to black South Africans: "*The Voice of Missions*, your Lordship sent us over, is a very, very important and instructive paper to a Christian community . . . its circulation among us has created an extraordinary revivification, which I suppose, will proceed on with no termination. . . . We desire much knowledge from it, procure more enlightenment, obtain more useful information, and it is a most sublime organ of the modern

3. Bishop Turner Diary, February 25, 1893, in "Enroute to Africa"; "Frederick Douglass," *Imvo*, April 25, 1895.

4. M. M. Mokone *et al.*, "Synopsis of the Early History of the African Methodist Episcopal Church in South Africa," in L. J. Coppin, *Observations of Persons and Things in South Africa, 1900–1904; Part Second, Letters from South Africa* (Philadelphia, 1905), 11.

ages, especially to the Ethiopians at large. Even an unconverted African takes much interest in it, and it leads him to a profound contemplation, marvelously." Xaba went on to say he was heartened to learn from the *Voice* that Afro-Americans regarded Africans as their kith and kin and that they wanted to evangelize Africa. Now that he had learned about this black brotherhood, Xaba was in a position to implore the AME church to think of the "southern extremity" of Africa, where the Christian gospel had merely been "half-baked, and left uncooked." This was a restatement of the Ethiopian Church's dissatisfaction with white missionaries' evangelism.[5]

The Missionary Department had hardly digested the imagery contained in Reverend Xaba's letter when another South African appealed to the AME church to come and minister among blacks. The author of this letter was John Tule, a Thembu from the Transkei, a chiefdom that had built up a tradition of protest since the days of Nehemiah Tile in the 1880s. Tule had had to leave his impoverished chiefdom in order to make a living as a laborer in Cape Town. Tule's appeal was persuasive, for he took the trouble to depict the black man's debilitating situation in South Africa in its political, economic, and religious manifestations.

Dear Brothers in Christ:—
I am trying to draw your attention to the following facts: Our people at home in Transkei are in a bad state; needing two principal modes of life; first, Christianity and civilization, but in the first place we are sinking down every year through the bad treatment of white men with our Kings or Chiefs. He, the white man, first, said I brought peace amongst you, the good tidings of God. Our Chiefs believed that to be the whole truth. The second thing they will see that ministers shall be appointed as commissioners or government agents: that is the first turn to cruelty, because [the missionary] is going to tell them now what the government wants them to do, not what that God whom he said he was sent by to publish the good news of salvation. Now, brethren, take great care what that government agent is going to do. He will convince one chief to fight against his own brother, promising that the government shall help and make you a paramount chief of the

5. Wright *et al.* (eds.), *Encyclopaedia*, 318; Coan, "The Expansion of Missions," 101–102, Appendix II, 442; Mangena Mokone and J. G. Xaba to Turner, September 18, 1895, quoted in their "Ethiopian Mission," *VOM*, December, 1895; Xaba to Turner, October 26, 1895, in his "South African Letter," *ibid.*, December, 1895.

tribe, and by this instigation, nations have risen against nations, king-doms against kingdoms.

Now, my honest brothers, this is a cry from Rama; send us ministers. I have found your address in your paper. I am Tembu Kafir, who came here to earn something for my country.

Brethren, hark to this cry from Macedonia and harden not your hearts. When I saw in your paper, your freedom, I could not help shedding tears for my poor native country. You are born of God (as Moses in Egypt). Brothers, consider that clearly. Don't put those talents in safes . . . use them . . . to purchase the freedom of your brothers in South Africa, or in the whole of Africa. I shall await your favourable reply.

Tule's letter had some effects on the editor of the *Voice*. Although Bishop Turner had not taken the initiative to evangelize South Africa, he called upon the AME church—as a matter of urgency—to send missionaries. With his now typical flair for exaggerating his church's obligation to evangelize, Turner asserted that Tule's letter was

a heavy indictment against the white missionaries in South Africa, and also presents a strong appeal to the A.M.E. Church to come and deliver them from the chains of sin, and the treachery of our brothers in white, who pretend to be very holy till they get to be government agents. Here is a field where five thousand of our young men could go and do well as preachers of the gospel, teachers, doctors, lawyers, and everything. And the climate is about the same as Georgia and Tennessee. No one can raise a howl about African fever in Cape Colony, for there they have snow, frost, winter and summer. And [Tule's] letter shows . . . that the young men of our race . . . can accomplish marvelous good by simply being advisors and councilors of the African Chiefs. The . . . letter is an appeal to the A.M.E. Church that should move the heart of every Bishop, Elder, Deacon, local preacher and member; and if somebody does not heed it, God have mercy upon the American Negro.[6]

In the meantime, Professor W. H. Councill of the Missionary Department of the AME church had written to Reverend Mokone, informing him that the church could help South African students who desired to study in America. Mokone was elated and wrote

6. John Tule to AME Church, November 12, 1895, in his "Letter from South Africa," *VOM*, March, 1896. For more views on missionary complicity in colonial schemes, see "The Missionaries and the Chiefs," in Nozipho Majeke, *The Role of the Missionaries in Conquest* (Johannesburg, 1952), 25ff.

back that the Ethiopian Church was most grateful for the assistance the AME church was willing to provide. Mokone, like the layman Tule, welcomed the brotherly solidarity evinced by Afro-Americans: "We never dreamed of you Americans thinking of us at all to be your people and that you work for our salvation." Mokone said that Councill's declaration of black brotherhood inspired South Africans to work harder to retain church independence: "Your favourable letter has been the cause of our revival and strengthening. We are always so strengthened when we receive letters from America, and feel as if we have been visited by an extraordinary being."[7]

Elsewhere in southern Africa, 1895 had been marked by the success of African initiatives to ward off European aggression. Chief Kgama and two other Tswana chiefs went to England toward the end of 1895 and successfully lobbied the British government against Rhodes's plans to annex their country to chartered-company territory (Rhodesia), and the chiefs became celebrities in the eyes of Africans.[8] By 1895, black South Africans were seeking an external helping hand to ameliorate their social and political situation. Once Charlotte Manye had provided them the link, the Ethiopians resolved at their third annual conference held in March, 1896, to affiliate with the AME church. Significantly, the preamble to the resolution on affiliation reflected the pan-African vision embodied in Mokone's declaration at the launching of the Ethiopian Church in 1893. "This Conference," said the preamble, "is strongly of the opinion that a union with the African Methodist-Episcopal Church will not only be hailed by our people, but would be the means of evangelizing numerous tribes of this vast continent."[9] Clearly, the delegates' mood was very much in line with the AME church's sentiment for evangelism.

The Ethiopian conference selected Reverend James Dwane and Reverend Jacobus Xaba to go to America to negotiate the affiliation. But the Ethiopian Church raised only enough money for one fare.

7. "Rev. Mokone of South Africa to President Councill," VOM, April, 1896.

8. Rhodes was described as the "Great Cape Opportunist" ("Khama's Success," Imvo, November 21, 1895). See also "Khama's Mission," ibid., December 19, 1895; and "Ukhama," ibid., December 27, 1895.

9. Berry, A Century of Missions, 76–78; Wright et al. (eds.), Encyclopaedia, 318–19.

Dwane alone left Cape Town on April 16. Even before Dwane arrived in New York, Turner informed readers of the *Voice* that the AME church would approve the proposed affiliation and that the Ethiopians were as justified in breaking with the Methodists as Richard Allen had been in leaving the predominantly white Methodist Episcopal church in Philadelphia in 1787 to form the AME church. Once in America, Dwane met Bishop Turner and other church officers. On June 19, 1896, the affiliation was effected, the Ethiopian Church of South Africa becoming the Fourteenth District of the AME church. This arrangement meant that the Ethiopian Church had come not as an equal partner but had compromised its independence. Dwane was appointed general superintendent and vicar bishop of that district and returned to South Africa in September. He later convened the first conference of the newly constituted Fourteenth District, which met at Queenstown in the Cape in April, 1897. At the meeting he reported on the success of his trip to America and that the AME Church's Council of Bishops, the highest governing body of the church, expected loyalty from all members of the new district. Dwane was also sending reports to America. In one, he complained that the white press was publishing articles damaging to him and the AME church. He urged the mother church to build an institution of higher learning, which blacks were eager to have. Dwane saw the school as a way of enhancing the church's prestige.

> Our great need in this country is a first-class institution of learning. . . . People in this country are very anxious about higher education. I hope the A.M.E. Church will soon take up this question in earnest. You have not the least idea, my lord, how much depends on this question. The failure of the white churches to do so is a source of much discontent and our church must take the matter up; for you can run a college here for one-third, if not one-fourth [of what it cost in America]. Everybody in Africa is watching how we the [A.M.E. Church] are going to deal with this great question.

Dwane went on to predict that the construction of the school could attract more church members, and he assured prospective teachers, just as Turner had done before him, that South Africa had a healthful temperate climate.[10]

10. Wright *et al.* (eds.), *Encyclopaedia*, 318–19. "Ecclesiastic Envoys from South Africa," *VOM*, July, 1896; Berry, *A Century of Missions*, 318–19; James Mata Dwane

The Missionary Department of the AME church was kept informed about events in South Africa by ministers as well as by laymen. In May, 1897, Reverend Marcus Gabashane wrote from the Transvaal and invited Turner to visit if he should come to South Africa. In the same month, Reverend Mokone wrote the senior bishop, recounting how he had moved an independent church of eighty to one hundred colored residents of Johannesburg to join the AME church, pointing out that the conversion augured well for the Fourteenth District. The same letter also shows that Mokone was becoming exasperated by blacks' inability to unite against whites and the AME church's tendency to talk about emigration schemes that were never carried out. Thus he could pose rhetorical questions to black Americans:

> Don't you weep when you remember Africa? When you sing those songs, when you are in [the United] States of America? Aren't you afraid when your right hand forgets Africa's wisdom and arts? . . . Here in Africa all the nations are gathered together except Negroes, my own people. English, Dutch, Germans, Hollanders, French, Russian, Jews, Swedish, Arabian, Indian, German Jews. All are doing the work but we are sleeping and [you] will not come to visit the fatherland and then when all is taken . . . we shall begin to cry like Esau.[11]

The activities of the Ethiopian Church were not passing unnoticed in South Africa. Not surprisingly, Reverend George Weavind, the Wesleyan superintendent who had reluctantly accepted Mokone's resignation in 1892, kept an eye on the new church and reported regularly to his superiors in London. In August, 1896, he was less restrained than he had been in 1892:

> You will remember that Mangena Mokoni, a former native minister, went out from us to establish a church of his own. It is called the Ethiopian Church and is somehow allied with these natives who left [the Methodist Church of] the South African Conference some years ago. This independent church has already created many difficulties in the country. The leaders have laid hands upon any native without respect to character, who had some little education, and in some cases

---

to Turner, February 22, 1897, in his "Our South African Superintendent Writes," *VOM*, May 1, 1897.

11. Marcus Gabashane to Turner, May 25, 1897, in "Letter from South Africa," *VOM*, July, 1897; Mangena Mokone, "Grand Letter from South Africa," Mokone to the Editor, May 22, 1897, *ibid.*

ordained him and in others placed him in positions of responsibility. These men, without control have as I said caused trouble and the government are beginning to see that Native Churches without a European head, will set the country in a flame if they are not suppressed. So they are moving in that direction.

Weavind noted that Ethiopians had collected some money to pay Dwane's passage to America and mistakenly welcomed the impending affiliation of the Ethiopian Church and American Methodists. He was apparently under the impression that the church in question was the predominantly white Methodist Episcopal church. Hence he could say: "I could have no possible objection to such union, if the control of Methodist Episcopal Church be an effectual one. Anything else would be a calamity to the native peoples, for it would only encourage the pride and ambition of a few native men, who owe their all to Methodism, and who are not yet morally or spiritually or intellectually fit to stand alone."[12]

The general criticism levied against Ethiopians, that they were recruiting members of questionable character and also that they tended to politicize their followers, was echoed by white American missionaries in Natal. The combined opposition of the British authorities and American missionaries had failed to throttle Mbiyana Ngidi's church. An 1894 report said the church was flourishing and that Mbiyana's followers were addressing him as "bishop" or "apostle." At Groutville, black members of the American Zulu Mission challenged a rule that required members to donate some money before they could partake of holy communion, a procedure they construed as tantamount to purchasing the Lord's sacrament. In Johannesburg, the Americans witnessed another secession when a faction at Table Mountain departed. The missionary there must have had little comfort from a visit by Dr. James Stewart of Lovedale, who predicted that the church schism would last for another twenty years.[13]

Nor were Methodists the only ones concerned about the so-called Negro influence on South African Ethiopians. In 1897 the *Christian Express* published an article in which it was asserted that black South Africans' views of Afro-Americans were still affected

12. Weavind to Hartley, August 29, 1896, in Transvaal Box, 1891–1896, WMMS.
13. W. C. Wilcox, "Report of Mission Work on Umvoti and Mapumulo Mission Station for Year Ending June 30, 1894," in American Zulu Mission, 1890–1899, Vol. I, Documents; H. D. Goodenough to Judson Smith, October 17, 1896, ABC, 15.496, Vol. IV, *ibid.*

by the Jubilee Singers' 1890 tour of South Africa. Segregation laws had had to be relaxed then to allow the black singers to move about unencumbered, and that engendered a feeling among Africans that they too "might become more than 'hewers of wood and drawers of water.' " [14] The article could have added that the historical writings of George Washington Williams, the political activities of Frederick Douglass, and the aspirations of Afro-Americans generally had their effects on black South Africans. This indicates that when Bishop Turner visited the recently constituted Fourteenth District in 1898, he went to a people who were not wholly ignorant of the existence of America and Afro-Americans.

By the time of that visit, Turner had taken to heart a doctrine of belligerent pan-Africanism, which asserted that Africa in fact belonged to black Africans ("Africa for Africans"), and the corollary that Afro-Americans return to their ancestral home (back-to-Africa movement). Yet the Turner who subscribed to these radical ideas had come a long way. Born a free Negro in South Carolina in 1833, he found out to his horror that a free black in a slavocracy was in some respects unfree. He became a member of the AME church and was baptized in Abbeville, South Carolina, in 1848; he was licensed to preach in 1853 and became a traveling preacher the same year. Turner was ordained a deacon in 1860 and consecrated bishop in 1880. He had been awarded an honorary LL.D. by the University of Pennsylvania in 1872 and a doctor of divinity by Wilberforce University in 1873. In 1876, Turner was elected by the General Conference of the AME church as manager of the Publication Department. In 1893 he started the monthly *Voice of Missions;* as editor, he wrote several articles and editorials on his passions: emigration of Negroes to Africa, Negro missionary movements, and black consciousness (or pan-Africanism). To Turner, the solidarity of black people was not negotiable; it was a sine qua non for survival. Turner acquired at an early age a penchant for emotive language. He used this freely to criticize people who disagreed with him on what he believed was the proper path for Afro-Americans to follow. A Methodist publication said of his writing: "The missiles he would throw from his pen would rarely ever fail their mark." [15] Turner had flirted with active politics for some time: he had served, for example, as a representative in the Georgia Re-

14. See "The Colonial Native and the American Negro," *CE*, September 6, 1897.

15. M. M. Ponton, *Life and Times of Henry M. Turner* (Atlanta, 1917; rpr. Westport, Conn., 1970), 33; "Resolutions on Death of Bishop Henry McNeal

construction Assembly in 1868 but was soon expelled along with other blacks.[16]

As early as 1870, Turner was promoting black emigration to Africa, arguing that Africa was the only safe place for Afro-Americans who had become disillusioned with American racism, which seemed to intensify in the wake of emancipation. The interest Turner's emigration schemes sparked among blacks persuaded him to visit West Africa in 1891 and again in 1892. A plan to send three hundred blacks to Liberia in 1892 led to great disappointment—the chartered ship had room for only fifty emigrants. Yet the euphoria generated by Turner seems to have been considerable. Edwin S. Redkey has observed: "So eager were they to flee to a place where they would have land of their own and find economic and political independence that over 300 Blacks, mostly from Arkansas and Oklahoma, arrived in New York expecting transportation to Africa. Most were penniless, ragged, and uneducated—typical of Southern Black farmers—but like many others, they believed that life could only get worse in the United States."[17] Their enthusiasm to get to a better country no doubt outweighed any obstacles to emigration and spurred Turner to press on with renewed vigor.

It was against this background that Turner reaffirmed his belief in emigration before he left for South Africa in 1898.

> I would not be understood as saying that the Black man cannot exist here as a mere individual. That he is doing very well, but if he would ever become anything in the way of a power and force in the world, ever reach the condition where his influence and commerce would be courted and turned to his own advantage, he must have a country and a government of his own that is a success. Why, if we had a Negro nation in Africa, though it did not contain over ten millions of people, and if we had active and prosperous cities, had cars and telegraph lines,

---

Turner, D.D., from the Baltimore A.M.E. Preachers' Meeting," *VOM*, July, 1915; "An American Bishop at the Opera House," *Cape Argus*, April 25, 1898. See Appendix F.

16. See Ponton, *Life and Times of Turner*, 57; Edwin S. Redkey, "The Flowering of Black Nationalism: Henry McNeal Turner and Marcus Garvey," in Nathan I. Huggins *et al.* (eds.), *Key Issues in the Afro-American Experience*, Vol. II, *Since 1865* (New York, 1971), 110.

17. Redkey, "The Flowering of Black Nationalism," in *Key Issues*, II, 111; Redkey, *Black Exodus*, passim.

schools and factories, newspapers and ships, and numbered among our population statesmen, writers and soldiers of recognized ability, and, more especially, if we had a substantial currency and commerce of our own—made and carried on by our own race, the condition of the Black man would be elevated all over the world. Those things I have just mentioned constitute the very nest-egg of civilization and only their successful and permanent development out of a people's own resources can ever bring national vigor and strength.

Turner advised young men to emigrate to South Africa, where, he surmised, one's ability, not color, determined one's advancement in society.[18]

Turner's views on emigration, though enjoying a measure of support, did not go unchallenged. Opponents ranged from the hard core, those who thought even domestic migration from southern to northern states was a grave mistake, to fairly articulate spokesmen who feared the consequences of shipping blacks to a continent they had long since lost contact with and where the unfamiliar environment boded ill for the prospective settlers. The historian George Washington Williams had in 1884 issued one of the most compelling statements against emigration: "Emigration has virtue in the judgement of some of our discouraged and gloomy brethren. This is an error of judgement. America is the theatre of the Negro's noblest acts. The graves of his ancestry are here. He was married and was given in marriage here. His children were born here; and, while undergoing the crucial test of manhood and citizenship, he cannot afford to withdraw." Yet Turner remained unmoved by such reasoning. In 1893 he chaired a national convention in Cincinnati at which the question of repatriation of Afro-Americans was not well received. A subsequent report on the convention appeared in an AME Zion publication: "The pet idea of Bishop Turner, for the race to be expatriated to Liberia, found but few followers, and failed of endorsement. The scheme to seek shelter in Mexico, met quite as welcome a rebuff. The sentiment, therefore, seemed to prevail that the Afro-American must remain here and manfully fight for those rights which are his by the Constitution and the laws, and work out his own destiny as an American citizen." Nor was that the end to criticism of Turner's views. After the Atlanta *Evening Journal* quoted the bishop on

18. "Bishop Turner's Views. He Will Visit Dutch and British South Africa," *Imvo Extra* (*Itole le'Mvo*), April 20, 1898 (excerpt from the Atlanta *Evening Journal*).

merit as the criterion for promotion in South Africa, an Afro-American paper the *New York Age* took issue with Turner's views on South African race relations. The paper pointed out that the African press in South Africa published stories that suggested that racial discrimination was practiced there. Hence it was contended that "Bishop Turner will find on closer inspection that the Afro-American possesses advantages in the United States which he nowhere possesses in South Africa. As we understand it, the Native African has no honourable part in the citizenship of the Dutch or British rule of South Africa, and his industrial status borders upon a species of slavery." The article went on to point out that Haiti and the Dominican Republic might, as sovereign states, impose restrictive conditions on Afro-American immigration, but Liberia, "an Afro-American state pure and simple," could be more receptive to black settlers. The paper ridiculed the idea that Bishop Turner alone knew God's plan to let Afro-Americans return to their ancestral home.[19] Yet neither subtle rebuke nor hostile criticism could move Turner, who championed emigration causes without compromise to the very end of his life.

The Turner who landed in Cape Town in April, 1898, evidently had a grand plan to change with great dispatch the status quo in the religious life of South African blacks. On arrival he declared that he was "mighty glad to get my feet once more on the soil of renowned Africa—My Master's business requires haste." Turner was dismayed to find that "no coloured minister, till a year ago, was found in Cape Town. All the ordained ministers at least were white." This was certainly an exaggeration on the bishop's part. Turner welcomed the Ethiopian spirit that had led black South Africans to "discover that churches of their own race . . . would be of far more benefit in a pragmatic measure than worshipping among whites all the time, where they are compelled to occupy a subordinate status." He ordained as AME ministers thirty-one elders and twenty deacons, and he reordained at their own request

19. G. W. Williams, *The Negro as a Political Problem*, 34; Douglass, "Oration," 174–75; "The Turner Convention," *AMEZ Quarterly Review*, IV (January, 1894), 181–82; *New York Age*, February 10, 1898, excerpted in "Bishop Turner and Africa," *Imvo Extra*, April 20, 1898. For earlier emigration schemes to Haiti, see Floyd J. Miller, *The Search for a Black Nationality: Black Colonization and Emigration, 1787–1863* (Urbana, 1975), 15–18.

all eight ministers who had been consecrated in the Ethiopian Church. He promoted Reverend Dwane from superintendent to vicar bishop of the Fourteenth District.[20]

A closer look at Turner's activities suggests that the former Georgia legislator inched his way through South Africa with the shrewdness of a seasoned agitator. It appears also that for the greater part of his six-week visit, Turner concealed from whites his political activities. He was able to do so by judiciously choosing his topics whenever he addressed gatherings at which whites were present. For example, when on April 24, 1898, he spoke before a public meeting in Cape Town, his subject was the impending spiritual crisis threatening mankind and the need for Christian denominations to work together in harmony, "not shouting each other down and cutting each other's throats." He portrayed himself as a loyal American and merely regretted the outbreak of hostilities between Spain and the United States in 1898; he did not mention who might have been at fault. Turner then spoke on an issue that must have pleased whites. "He compared the American coloured man with the South African coloured man and urged the latter to improve themselves morally and intellectually, for only upon education could they depend to rise from ignorance and sloth." By appearing to imply that black South Africans were to blame for the colonial situation that oppressed them, Turner reinforced a theme that the white press had been harping on since the 1870s. Little wonder the *Cape Argus* could describe Turner as "a powerful man with an equally powerful voice" who spoke in a "very interesting and a very telling manner." During the same tour, Turner reportedly had an interview with Paul Kruger, president of the Transvaal, and the Afrikaner leader conceded, "You are the first black man whose hand I have ever shaken." Kruger is said to have commended the AME church on its missionary work. However, in the South African context, Kruger must have welcomed the AME church more for political reasons: he no doubt thought that the American group could counterbalance the influence British missionaries—his perennial rivals—wielded in African communities. It took Turner some time to grasp Kruger's

20. Wright *et al.*(eds.), *Encyclopaedia*, 319; "Bishop Turner Renders His Report," *VOM*, June 1, 1898.

motives, but in due course he was able to interpret correctly Kruger's contrived hospitality.[21]

If Kruger's reported commendation marginally enhanced the AME church's mission work, the African response to Ethiopianism in general and to Turner's visit in particular was mixed. Again, *Imvo*, by now deeply imbued with Jabavu's integrationist philosophy, commented on both issues and typically provided a forum for its readers to air their views. In April, 1898, *Imvo's Itole le'Mvo* carried a lead article on Turner and Ethiopianism. The editorial reiterated the story of the formation of the Fourteenth District of the AME church in South Africa and portrayed Turner as a man who believed in and espoused racial segregation in his country. That practice had no foundation in Christian doctrine and bred animosity between races. The paper therefore urged that segregation be rejected, as it boded ill for the future happiness of black South Africans. In May, 1898, *Imvo* endorsed a report in the *Christian Express* that criticized the Ethiopian movement for playing on two volatile issues, race and religion:

> Among the influences that move men in large numbers, there are none more powerful than those of Race and Religion, and when they are combined the motive force is a very considerable one. The Pied Piper of Hamelin could not have piped with a note more attractive or irresistible. And the leaders of this new movement, the Ethiopian Church, are making skillful use of these two powerful influences on human conduct. By the former that of race or colour, they make an appeal to certain instincts, of which all are more or less conscious; and to which all, young and old, religious or not, are more or less susceptible. By the other motive of religion they appeal to higher feelings to give stability and sanction and a non-worldly aim to the movement in question.

The article expressed some alarm that the document signed by Turner during his tour of South Africa to complete the formalities affiliating the Ethiopian Church and the AME church had been countersigned by the governor of Georgia: the implication was that the governor had acted improperly. Finally, the *Christian Express*

---

21. "An American Bishop at the Opera House"; Wright *et al.* (eds.), *Encyclopaedia*, 319; H. M. Turner, "My Trip to South Africa," AME Church Review, April, 1899, pp. 809–13. *Cf.* John W. Cell's unconvincing characterization of Turner's visit, in *The Highest Stage of White Supremacy*, 39. Significantly Cell relied on thin evidence for his comments.

article deplored the fact that Kruger and other leaders of the Afrikaner republics had given Turner an audience at all.[22]

Nor did *Imvo*'s editors monopolize the debate on Ethiopianism. At Blythswood, a Free Church of Scotland school in the Transkei, students reportedly debated the question, "Has the time come that we should have churches and schools of our own?" Amos Qunta took the affirmative side, saying Africans now had a sufficient number of qualified churchmen to take over from white missionaries. Qunta drew parallels with the United States, where, he said, schools and churches had orginally been dominated by Europeans, but Americans had eventually taken over control of those institutions: "Today they have their own churches and universities ruled and financed by them only. They have Bishops and Professors of their own nationality." He maintained that no country could rightfully lay claim to nationhood until it had set up and could support its own churches and schools. Qunta also drew examples from Europe, where, he said, there were ample precedents to show that independence in such institutions had historically always conferred a sovereign personality on the countries in question. J. B. Luti opposed the motion, saying that the time had not arrived when Africans could run churches and schools by themselves. He maintained that there was a lot of petty jealousy among blacks, which hardly enhanced their claims to independence. There was neither the unity nor the money with which to maintain independent institutions. "We are still in a very low stage in civilization; we have no trades of our own which is the only thing that improves and raises up a nation. Let us not be in a hurry to separate ourselves from our fathers the European missionaries. We must take time to do this. Then there will come a time when civilization will have reached its maturity. Great things can never be accomplished in one day." England's history illustrated his observations, Luti said. He predicted the fall of the Ethiopian Church: its leaders were mere rebels who had not taken the trouble to study theology.[23] In November, 1898, *Imvo*'s long editorial criticized the Ethi-

22. "Our Negro Visitor," *Imvo Extra*, April 20, 1898; "Race and Religion," *ibid.*, May 11, 1898.

23. See "Natives and Independence. At a Debating Society," *Imvo Extra*, May 18, 1898. In this article an anonymous author criticized Amos Qunta for not distinguishing between American Indians and white Americans.

opian movement's theology as devoid of content and denounced Ethiopians as misguided rebels.[24]

The adverse publicity that *Imvo* and the South African press generally accorded the Ethiopian movement does not seem to have seriously deterred new members. The AME church had 10,800 members by 1898. It is also evident that Turner's visit gave an impetus to Ethiopian activities in South Africa as well as in neighboring territories.

In Botswana the Ethiopian spirit was bubbling to the surface in the aftermath of Turner's visit. At Kanye an LMS agent reported in 1898 that an evangelist there had been ordained an officer of the AME church by "a black American Bishop." Later that year, two Ethiopians from Kunwana in the neighboring chiefdom of the Rolong visited Chief Bathoen at Kanye and tried to get permission to start an Ethiopian church. Bathoen convened a *pitso* (assembly) at which the Ngwaketse nation rejected the Ethiopian overture on the ground that the LMS, which had had its mission at Kanye since 1871, was serving them well.[25] But this turned out to be only a respite, as Kanye was embroiled in belligerent Ethiopianism from 1901 onward.

In the meantime, generally unfavorable responses to Ethiopianism were building in the white community. And in this respect, both lay and church papers took the offensive. One of the earliest publications (besides the *Christian Express*) to come out against Ethiopianism was the *South African Congregational Magazine*. In the middle of 1898, one of its articles used military imagery to describe Ethiopianism and criticized its adherents for allegedly expressing a theology exclusively for blacks ("cut in ebony," as the magazine put it). Reverend Dwane was said to possess tricky canine traits (the "curly paw"), on account of the role he played in affiliating the Ethiopian Church and the AME church. The magazine, apparently unaware that the AME church had seceded from the Methodist Episcopal church in America in 1787 and that it was determined to be more effective than white missionaries were, criticized the Methodists for supporting Ethiopians who had broken with Methodist Episcopalians.

24. "Native Churches," *Imvo*, November 14, 1898. See Appendix D.

25. Rev. James Good to Foreign Secretary R. Wardlow Thompson, November 11, 1898, in Box 55, Jacket D, Folder Two, LMS Archives.

It is somewhat difficult to understand the action of the Negro Methodists in this connection. Their church is professedly identical with the Wesleyan body throughout the world. The Episcopal system is only an expediency, the bishops exercising no other greater authority than that of superintendents of circuits in England and Africa. Yet the American Negro Methodist Church has apparently decided to enter the mission field in Africa in open rivalry with the existing Wesleyan Missions, and in a manner that most inevitably tends to the injury of these Missions throughout the native districts. Surely there must be some effectual means of convincing the authorities of the American Church that they are thus entering on a policy that must be attended with all the disastrous results of a house divided against itself.

Toward the end of 1898 the *South African Congregational Magazine* sharpened its attack on independent African churches and the role black Americans were playing in the new movement. They were criticized for allegedly politicizing South Africans and encouraging the latter to discard the supposedly civilizing influence of European missionaries. Afro-Americans were accused of polarizing the races in South Africa and of fomenting secession in order to recruit the disaffected members into the AME church. After some rhetorical questions implying that Congregationalists were not opposed to self-determination per se in church government, the article condemned Ethiopianism for apparently doctrinal reasons:

To have seen the spirit of native devotion resulting from the bondage of European formalities and breaking forth into fresh, free manifestations of its own distinctive life and power—that would have been a most interesting spectacle, worthy of the most generous interest and sympathy of all to whom religion is an inspiration and not a mere dead and dry tradition. But there is not a vestige of spiritual originality in this movement. In connection with it the Ethiopian does not change the skin, nor the leopard his spots but only his ministerial diet. He is taking black missionary from America instead of white missionary from England. That is all the difference. He turns English Methodism out of the door to bring Negro Methodism down the chimney. He bites the white hand that has ministered for so many years to his spiritual destitution and kneels to kiss the black hand whose opening promises to make him a bishop.

In another article the Ethiopians were accused of preaching a gospel of "white for white" and "black for black" and calling on Africans to escape from their spiritual bondage in white churches.

The same article estimated the members that white churches had lost to the Ethiopian Church: Wesleyans, four thousand; Anglicans, one thousand; Presbyterians, one thousand; Congregationalists, forty.[26]

The secular press joined the refrain that was being chanted against Ethiopianism. Once the consequences of Turner's ministry started unfolding after the bishop's return to America, the *Cape Argus* did an about-face hardly a year after it had praised Turner: "This [Ethiopian] movement has been fostered and encouraged by that arch-mischief maker the Black Bishop Turner of the [African] Methodist-Episcopal Church in America." The same article also blamed the spread of Ethiopianism on Africans who studied abroad and ministers who paid short visits to countries overseas.

> A native minister who has always implicitly accepted the control of the European missionaries perhaps visits England, and is utterly spoilt. Many a good native has gone wrong as a result of six months' social dissipation and moral molly coddling in the old country. He comes back to the Cape suffering from what is vulgarly known as a swollen head, and chafes at the old trammels. He becomes possessed of the idea that he is absolutely civilized up to, if not above the level of those under whose mild authority he is placed, and that he is capable of standing alone. He is also apt to become impregnated with an anti-European spirit. "Why," he argues, his memory fondly dwelling on the holiday delights of the homeland, "why because I happen to have a dark skin should I be relegated to a secondary position? I am just as good as these white men, and I will show them that I can break away from their guidance and control, and take my people with me."[27]

That the *Cape Argus* should deplore the relatively humane treatment accorded African ministers during their stay abroad is indicative of the racist posture that white South Africans had assumed at the beginning of the twentieth century. It is also reminiscent of the attitude displayed by Reverend Robert Moffat in the 1840s when he discovered that his servant Mokotedi expected to be treated with the same civility he had experienced during his stay in Britain.

26. "The Future of Our Native Churches," *CE*, August 1, September 1, October 1, 1898 (excerpts from the *South African Congregational Magazine*). Apparently the article overlooked Reverend Mzimba's large following.

27. *Cape Argus*, February 28, 1899, quoted in "Native Disruption," *CE*, March 7, 1899.

Bishop Turner did not let the tirade against his church pass unchallenged. Fully informed about the white reaction to Ethiopianism (AME church officers in South Africa reported to him, and he himself read South African papers), Turner could refute some of the allegations against his church and he characteristically gave his own assessment of what was wrong with Christianity in South Africa. In December, 1898, Turner criticized an article in the August issue of the *Christian Express* that had berated Ethiopians and black American missionaries for being devoid of Christian virtues. The bishop said the white authors had pandered to racism. Turner could well understand the causes of Ethiopianism. "We can now understand why our Ethiopian brethren desired unity with a church of their own kith and kin, with whom they could worship God on fraternal conditions and not be looked upon and regarded as religious scullions."[28]

However much white opinion might have exaggerated the influence of Turner's visit on potential Ethiopians, it is significant that some of the secessions were sparked by issues arising from monies that black ministers had collected abroad. In 1895, Reverend Dwane broke with the Wesleyans for several reasons. One involved the question of whether an ordained minister should be required to surrender to the Methodist Conference money he had collected abroad on behalf of his parish. Dwane took the view that the conference was not entitled to the funds he had raised in Britain for the purpose of building a school in his parish. Dwane had hardly left the Wesleyan church when Mokone invited him to join the Ethiopian Church, where his rise to the top was meteoric.[29] Nor was Dwane the only one to join the ranks of irredentist Ethiopians. Reverend Mzimba left the Free Church of Scotland in 1898. He was driven to do so by racial discrimination, and subsequently he quarreled with church officials over some parish property and money he had collected in Scotland in 1893.

Mzimba, a Mfengu, was born in the Cape in 1850 and entered Lovedale in 1860. From 1865 to 1871 he was apprenticed in the Printing Department, where he commended himself to school authorities. At the completion of his course in 1871, they praised him for what a Lovedale publication called "the general moral

28. See "South African Christianity," *VOM*, December, 1898.

29. See Skota (ed.), *The African Yearly Register*, 337–44; "Vicar Bishop Dwane of South Africa Visits This Country by Special Orders," *VOM*, December, 1898.

influence which they believed his character has exerted on others, and also their satisfaction with the manner in which he has endeavored to promote the interests and welfare of the Institution by spontaneous and ready activity and uniformly unselfish conduct."[30] Mzimba entered the Theology Department at Lovedale in 1872 and was ordained in 1875, the second (after Tiyo Soga) black South African to become a Free Church of Scotland clergyman. He was appointed minister at Lovedale and in 1893 he was chosen to go to Scotland to represent South African Presbyterians at the jubilee celebrations of the Free Church. During his stay, Mzimba solicited funds for his Lovedale parish. In May, 1893, he informed church authorities why he needed the money: "The Lovedale Congregation in numbers is the largest in the Free Church Kaffraria (it being the name given to the Free Church district of South Africa) Mission but it is very poor. It is chiefly made up of widows and women who have no way of supporting themselves but are maintained by their male relatives and heathen husbands." The congregation also supported its minister. Mzimba's appeal brought some results—he collected about £1,500, which he took with him to South Africa.[31]

In the meantime, Mzimba was slowly becoming alienated from the white clergy in Kaffraria. Part of his disenchantment was no doubt caused by the entrenchment of minority white rule throughout southern Africa, but some of his resentment arose from his fellow clergymen's paternalism and discriminatory practices. The success of Mokone's Ethiopian Church seems to have also influenced Mzimba. The political casuist of 1886, the one who had urged his Lovedale congregation to accept white representation in the Cape legislature, was himself now agitating for self-reliance and independence in church government. Mzimba resigned from the Free Church of Scotland on April 6, 1898, and subsequently issued several pamphlets in which he justified his secession. Mzimba, like his contemporary the Blythswood student Amos Qunta, asserted that time was ripe for the black man to stand on his own feet in religious matters and stop relying on white missionaries.

30. Shepherd, Lovedale, 246; Skota (ed.), The African Yearly Register, 75; "The Late Rev. Jeremiah Mzimba," Imvo, July 4, 1911. See the biography by Mzimba's son Livingstone Ntibane Mzimba, Ibali Lobomi Nomsebenzi Womfi Umfundisi Pambani Jeremiah Mzimba (Lovedale, South Africa, 1923).

31. See Mzimba to Smith, May 11, 13, 29, 1893, No. 7798, in Free Church of Scotland Archives; Shepherd, Lovedale, 246–57.

Further, Mzimba posited that church independency and evangelism had been sanctioned by God and the African was therefore
obligated to work toward those ends. On another occasion, Mzimba
said that church independency made Africans more persevering
workers.[32] To give more weight to his secession, Mzimba stated
that his senior position among the black clergy compelled him to
take the lead in setting up an independent church, which he called
the Presbyterian Church of Africa. He was supported by the majority of Lovedale deacons as well as by three-quarters of the congregation, who joined his new church. In the aftermath, Dr. James
Stewart and other missionaries tried to persuade Mzimba to change
his mind. So did Reverend and Mrs. Elijah Makiwane, a conser-
vative African couple who opposed Ethiopianism for the rest of
their lives. In May, 1899, Reverend Makiwane's wife wrote: "Last
year has been a time of great anxiety—so many denominations
have dropped into Africa that go by the name of 'The Ethiopian
Churches,' which exercise their influence over other churches so
as to draw them to themselves. You will have heard of the Rev. P.
J. Mzimba separating himself from the Free Church of Scotland.
Oh, we feel it very much. . . . Mr. Makiwane did his best to urge
Mr. Mzimba to change his opinion." Mzimba's success as a secessionist rested largely on his unflinching determination.[33]

The advent of Ethiopianism at Lovedale, the home of the *Christian Express*, took Free Church of Scotland agents by surprise.
Missionaries there had viewed secessions from the Wesleyan Methodists with a certain sanctimoniousness; now the ball was in their
court. Even a Free Church organ published in Edinburgh expressed
alarm that Ethiopianism had spilled over to their mission, but the
paper blamed Boer racism and Afro-American missionaries: "As if
the local disintegration were not enough, two United States so-

32. Sheila M. Brock, "James Stewart and Lovedale: A Reappraisal of Missionary
Attitudes and African response in the Eastern Cape, South Africa, 1870–1905"
(Ph.D. dissertation, University of Edinburgh, 1974), 386; testimony of Mzimba,
SANAC, II, 794.

33. *SANAC*, IV, 906–907; "The Case of the Rev. P. J. Mzimba, II," *CE*, March
7, 1899; Rev. John D. Don to Dr. Lindsay, September 5, 1898, No. 7798, in Free Church
of Scotland Archives; "Mr. and Mrs. Makiwane," *Free Church of Scotland Monthly*,
May 1, 1899, p. 113. See, for example, an assessment of Mzimba by his contemporary,
Reverend Thomas Chalmers Katiya, in "Letter from South Africa," *Lincoln University Herald*, January, 1912, p. 2: "He was a unique figure in the Bantu community,
and was among its foremost ecclesiastics—He was tried as few men are tried. He
passed through the fire."

cieties hastened to fan the flame. A 'Negro Missionary Society,' proposing to represent the Negro Baptist Churches of America, sent an emissary with a Scottish name into the heart of the Scottish mission field around Lovedale, and baptised 160 natives right away. That is nothing, however, to the action of the 'Right-Rev. Bishop Turner, from the African Methodist Episcopal Church of the United States.' He made Pretoria his headquarters, and gave the new church the basis it wanted by ordaining a large number of native preachers [including a former Lovedale student]." Not surprisingly, the *Christian Express* said Mzimba's reasons for resigning were unconvincing and that he ought to have surrendered parish money and property to the Free Church of Scotland at Lovedale. It ascribed the birth of the Presbyterian Church of Africa to racist motives: "This movement is simply an attempt to organize a church upon colour basis."[34]

The Free Church of Scotland at Lovedale subsequently took Mzimba to court and was awarded £1,361, six buildings, regular books and documents of the African section of Lovedale, and six title deeds to some garden plots. Mzimba reluctantly complied with the court order after several contempt-of-court citations. After the judgment against Mzimba, the *Cape Argus* seemed satisfied with the ruling and reported that "the Mzimba bubble has now burst as far as the immediate legal proceedings are concerned. . . . It is to be hoped that one result will be the return to the fold of many of the seceders when they realize that the 'game is up.'" On the contrary, Mzimba's church by 1902 had spread to Natal, the Orange Free State, and the Transvaal; there were twelve ordained ministers, sixty-five hundred members, and more than twenty thousand adherents.[35]

The metropolitan societies were disturbed by the turn of events in southern Africa. In November, 1898, the Free Church of Scotland sent a pastoral, if somewhat paternalistic, letter to its South African members, imploring them to stop factionalism: "You are children. A mother weeps when her children are hungry. She can-

34. "Schism in Kafraria," *Free Church of Scotland Monthly*, November, 1898, pp. 267–68; "South Africa. Unrest," *ibid.*, June, 1899, p. 130; "The Case of the Rev. P. J. Mzimba, II."

35. "The Lovedale Native Congregation versus Mzimba and Others," *Supplement to CE*, March 7, 1899; "South Africa. Unrest," 130; "Native Disruption"; testimony of Mzimba, *SANAC*, II, 794.

not sleep when they are lost in the forest. She goes to seek them and calls to them." And the letter contained this admonition: "Moreover, if wrong has been done anyone, or brethren have thought that wrong has been done them, is there no remedy but division and strife? Has not our lord Jesus Christ taught us how to act? Are we not to tell it to the Church?" The London Missionary Society was equally anxious to pacify the rebellious evangelist Seile in Botswana. Foreign Secretary R. Wardlow Thompson accordingly wrote the resident missionary at Kanye, saying Seile and other evangelists ought to be allowed to perform some of the duties normally reserved to ordained ministers:

> The question of administration of ordinances by native teachers is confessedly a very perplexing one: Theoretically it is hard to see what objection we . . . can raise against the wish of a native evangelist to undertake such duties. My own belief is that wherever a company of the followers of Christ meet together in His name and in His worship, they are perfectly free to celebrate together the Lord's supper without the intervention of any priest or parson. As a matter of decency and order they should choose amongst them the one who is most trusted and ask him to be their president. . . . I don't myself like the tinge of ecclesiasticism and sacramentarianism which still alludes in our methods in refusing to allow properly qualified evangelists to undertake these services for the church.

Thompson asked missionaries in Botswana to weigh his recommendation in light of their experiences in the field. However, neither the LMS initiative from London nor the pastoral letter from Scotland could conciliate the protagonists in church schism. Instead, these directives tended to harden the attitudes of Ethiopians and members of orthodox churches. By 1899, some observers were predicting that Ethiopianism could well turn into an African Reformation. One writer described it as "a veritable revolutionary movement."[36]

Reformation or no, the AME church was determined to make a success of its work in southern Africa. So in October, 1898, Turner invited Dwane to come to America, this time to acquaint the

36. "Pastoral Letter from the General Assembly to the Ministers, Elders, Deacons and members of the Free Church of Scotland in the Synod of Kaffraria," November 30, 1898, No. 7798, in Free Church of Scotland Archives; CE, February 1, 1899; Thompson to Edwin Lloyd, January 21, 1899, in Box 3, LMS Archives; "Will a Reformation in Africa be Necessary?" CE, November 1, 1899.

newly appointed vicar bishop with AME church doctrine and also to enable him to learn techniques of running the Fourteenth District. He arrived in New York on October 26 and, during the next three months, traveled extensively, giving lectures about his own life and about Africans' living conditions in South Africa. In Atlanta, Dwane informed his audience that "the Africans would never allow the white man to ride roughshod over their country. Africans were rapidly imbibing civilized habits and would soon be able to run great civilized governments. Then they would say to the European nations, 'Hands Off.' " Dwane seems to have impressed his audiences and newspapermen alike. The latter invariably described him as a learned man and an accomplished linguist; black audiences were delighted to "see and shake hands with a real pure African." Some parishes renamed their churches after the vicar.[37] It was certainly a measure of the man's influence that "Dwane" missionary societies were formed in several AME church districts. Dwane took advantage of his popularity to solicit funds for the proposed school in the Cape to educate AME church members as well as to serve notice to white missionary societies that the Afro-American mission was going to outstrip them in effectiveness. A December, 1898, report said of Dwane: "He says education is a burning question in Africa, and that our success in mission work depends a great deal on this matter. The Vicar is desperately in earnest about this subject, and hates returning to Africa without being satisfied that something has been done to give good education to our youths in South Africa. Before he left Africa he says his soul was eased and gladdened by the ladies of the W.M.M. [Women's Mite Missionary] Society of Ohio, who wrote him encouraging letters [about the school]." Estimates of the cost of the school ranged from $10,000 to $30,000.[38]

Reports published in the *Voice of Missions* suggest that before he left America in January, 1899, Dwane was given assurances that money for the proposed school would be forthcoming. In addition, officers of the Missionary Department of the AME church justified

37. "Vicar Dwane Visits This Country"; Edward Roux, *Time Longer Than Rope* (Madison, Wis. 1966), 81; see, for example, "Vicar Bishop Dwane, the Connecting Link," *VOM*, March 15, 1899; Wright *et al.* (eds.), *Encyclopaedia*, 318–21.

38. Nannie Bush, "Dwane Missionary Society," *VOM*, November, 1898; "Dwane, the Connecting Link"; H. B. Parks, "Kaffir University," *VOM*, March, 1899; "The Queenstown College," *ibid.*, March 15, 1899.

the construction of a "Kaffir University," not just a high school, by saying that it was the only effective way to prepare the African for the expanding British Empire's demand for skilled manpower. In this connection, Bishop H. B. Parks wrote:

> The Kaffir University, industrial and religious, at Queenstown, South Africa . . . has a good, straightforward proposition to back the request. Cecil Rhodes will have his railway running from Queenstown to Cairo in a few years, and the whole of interior Africa will be opened up. Civilization can sometimes travel too fast for the civilizee. If the African resists, he will be exterminated. If he takes to whisky and miscellaneous vice, he will meet the fate of the American Indian. If he gets his industrial training first, and meets civilization in the right spirit, he may become a strong and useful member of society. That is the mission of the Queenstown School.[39]

Nevertheless, Vicar Dwane returned to South Africa empty-handed. He continued to organize the Fourteenth District, and in March, 1899, membership had risen to 12,500 souls. By that time also, there were sixteen South African students enrolled at Wilberforce University, and another student was studying at Meharry Medical College in Tennessee. The cost of educating South Africans in America was, as Dwane had indicated to Turner in 1897, depleting the coffers of the AME church. The need to provide school facilities in South Africa in order to reduce expenses for the church was becoming increasingly apparent. Bishop Parks, the secretary for missions, kept harping on the importance of building a school in the Fourteenth District. He drew parallels between the plight of South Africans and Afro-Americans, saying that a college in Queenstown would serve the same purpose that Wilberforce University filled for Negroes: "What would the condition of the American Negro be today if at the close of the Civil War [1865], there had been [no] Wilberforce in existence? This school is to be the Wilberforce of South Africa, will we let our brothers wait as long as we did? Or knowing how great a boon we grant will we give it when it will do most good?"[40]

In the event, all the carefully reasoned arguments for the proposed college came to nought—or were not implemented at a pace

39. See, for example, H. B. Parks, "Redemption of Africa, the American Negro's Burden," VOM, September, 1899; Bush, "Dwane Missionary Society"; "Dwane, the Connecting Link"; and "The Queenstown College"; Parks, "Kaffir University."
40. "Dwane, the Connecting Link."

satisfactory to Dwane. The official history of the AME church states that the delay in funding the school was deliberate: the church was reluctant to entrust large sums of money to a vicar who was new at the job. The upshot was that Dwane, who evidently had staked his prestige on the school project, lost face. The insult came at a time when he was pondering two issues concerning the AME church. One arose from his reading of the church's *Book of Discipline*, which seemed to him to highlight the presence of an Anglican minister at the consecration of the church's founder, Richard Allen. Dwane concluded that the AME church derived its ecclesiastical authority from the Anglican church. Although Dwane's logic was questionable, he nevertheless concluded that the AME church was founded on an unsound theological basis and that all holy orders from such a source were doctrinally fraudulent. The other matter Dwane was considering had to do with the apparent discriminatory practice he had observed during his stay in America, where he found out that most Afro-American parishes preferred light-skinned ministers to dark-skinned ones. Consequently, Bishop Dwane decided to sever his connection with the AME church.[41] He called a special conference at Queenstown; approximately thirty-nine officers were there. According to loyal AME elders who attended that fateful October 6 meeting, Dwane said a lot more than he was willing to concede before the South African Native Affairs Commission in 1903. At the October meeting, Reverend J. Z. Tantsi, an elder and a member of the Cape Conference, charged Dwane with several procedural errors, which the vicar was unwilling to correct. The peremptory manner in which he conducted the meeting was also criticized. For example, Elder Tantsi challenged the constitutionality of holding a meeting while delegates from the Transvaal Conference were unable to attend (martial regulations had been imposed because of the Anglo-Boer war). Yet Dwane was determined to proceed.[42]

He was reported to have started his address by extolling the validity of the episcopacy of the Church of England in contrast to the alleged irregularity of the AME church episcopacy, a stance no

41. Wright *et al.* (eds.), *Encyclopaedia*, 319–20; testimony of Dwane, *SANAC*, II, 708–709. For Dwane's effort to set up the college, see Parks, "Redemption of Africa." See also the bishop's letter, "The Episcopal Church of the Province of South Africa," *CE*, October 1, 1900.

42. "The A.M.E. Conference at Queenstown," *CE*, March 1, 1900.

doubt designed to pave the way for his joining the Anglicans. He criticized Turner for failing to fulfill his promise to build a training school in South Africa. In doing so, Dwane was said to have "rehearsed nearly every point of [Turner's] failure and weakness" before calling for a motion to secede from the AME church. At this point Tantsi dissented: "I cannot help, I must attack your address. Such an address is unconstitutional. I cannot tolerate it. Now, you have already passed your decision without allowing the motion to be discussed by the Conference. You have taken [adopted] an unusual policy." Tantsi was overruled, and the motion was read by Reverend Henry R. Ngcayiya and passed, despite another objection by Tantsi, who was seconded by Reverend Mpumlwana. Before the vote was taken, Reverend P. S. Kuze asked the vicar bishop if the act of secession did not abrogate the oath of allegiance he had sworn before Bishop Turner. Dwane reportedly denied ever having taken such an oath. Yet Turner's report of 1898 contains a copy of Dwane's April 18, 1898, letter:

> The Rt. Rev. H. M. Turner, D.D., LL.D., Your Grace—
> Having heard the request made of you by a resolution of the two Annual Conferences, I most humbly and respectfully beg to inform you that I am a loyal minister of the African Methodist Episcopal Church, and am determined to live and die so.
> If it will be in keeping with your judgment that I should be the Chief representative of the A.M.E. church in this country, I shall be obedient and loyal to the regular Bishop of Africa, whoever he may be, or any other ruling power of the Church, and do all in my power to unite our people and build up a great wing of our church in South Africa, and should I be directed to cease exercising the functions of the office, I will comply without a murmur and fill any appointment assigned me. While I may not be the man for the place, nor do I covet the hard work and travel, which the duties will involve with its sacrifices, yet I see that such an arrangement is an absolute necessity in our present conditions, if it is possible to make it.

Nevertheless, Reverend Tantsi and other loyalists overlooked the fact that church reformers, like political revolutionaries, hardly ever respect the conventions of institutions they seek to overthrow. Dwane simply denied ever making pledges to Turner and proceeded to influence the conference to approve the motion on secession. He even succeeded in getting the support of Reverend Mangena Mokone, the founder of the Ethiopian Church. However, four ministers refused to join the rebellion: P. S. Kuze, Abraham Magqibesa, William G. Mashaloba, and J. Z. Tantsi. They wrote to Bishop Turner, restating their loyalty to him and the AME church. They urged Turner to appoint a bishop to replace Dwane, as the latter had refused to surrender the seal of the Fourteenth District, without which they could not function. They also urged Turner to repudiate Bishop Gaines's contention, which had appeared in the *Voice of Missions*, that the district did not have valid links to the mother church in America: ''The strong presumption is that we hold no connected links with America, and that we should produce minutes of the meetings of [the] House of Bishops, approving of action of Bishop Turner in ordaining Vicar Bishop J. M. Dwane. This the prime minister [of the Cape] has demanded previous of Rev. J. M. Dwane's withdrawal, and hence the refusal of our holding marriages in our churches in Cape Colony. This also we take as one of the reasons of Vicar Bishop Dwane's withdrawal from our church.''[43] In November, 1899, the four ministers met with four other loyal ministers to chart plans for preventing secessions. They wanted to reinforce the faithful and to try to persuade secessionists to come back to the AME church fold. Although Dwane stood his ground, the loyalists succeeded with Mokone, who rescinded his resignation.

In the meantime, Reverend Francis Gow, one of the loyalists, had written to Bishop Turner about the turn of events. Gow's letter dealt at great length with Dwane's reasons for withdrawing from the church, stating more or less what was contained in the loyalists' letter to Turner. When Turner learned of the secession of Dwane and others, he was particularly disturbed to find that Mokone had joined the rebellion: ''We are equally surprised that Rev. M. M. Mokone should join the revolting crusade, for we had intended to recommend him to the General Conference for a position of honour and trust, as he was the founder of the Ethiopian Church, and a man of transcendent virtues.'' It appears that even before Turner's letter reached South Africa, Mokone, who had already withdrawn his resignation from the AME church, had written Turner about the October 6 meeting and why he had changed his mind: ''Of course, I was one of the 30 who were in favour of it [secession]. But now I change my mind, for I feel not justified to treat you in this

43. *Ibid.*; ''Bishop Turner Renders His Report''; ''Another Account of the Conference,'' *CE*, March 1, 1900.

manner, to let your gray hairs go to the grave with tears and sorrow caused by me. I rather suffer with you if there is any thing for suffering. Therefore, Holy Father, I wish you to accept for 'bona fide' this, my seeing my folly for attempting such steps as that to pain you and your good men.'' Mokone then recalled his role in the creation of the Fourteenth District: ''For it was I who sent you a letter in 1895 to ask you for your discipline, which you did and with great pleasure. It was I who sent Vicar Bishop Dwane from Ethiopian Church in 1896 to amalgamate with the A.M.E. Church. It was I who sent for you to come over here, which you did in 1898. I therefore, withdraw from all, I have thought of it before and even for the future. I wish you to forgive and forget and treat me as before. I promise faithfully before our living God and men to be faithful to the Methodist Episcopal Church for the future.'' Mokone pleaded with Turner to send a representative to South Africa and also recommended that Afro-American officers working in South Africa be paid by the church in America.[44]

In a postscript, Mokone elaborated on his reasons for rejoining the AME church. He feared that the world would ridicule Turner for an apparently triumphal tour of South Africa that crumbled in a morass of rebellion hardly twelve months after the bishop returned to America. Bishop Gaines, the critic of Turner's tour, might well be vindicated and triumph over Turner. Further, the rebellion was creating the unfortunate impression that black people could not work together. Finally, his own integrity compelled him not to act in bad faith by resigning behind Turner's back.[45]

Some parishes criticized their delegates for having supported Dwane. At Rondebosch, Cape, Reverend Adriaanse was censured for speaking in favor of the motion to secede. Minutes of a meeting held at Rondebosch on October 30, 1899, show that Reverend Adriaanse apologized. The following question was asked: ''Did you not move at the Conference that America misled us with money, etc., and you would sever your connection with this [AME] church and join the English Church?'' Reverend Adriaanse replied: ''I did; but am sorry, as Bishop Dwane told me a lie and misled me; Mr. F. Gow has explained the whole thing to me.'' The meeting nevertheless resolved to suspend Adriaanse, pending a decision from

44. Francis Gow, ''Dreadful Letter from South Africa,'' *CE*, February 1, 1900; ''Subsequent Proceedings in the A.M.E. Church,'' *CE*, March 1, 1900.

45. ''Subsequent Proceedings in the A.M.E. Church.''

Turner. This action angered Adriaanse, who reportedly left "behaving more like a madman than a minister of religion."[46]

For his part, Dwane moved swiftly to implement the October 6 resolution. He had shown his displeasure.[47] In fact, he had taken preliminary steps to affiliate his group and the Anglican church long before the secession. He had held several secret meetings with the Anglican archbishop of Cape Town, the Most Reverend W. W. Jones. The Anglican church encouraged Dwane to secede. When he did, the first crack in the hitherto apparently united Ethiopian movement elated Anglicans and Protestants who had long accused the group of being "sheep stealers" and "missionary raiders," that is, luring members from orthodox churches to the separatist group. In the aftermath, the archbishop and the bishops of the Anglican Church of the Province of South Africa could inform their members in 1900:

> In the early part of the last year the leaders of that body [Dwane's group] began to make approaches to members of our church with a view to securing for their organization a more stable foundation of ecclesiastical order. The "Ethiopian" movement had originated with certain natives of this country who, having left all religious bodies to which they generally belonged, subsequently allied themselves with the A.M.E. Church of America. On further study and investigation the leaders became dissatisfied as to the historical continuity of that church and the orders which it professed to confer. They then spontaneously sought for further instruction at our hands; and the result of the intercourse and correspondence with Bishops and clergy of the Province . . . was the conviction on the part of the leaders of the Ethiopian community that they ought to seek in the church of the Province for that security in Catholic and Apostolic order which they had sought in vain elsewhere.

In August, 1900, Dwane's group, Ibandla Lase Tiyopia (the Order of Ethiopia), was formally accepted into the Anglican church; the group retained its distinct identity within the province of South Africa. In December, 1900, Reverend Dwane was ordained follow-

46. *Ibid.*; "Another account of the Conference."

47. See, for example, a statement attributed to Bishop Turner in "The A.M.E. Conference at Queenstown": "We knew before he [Dwane] left that he was smarting under what he regarded an insult, both to himself and his people in South Africa. . . . The truth is Brother Dwane left this country with revolt in his heart, and he carried out his contemplated scheme." Turner was probably referring to Dwane's anger at the church's failure to build a school in South Africa.

ing his success at an examination in theology that was conducted by two Anglican priests. The Anglicans signed a compact with Ibandla Lase Tiyopia in which both groups spelled out their special relationship.[48]

At about the time Dwane was hatching his plans for secession, another Afro-American church group sent an outspoken minister to South Africa. The National Baptist Convention sent Reverend Charles S. Morris in 1899. The Baptists had planted their mission in South Africa in 1894, when Reverend R. A. Jackson started a church near Cape Town. But they had had relatively little impact on South African life until Morris arrived in July, 1899. Morris visited many parts of the country, including Lovedale, and baptized more than one thousand converts during his short stay. In September, 1899, he sent a report of his activities, the potential for missionary work, and his personal observations on African life in South Africa to the *Voice of Missions*. Morris recognized the quality of leadership provided by Ethiopians, such as Gow, Mzimba, Walter Rubusana, and Jonas Goduka, who succeeded Tile as the leader of the Thembu church. The African evangelists who manned several European and white American missionary societies' schools also impressed Morris. He described them as the backbone of mission work, though the effectiveness of their service was minimized by the white missionary:

> Our White brother has sent them out. They have gone into the highways and byways and preached the gospel to every creature. They have taught the little schools. They have done the most towards building all the churches. They have contributed most towards translating the Bible. But when reports go in to be published to the World, alas! they are ignored and unmentioned, and White Missionaries—especially these latter-day apologies for their grand old predecessors, who were missionaries indeed—get all the credit for all this hard work, although many of them do precious little except dress in fine linen, fare sumptuously and lay schemes to keep the really able native ministers and missionaries out of places they ought to have and which the natives desire to see them have, but which it is the growing policy of the younger set of men to hold for European friends.

Morris asserted that Ethiopian secessionists were justified in breaking with established churches. He lamented the paternalism of

48. "The Episcopal Church of the Province of South Africa"; "The Ethiopian Order," *CE*, October 1, 1900. See Appendix E.

European and American philanthropists who failed to "realize that black 'boys' ever become 'of age.' "[49]

Reverend Morris wrote an article for the *New York Age* about his observations in South Africa and urged blacks to go there as missionaries. The paper endorsed this part of Morris' article but cautioned that young blacks be trained first. Toward the end of 1899, Conrad A. A. Rideout arrived in South Africa. He was previously a district judge in Pennsylvania before he went on a seafaring adventure with his family. In South Africa he became a free-lance missionary of the AME church and, together with another Afro-American adventurer called Harry Dean, seems to have had the financial resources to enable him to proselytize without the help of the church. He performed that task to some effect. *Imvo*, which had had a lull in its adverse comments on Ethiopianism, had its penchant for criticism reactivated by the arrival of the extroverted Morris and Rideout. And again, the editor of *Imvo* displayed some familiarity with what the Afro-American press was currently reporting on southern Africa. *Imvo*'s December 4, 1899, editorial entitled "Negro Immigration" was clearly at variance with Turner's immigration schemes. It also opposed the modest pleas by Ethiopian officers that more qualified Afro-Americans be sent to South Africa to help start new schools. The editorial criticized Reverend Morris' report to the *New York Age* for its intemperate language, especially Afro-Americans' being challenged to accept missionary work in South Africa or continue to "cling like a drowning man to the coat tails of the white man." *Imvo* objected to the bitterness that characterized race relations in America but prayed that it should not be transplanted to a supposedly tolerant South Africa. Morris was also criticized for suggesting that whites could not be effective missionaries because, he alleged, they could not empathize with the African soul. Finally, Afro-Americans in South Africa were criticized for their Ethiopian sympathies and their apparent ingratitude to American whites who, *Imvo* claimed, had provided them opportunities for advancement.[50]

49. Jordan, *Up the Ladder in Foreign Missions*, 21–23; J. Dexter Taylor (ed.), *Christianity and the Natives of South Africa* (Lovedale, South Africa, 1928), 79; see also W. L. Williams, *Evangelization*, 71; Charles S. Morris, "South Africa and Her People," *CE*, February 1, 1900.

50. "The Negroes and the Native," *Imvo*, December 4, 1899 (excerpt from *New York Age*); Dean, *The Pedro Garino*, 139–45; "Negro Immigration," *Imvo*, December 4, 1899. See Appendix D.

Nevertheless, as the nineteenth century was coming to a close, the AME church was drawing on its eighty years of experience in mission work in Africa, the Americas, and Haiti to refute the more excessive criticism coming from both religious and secular quarters. Another source of strength was a small group of white missionaries who were beginning to support the principle of self-determination in church government. Significantly, one missionary publication questioned the wisdom of "maintaining too long in a state of tutelage a native church already old, which would have been capable of exercising a certain control over itself." If this slight change in whites' attitude was salutary, the true source of resilience for the black missionary movement—and the AME church—was the persistence of the Afro-American's prophetic vision of ministering in Africa. This dream remained utterly impervious to adverse criticism. In the AME church the bedrock of this almost mystical connection between Africans of the diaspora and those on the continent was Bishop Turner himself, who, in addition to his familiar support for the South African mission, declared in 1899: "I confidently believe that as God prepared the heart of Simon Peter to receive and instruct Cornelius, and at the same time taught Cornelius where to find Peter, so He has moved upon our hearts here in America and theirs in South Africa, to the building up of His Kingdom among men."[51] Turner certainly captured the prevailing mood to minister in Africa, upon which clergy and laymen alike were determined to act.

51. "Will a Reformation in Africa be Necessary?"; Turner, "My Trip to South Africa," 809–13.

4/Growth of the AME Church, the Witch Hunt, and Its Aftermath

The beginning of the twentieth century saw an improved climate for the growth of the Ethiopian movement and the entrenchment of the AME church in southern Africa. But the new favorable conditions came after intense soul-searching, self-criticism, and bickering within all sections of southern African society. It was only after the publication of the South African Native Affairs Commission (SANAC) report in 1905 that the independent-church movement was absolved of subversive intent and grudgingly allowed to operate. The AME church benefited from the new dispensation.

The missionary zeal was kept alive in the wake of Bishop Turner's visit to South Africa. In this respect, AME church members in America must have been encouraged by a report published in the *Voice of Missions* early in 1900. A white American missionary stationed in Bulawayo, Rhodesia (now Zimbabwe), declared that black Americans were suited to evangelize the Ndebele and the Shona. Describing a group of workers she had watched, Mrs. van Blunk said, "I asked myself 'who is going to be the instrument in God's hands to touch and call into activity this latent power?' A voice seemed to say, 'no one will ever move them but they of the same rich, warm blood, who are already God's children—the Afro-American.'"[1]

Mrs. van Blunk was apparently unaware of earlier attempts to plant the AME church in colonial Rhodesia. In 1896, Reverend M. C. Ncube founded the first AME church station in Bulawayo. However, this pioneer mission suffered a setback in 1898, when Reverend Ncube joined the Dutch Reformed church. The Bulawayo mission was revived in 1900 when the AME church in South Africa

1. Mrs. J. M. S. van Blunk, "Letter from Bulawayo," November 24, 1899, in *VOM*, March 1, 1900.

sent Reverend S. J. Mabote to take charge of the ailing station.[2]
Even before Mrs. van Blunk had written to the bishop, Turner
received a letter from Reverend R. A. Jackson, pleading for selective
Afro-American emigration to South Africa.

Reverend Jackson, whose missionary activity was a little more
restrained than that of the flamboyant Turner, painted a rather
gloomy picture of Afro-American political life in the United States
and asserted: "Fellow Negroes, I believe that we are on an active
volcano today in America." In contrast, Reverend Jackson conveyed the impression that South Africa had rich resources and a
salubrious climate. "There are gold and diamonds here in innu-
merable quantities. Then ivory and ostrich feathers, coal and cop-
per, wool and wax, corn and wine, a land of milk and honey." He
warned that the scramble for South Africa was intense and that any
procrastination on the part of blacks might well jeopardize their
prospects of getting a share of this wealth because prejudiced white
Americans were settling in South Africa in large numbers. "Those
Negro haters come out here, amalgamate with the Dutch, pose as
Dutchmen and give the Boers a bad name." Reverend Jackson
might have added that the mining complexes, especially those on
The Rand, were attracting all sorts of whites, from America and
from Europe as well. And Johannesburg was indeed growing like
a mushroom. Still, he warned fellow Afro-Americans that they
might be prohibited from entering South Africa if they did not
immigrate in substantial numbers and whites by default became
the entrenched political power.[3]

Reverend Jackson proposed an imaginative emigration scheme
that would "leave the poor of the land behind" in America and
would set up an enterprise of four thousand well-to-do blacks.
These merchants would form two hundred subsidiary companies
capitalized at a little over $2.5 million.[4] This ambitious project,
which seems to have been inspired by the commercial syndicates

2. D. D. Khomela *et al.*, "Historical Sketch of the Zambezi Conference" (Ms
in Makokoba AME Church Archives, Bulawayo, Zimbabwe).

3. R. A. Jackson, "A Baptist Missionary in South Africa," *VOM*, November,
1899. By the late 1890s there were more than fifteen hundred Americans in South
Africa. See Manion to Acting State Secretary, January 15, 1896, in RG 59, Microcopy
T. 191, Roll 18; Keto, "Black American Involvements," 6–11; McAdoo, "A letter from
South Africa."

4. *Ibid.* The members would then be divided into four classes of one thousand

Reverend Jackson saw all over South Africa at that time, does not appear to have been implemented. But the idea of emigrating to Africa remained a lively, if mostly theoretical issue well into the twentieth century. In December, 1899, A. E. White, a black doctor who practiced in Media, Pennsylvania, wrote to the *Voice* in support of emigration, arguing that Africa was the only place on Earth where the black could hope to live in any meaningful way the precept "Government by the people for the people."[5] In the same month, Pamela M. Rideout, the eighteen-year-old daughter of the free-lance AME missionary Con. A. A. Rideout, wrote from Cape Town and said glowing things about South African blacks and the

---

each, and each group was determined by the amount of money to be deposited in a common fund.

Class A

50 Companies of 20 persons each; and each company designated as A1, A2, A3, A4, etc., up to the full number of 50.

Each person in Class A to deposit in the Company's treasury ....$ 1,000
Each Company in Class A to deposit in the Company's treasury   20,000
50 Companies in Class A to deposit in the Company's treasury 1,000,000

Class B

50 Companies of 20 persons each; and each company to be known as B1, B2, B3, B4, etc., up to the full number of 50.

Each person in Class B to deposit in the Company's treasury ....$ 800
Each Company in class B to deposit in the Company's treasury.........   16,000
50 Companies in Class B to deposit in the Company's treasury   800,000

Class C

50 Companies of 20 persons each; and each company to be known as C1, C2, C3, C4, etc., up to the full number of 50.

Each person in Class C to deposit in the Company's treasury............$ 500
Each Company in Class C to deposit in the Company's treasury   10,000
50 Companies in Class C to deposit in the Company's treasury   500,000

Class D

50 Companies of 20 persons each; and each company to be known as D1, D2, D3, D4, etc., up to the full number 50.

Each person in Class D to deposit in the Company's treasury............$ 250
Each Company in Class D to deposit in the Company's treasury   5,000
50 Companies in Class D to deposit in the Company's treasury.........   250,000

The Entire Enterprise

And you have 200 companies owned by 4,000 merchants with a capital of $2,550,000

5. A. E. White, "African Emigration," *VOM*, December 1, 1899. For contemporary views and schemes, see Box 359, Booker T. Washington Papers, Library of Congress; C. C. Scott, *Emigration, Submission, or What* (Columbia, S. C., 1907); Redkey, *Black Exodus*.

bright prospects for mission work in that country. She herself was going to teach in Natal. Of educational opportunities for blacks, she said:

> They are allowed little or no opportunity to attain the higher rudiments of education and knowledge. And why? Because the whites know that they are a race of people that have made vast progress, yes, for the past few years more than any other people upon the globe. I say again, if they were to be given just a third of the chances that our American boys and girls have had, there will be no race of people to surpass them. Dear Bishop, I would ask you that you impress again upon the minds of our brothers, sisters, sons and daughters of America to wake up and unite with our Bishop in redeeming the land of our fathers. . . . Let us all unite with one aim. . . for the redemption . . . of our people here, and by so doing . . . "Ethiopia shall have stretched forth her hands to God."[6]

Whatever indecisiveness the Missionary Department might have felt about its South African venture, the need for a representative in the Cape was repeated by so many clergy and laymen that by December, 1899, Bishop Turner had made up his mind to send someone to replace Dwane and reorganize the Fourteenth District. After consulting the Council of Bishops, Bishop Turner sent Reverend I. N. Fitzpatrick to South Africa early in 1900. Upon arrival, Fitzpatrick went about trying to bring some order to the district. He convened a meeting of the South African Conference on March 8, 1900, at which he reinforced the faithful clergy and laity of the AME church.[7] He also discussed with the Cape Colony government the matter of AME clergy being able to solemnize marriages, a privilege they had been denied because of unfavorable publicity the church had received and uncertainties about the church's legal standing. Fitzpatrick reported on his activities:

> On the very day of my arrival Mr. Dwane was holding his Conference [of the Order of Ethiopia] at Queenstown for the purpose of making inroads into our Church. My presence, however, has put a quietus on his movements and confidence is restored; hence a bright future is before us. . . . I called, with Mr. Francis Gow, on February 10th to see the American Consul, and asked an introduction by him to the Prime

6. "A Letter from Miss P. M. Rideout of South Africa," December 26, 1899, in *VOM*, March 1, 1900.

7. I. N. Fitzpatrick, "Letter of Great Interest from Elder Fitzpatrick to the Church, *VOM*, April 1, 1900.

Minister of Cape Colony. This honour . . . was conferred. The enclosed communication will explain itself. The subject matter, however, is the rights of our ministers to solemnize marriages. I do this because I want to submit a printed document covering all points at dispute, so his honour, The Premier, may have the matter set clearly before him, and I feel assured that justice will be done us.[8]

Fitzpatrick subsequently wrote to W. P. Schreiner, prime minister of the Cape Colony, acquainting him with the fact that the AME church was a legally constituted body in the United States, with one million members, seven thousand ordained ministers, and more than three million followers including those in Canada, the Caribbean, and West Africa. He enclosed a document from the governor of Alabama to support his contention that the church was duly recognized in America. In reply, the prime minister's office regretted that several issues compelled his government to defer recognizing the AME church. These ranged from the legal position of the vicar bishop in the AME church, which had not been resolved even before Dwane seceded, to the general cloud of uncertainty and suspicion that had surrounded the church in South Africa especially in the wake of Dwane's departure. The Cape government would have to await the General Conference of the AME church in 1900. Then they could determine the viability of the church with more certainty.[9]

Besides attending to administrative duties, Fitzpatrick devoted part of his stay in South Africa to preaching and converting new members. At Kalk Bay in the Cape, he led a service that resembled a revival, after which he reported that "among the many who gave us their hand was a German and Mohammedan. This German is truly converted, and desires to secure local preacher's license in our Church."[10] This indicates that the AME church was not exclusively for blacks, contrary to what some critics of the church persistently alleged.

At the same time, Dwane's secession, though not altogether

8. Fitzpatrick quoted in "The AME Church Movement," *CE*, June 1, 1900, pp. 88–89.

9. I. N. Fitzpatrick to Prime Minister W. P. Shreiner, February 26, 1900, *ibid.*; L. J. Coppin, "The Outlook in the 14th District," *AME Church Review*, January, 1904; A. Dale [for Schreiner] to Fitzpatrick, March 3, 1900, in "The AME Church Movement," 88–89.

10. Fitzpatrick to Turner, February 28, 1900, in Fitzpatrick, "Letter of Great Interest," *VOM*, April 1, 1900.

catastrophic, had its effects throughout the Fourteenth District. Parishes debated several issues arising from it, and some reluctant secessionists stopped their temporary flirtation with Dwane's brand of Ethiopianism. For example, early in 1900, leading members of the AME church in the Pretoria District met to reassess the impact of Dwane's secession. They declared that Dwane's convening the October 6, 1899, meeting was illegal. And they resolved, among other things:"(1) That they protest most emphatically against the revolt led by Vicar Bishop Dwane and Brother M. M. Mokone; (2) That they continue to remain true and loyal to their mother Church in America; (3) That they record their feelings of intense surprise and deep regret at the action of Brother Mokone, the founder of the Ethiopian Church; (4) That Senior Bishop H. M. Turner be requested to kindly use all his influence at the approaching General Conference to obtain its sanction to the appointment of an American Bishop or general superintendent over South Africa." Nor was that the end of accusations against the leader of the Order of Ethiopia. Dwane was further discredited by Reverend Fitzpatrick, who depicted him as a swindler, alleging that during his two visits to America, the vicar had received "large sums of money," which he misappropriated. Fitzpatrick did not say how much money was involved, so he was probably out to smear Dwane. Nevertheless, several church members wrote Turner, commending Fitzpatrick's work and criticizing Dwane's secession and his character. One correspondent regretted that an indigenous bishop had let the church down and suggested that the Fourteenth District would be better served by an Afro-American bishop. This view had prevailed at the January, 1900, meeting of the Transvaal Conference.[11]

The General Conference of the AME church met in Atlanta in 1900, and South Africa was represented by five delegates, Reverend Mangena Mokone and Reverend Francis Gow among them. The General Conference elected Bishop L. J. Coppin to serve as the first Afro-American resident bishop in South Africa. Coppin's impending departure early in 1901 provoked yet another spate of calls for more vigorous missionary and new emigration schemes by black

11. "Resolutions of the Pretoria District of the AME Church," CE, July 2, 1900; I. N. Fitzpatrick, "The Eloquent and Timely Address Before the South African Conference," [March 14, 1900], in VOM, May 1, 1900; "Notes on the AME Church," CE, July 2, 1900. Mokone had in fact rejoined the AME church.

Americans. Not surprisingly, the occasion provided Bishop Turner a convenient platform for pronouncing his now familiar views on emigration, for extolling African culture, and for impugning racism in America. In his view, Coppin's departure

> was not only a unique and unprecedented event in the history of [the AME] church, but the respect shown by all classes and grades of our people and the farewell receptions that were given a manifestation of the high regard our people entertain for Africa. Though many pretend considerable opposition to African emigration they admire the man or woman who is willing to make what they call a sacrifice for the enlightenment of that benighted continent, which, after all, is not near so benighted as many would have us believe. Some of the world's finest scholars, greatest linguists and brainiest men are Africans. Yet we grant that millions and hundreds of millions are in heathen darkness and do not possess the customs and habits of what we regard as civilization. But with all the charges of barbarism and savagery that we bring against them, and the further fact that they do not worship God as we do and conform to our civilized modes and habits, they are too enlightened to form themselves into mobs and hang, burn, butcher and kill men by the thousand because they are the victims of drunkenness and passion and possess a religion that judges men by the colour of their skin and the texture of their hair.

Turner maintained that his assertions were factual and that they were based on his personal investigations in Africa and the United States.[12]

Turner's rather favorable appraisal of African culture and his conception of the role he thought Afro-Americans ought to play in Africa were supported by Reverend A. Henry Attaway, who in 1901 joined Reverend Coppin's missionary staff in Cape Town. Attaway advanced the view that American technological expertise ought to be made available so Africa could exploit its resources to the fullest. An opponent of mass emigration to Africa, Attaway was convinced that only qualified Afro-Americans should enter the missionary field. But, like Turner, Attaway minimized the effectiveness of white missionaries, asserting that they were ill-suited for mission work in Africa, or at least they were not as efficient as black Americans were. Also like Turner, Attaway justified his assertion with historical and divine reasons, arguing that when Afro-

12. Bishop H. M. Turner, "Bishop L. J. Coppin D. D., Departs for South Africa," *VOM*, February 1, 1901. See Appendix G.

Americans were enslaved, they had in fact served an apprentice-ship, which whites had not, to enable them to go back to Africa as skilled workmen. He further observed that slavery had engendered in the Afro-American love, joy, peace, gentleness, faith, and tem-perance, which were a sine qua non for any successful missionary, but which were wanting in whites.[13] While this assessment has a tinge of bias and even racism, there is little doubt that the majority of black missionaries were spurred by a reverse sense of superiority to join the missionary movement. It was a lowly man's way to assert himself in a white-dominated world that denied the black man his human dignity.

The AME church was building up its mission in an environ-ment in which church independency was on the rise. Sects were multiplying all over South Africa as groups broke away from white or black parent churches to pursue unfettered religious existence. Yet what was striking to white observers was the secession of blacks from white-dominated churches; whites seemed to fear the potential for African political revolt. In Natal, Reverend Mbiyana Ngidi's sect survived in spite of a concerted effort by American Zulu Mission agents and Natal government officers to stamp it out. The American Zulu Mission had other problems to contend with, namely, two other Ethiopian cells, one in Natal at Table Mountain led by Simungu B. Shibe, and the other led by Reverend Sungusa Nyuswa in Johannesburg. Nyuswa had orginally worked in the American Zulu Mission in Natal, but accepted an invitation to lead the Johannesburg faction after its founder, the evangelist Fokoti, died. In 1897 both cells withdrew from the American church, tak-ing with them about half the membership at each place. The seceders joined hands to launch the "Zulu Congregational Church." Subsequently, both sides attempted to reconcile seceders and the American Zulu Mission, and some measure of success was achieved. Part of the reason was that some white missionaries did some rethinking in an effort to come to terms with Ethiopianism. As a result, in 1900, Reverend Pugh, who had hitherto been a hard liner on seceders, could inform his superiors in Boston: "Experi-ence and knowledge of the whole history of the independent move-ment have enabled me to recognize the fact that had I known what I know now I should have acted differently in respect to uSimungu

13. A. Henry Attaway, "The Part the Twentieth Century Negro Will Play in the World's Civilization," *VOM*, February 1, 1901.

at the outset. There are some things I have done during my time at Table Mountain believing then that I was acting for the highest good which I now wish I had not done." This change of attitude paid off: in 1901, American missionaries succeeded in bringing back to their church most of the seceders at Table Mountain and a sizable number in Johannesburg. However, the church was unable to bring back Shibe, whose sect flourished in spite of government opposition. Natal government officials looked on Shibe with disfavor, believing that the Ethiopian politicized the Zulu. He was known to sympathize with Afrikaners during the Anglo-Boer war (1899–1902) and he therefore was closely watched. But the government was unable to find sufficient incriminating evidence to bring a charge against him.[14]

In the Cape, Reverend Mzimba continued to wield influence. Shortly after his break with the Free Church of Scotland in 1898, he was joined by Reverend John Sibiya, who, like Mzimba himself, had served for many years as a minister at Lovedale. Reverend Sibiya became disillusioned and sought refuge in Mzimba's Presbyterian Church of Africa. Mzimba also ordained Moses Mbele, who left the Dutch Reformed church in the 1890s and subsequently formed his own church, the Ibandla lika Mosi (Church of Moses), in the Umvoti area in Natal. The Free Church of Scotland in northern Natal experienced a schism when a group of blacks banded together and left the parent church. In 1903 an American missionary reported to the Natal Missionary Conference his findings on this self-styled Uhlanga Church (National Church): "The purchase by natives of thousands of acres in open competition with Europeans, thus perhaps giving a sense of superiority, the exemption of many from Native Law, tribal politics, questions of discipline and consequent friction with missionaries, were all contributing causes to the schism." The sect was said to preach self-determination in government and was suspected of sympathizing with Afrikaners during the recent Anglo-Boer war.[15]

In Natal, Reverend Charles S. Morris of the National Baptist Convention was making good use of his time in South Africa, combining evangelism with politics. In 1900 he informed an ecu-

14. Shula Marks, *Reluctant Rebellion: The 1906–8 Disturbances in Natal* (Oxford, 1970), 63–64; "General Letter of the American Zulu Mission, June 1898," in American Zulu Mission, 1890–1899, Vol. I, Documents.

15. F. B. Bridgman, "The Ethiopian Movement, I," *CE*, October 1, 1903.

menical conference in New York City that South African Ethiopianism was justified on several grounds and proceeded to recount an
incident that he judged typical of the white missionary's hypoc-
risy. "A pastor in one of the large Wesleyan Churches told me that
when he went to visit his superintendent, when they had prayers
he was not even invited in. When the family had their food served
in the dining-room he had his meals sent out to him in the kitchen.
Now, what would be the result of native ministers and native
church members suing and smarting under these things? There is
but one thing they can do if they have any self-respect, and that
is to leave the churches that insulted them in that way." Reverend
Morris reported that racial prejudice was increasing in South Africa, and so he saw the need for black missionaries to go to South
Africa and counter white racism. During his stay in South Africa,
Reverend Morris opened seventeen congregations in which he received twelve hundred new members. One of his first converts was
Johannes Zondi, who later formed his own sect. The Cushites, or
Blind Johannies, practiced foot washing and open-air baptism. The
Cushites were disliked by government officials for promising their
followers that agitation would lead to a bright future and for stress-
ing their contempt for white authority. A white official in Natal
gave an account of how they dealt with Zondi.

> Some years ago, a blind preacher came first of all, and went about
> amongst the tribes in Alfred County. He received three or four terms
> of imprisonment, and eventually I received instructions from the gov-
> ernment to find him. We made a long search, and he was found even-
> tually on Table Mountain, east of Maritzburg, and he was sent away
> by the government up to the Lebombo and kept in [the] charge of the
> police. We had men on several occasions present when he was preach-
> ing; he was blind and could not see who was attending his services. On
> several occasions he preached "Africa for the Black man"; that was the
> principal subject of his sermon.

In 1898, Zondi was sent to jail for the political import of his teaching. In 1901, Natal authorities sought to silence him by deporting
him to remote Ubombo in Zululand.[16] By 1903 the Cushites

---

16. Charles S. Morris, "A Work for American Negroes," in *Report of the Ecumenical Conference*, I, 469–70; W. L. Williams, *Evangelization*, 71; Marks, *Reluctant Rebellion*, 65; testimony of W. J. Clarke (Chief Inspector, Criminal Investigation Department, Natal), in SANAC, III, 615.

(Amakusha) had divided into several sects, as was almost fashionable at the time.

The proliferation of sects was very much in evidence throughout southern Africa. Shula Marks has indicated that there arose at this time in Natal several sects and prophets. Visionaries promised in the tradition of Nongqause, the Xhosa prophetess of the mid-nineteenth century, that blacks would have a millennium of bliss. But Marks misses the existential import of these Ethiopians when she ascribes their visions to lunacy and fantasy, having no doubt employed a rational yardstick to judge what was a complex metaphysical phenomenon. Instances of the emergence of "prophets" in southern Africa at this time and elsewhere in Africa during the first quarter of the twentieth century suggest that this genre of Ethiopianism, some of whose members called themselves "gods" or "Jesus," was an ecstatic attempt to use spiritual contemplation to solve the social and economic difficulties of their communities. In northern Botswana, there were several such prophets at the beginning of the twentieth century.[17]

In 1901, Chief Kgama of the Ngwato, a ruler who displayed consistent hostility to Ethiopianism of any kind, found himself dealing with a more daring crop of Ethiopian visionaries. Five prophets claimed to possess the power to solve all the ills of the tribe. The fact that they commanded some following among the Ngwato annoyed Kgama. The chief convened a *phuthego* (court) on April 15, 1901, to try the prophets on charges of false pretenses. In the course of the trial, one prophet is reported to have "confessed that he had commanded the people to worship him." The court found them guilty and ordered that their houses be burned down. Those who had given them some presents were fined twice the goods' value. Ngwatoland was destined to see more of prophetism, as long as hunger and other hardships plagued the chiefdom, for people pursue the millennium in times of dire need.[18]

17. Marks, *Reluctant Rebellion*, 65; testimony of W. J. Clarke, in *SANAC*, III, 615. *Cf.* "The Messianism of the Disoriented Poor," in Norman Cohn, *The Pursuit of the Millennium* (New York, 1970), 53ff., for parallels in European history. For African parallels, see Gordon MacKay Haliburton, *The Prophet Harris: A Study of an African Prophet and His Mass Movement in the Ivory Coast and the Gold Coast, 1913–1915* (New York, 1973), 26ff.; and Marie-Louise Martin, *Kimbangu: An African Prophet and His Church*, trans. D. M. Moore (Oxford, 1975), 37ff.

18. W. C. Willoughby, "Worshipping the Daft" (MS in Folder 770, W. C. Willoughby Papers, Selly Oak Colleges Library, Birmingham, England); Chirenje, *A History of Northern Botswana*, Chap. 6; Cohn, *The Pursuit of the Millennium*, 53ff.

If Kgama was able to curb the growth of Ethiopianism in his chiefdom, his neighbor to the south, Chief Bathoen of the Ngwaketse, had a hard nut to crack in the person of evangelist Mothowagae Mohlogeboa. Mothowagae joined the Kanye mission of the LMS in 1874 and, except for the period from 1880 to 1884 when he was a Bible student at Kuruman, remained at that station until 1901. He entertained some hope of being ordained a Congregational minister, but the LMS mission to southern Africa deliberately kept blacks out of the ministry. Trouble flared at Kanye in 1901: Mothowagae refused to work as an evangelist at a mission station in the Kgalagadi (Kalahari) Desert, and a committee of white missionaries dismissed him from his post. But the disciplinary action was criticized by many members of the Kanye church. They demanded that Mothowagae be ordained a minister of religion and replace the white minister at Kanye. Chief Bathoen's brother also supported Mothowagae, thus strengthening the Ethiopian's hand in his quarrel with the chief and the missionaries.[19]

Early in 1902, white missionaries invited Mothowagae to a meeting at Palapye, where they tested him to find out if he was knowledgeable enough to be considered for the ministry. The missionaries and Chief Bathoen all said that Mothowagae failed, though they did not say what sort of test they administered. But Mothowagae maintained that it was irrelevant to the ministry: "I attended in 1902 at Palapye a Conference held there and on my presenting myself for ordination I was given a Latin Book and asked to read same. I informed them that they had not taught me this language in their schools and they refused to ordain me." For some time, Chief Bathoen sympathized with Mothowagae and wrote to the British administrators in Botswana, asking them to allow the evangelist to baptize children and to solemnize marriages. But, as was the case in Natal, white missionaries and government officials collaborated. And Bathoen's intervention was to no avail. The situation was exacerbated by Reverend James Good, a former Kanye missionary, who wrote from Cape Town to inform British officials that Mothowagae and other church secessionists were under the influence of South African Ethiopianism, the main aim of which was "to cast off the [white] tutelage in which they have lived up

19. Chief Bathoen to Acting Assistant Commissioner, June 27, 1902, in "Church Dispute at Kanye," 410, R.C.7/8, BNA Gaborone; Mothowagae *et al.*, "Petition of King Edward Bangwaketse Mission Church to Resident Commissioner," October 19, 1903, no. 715, R.C. 10/11, *ibid.*

to the present." Reverend Good identified agents of the spread of Ethiopianism as Tswana migrant workers who, after a spell in the Johannesburg and Kimberley mines, where they mixed with Ethiopians of all sorts, became dissatisfied with their home church. Another group was composed of Tswana students who attended Lovedale. Reverend Good observed that students and migrant workers brought back "the most wonderful stories about the Churches and their methods in the colony . . . the Ethiopians in particular."[20] This aided the growth of Ethiopianism.

Toward the end of 1903, Mothowagae's following totaled seven hundred, most of them coming from the LMS churches at Kanye, Moshupa, and Moshaneng. The Bechuanaland District Committee (BDC) tried to pacify Mothowagae's faction by sending to Kanye a delegation of two white ministers. But they did not get to see Mothowagae and could only give an unfavorable report. Bathoen complained to the London directors of the LMS about the irregular manner in which LMS agents tried to investigate the Kanye dispute and recommended that the Kanye missionary Reverend Edwin Lloyd be removed. Foreign Secretary R. Wardlow Thompson then informed the chief that he was needlessly meddling in church affairs.

> Of course you clearly understand that while we gladly recognize your position as the ruler of your people in all secular matters, and while we gladly attach great importance to your views as a member of the Church, we do not recognise that the secular ruler has any more right than any other member of the Church to decide about matters which are purely spiritual and that if any missionary enjoys the confidence of, and is successful in his work amongst the members of his Church as a whole he cannot be removed from that position simply at the request either of the Chief or of any British Official. The spiritual independence of the Church of Christ is a matter of such importance that we are obliged to maintain it even in opposition to the judgment and the wishes of secular rulers.

This cold reply seems to have been a boon, for Bathoen gave permission to Mothowagae's followers to build a church at Kanye in spite of opposition from the LMS. Mothowagae had by the

20. "Mothowagae's Declaration," 715, *ibid.*; W. C. Willoughby to R. W. Thompson, December 17, 1902, in LMS Archives; Bathoen to Assistant Acting Commissioner, June 12, 27, 1902, James Good to Ellenberger, June 30, 1902, all in 410, R.C. 7/8, BNA.

beginning of 1903 enhanced his prestige by administering holy communion according to his own articles of faith.[21]

In the meantime, the dispute at Kanye was becoming more complex. Five major players were involved at various times: LMS missionaries; Mothowagae and his faction; Chief Bathoen; British protectorate officials; and an unknown number of Ethiopians who seemed to come from South Africa to provide Mothowagae with legal counsel. The presence of Bathoen's brother in Mothowagae's camp, in addition to the Ethiopian's growing popularity, engendered some arrogance in the secessionists and tipped the balance of power at Kanye in their favor. This development clearly threatened the chief's position. In November, 1903, Bathoen complained to protectorate officials that Mothowagae was disregarding his authority as chief of the Ngwaketse, a charge that smacked of conspiracy to a law-and-order-disposed British administration. Consequently, Commissioner Ralph Williams instructed his juniors to advise Chief Bathoen that the chief would be justified in punishing Mothowagae if there was any evidence of insubordination.[22] But the course of Ethiopianism at Kanye was becoming a difficult tangle through which Mothowagae alone seemed able to wend his way—he relied on Tswana customary law and a rudimentary knowledge of English law. At the height of his quarrel with Chief Bathoen, Mothowagae named his group "King Edward Bangwaketse Mission Church," a ploy apparently calculated to flatter British officials, for the reigning monarch was Edward VII. When in November, 1903, Bathoen established that Mothowagae had committed acts of insubordination and also insulted the chief, the British commissioner approved Bathoen's request to banish the Ethiopian. But before the order of banishment could be enforced, Mothowagae sought refuge in the "belly" of Bathoen's deceased father, a desperate plea for mercy in Tswana customary law. Later, Williams and the chief pardoned Mothowagae and rescinded the order of banishment.[23]

21. "Petition of King Edward Church," October 19, 1903; John Brown and W. C. Willoughby, "Report of a Visit to Kanye," February 14, 1903, no. 715, R.C. 10/11 BNA; Bathoen to Thompson, February 19, August 27, 1903; Thompson to Bathoen, March 28, 1903, all in LMS Archives.

22. Bathoen to Ellenberger, November 4, 1903, Williams to Ellenberger, November 2, 1903, both 410 R.C. 7/8, BNA.

23. Resident Commissioner [Williams] to Assistant Commissioner, November 20, 1903, Minutes, November 19, 1903; both no. 715, R. C. 10/11, BNA.

Elsewhere in southern Africa the AME church was consolidating its mission in spite of the obstacles created by white missionaries and government officials. Soon after his arrival in Cape Town in January, 1901, Bishop L. J. Coppin, the first AME resident bishop in southern Africa, began acquainting himself with the affairs of the Fourteenth District. He also worked on the plans for the proposed college in Cape Town, having collected more than $1,400 before he left Philadelphia. The bishop successfully negotiated with the Cape government to have the AME church recognized; the authorities did so on March 12, 1901.[24] The church's legal standing and the completion of Bethel Institute in 1901 were important landmarks in the history of the AME church in southern Africa; the church had now been firmly planted.

Bethel Institute was completed at a cost of $22,000 and was dedicated on December 1, 1901. The opening ceremony resembled an ecumenical exercise, as Coppin's enthusiastic report from Cape Town suggests. He was gratified to note that all races were represented and that Jews and Christians wished the new center success. Typical of this spirit was Harris Growman, who said, "I am a Jew but we all worship the same God." He donated £5 to the institute; gifts totaled £62 11s. 6d. that day. This race mixing, which Coppin tended to exaggerate, was reinforced by the students who enrolled when the school opened on February 3, 1902. Thus he could report: "Among the first to apply for studies in the higher branches was a representative from the Mohammedans." At that time, the institute staff consisted of the principal, Reverend A. Henry Attaway, and Reverend Msikinya, a South African black trained at Wilberforce University. Bethel was strong in religious studies, and instruction was in Afrikaans, English, and a few African languages. Reverend Coppin saw several advantages in training African students at Bethel on South African soil.

> Hitherto the native students, boys and girls, who wished to prepare themselves for teachers and missionaries in the A.M.E. Church in South Africa were obliged to come all the way to America or else be prepared in other Churches. To this there are two valid objections; first, it is too expensive to come all the way from South Africa to America to get an education, and especially when it was necessary to do preparatory work for the student before giving the higher studies.

24. "The South African College," *VOM*, October 1, 1901; Coppin, "The Outlook in the 14th District."

Such a course requires so many years as to make the work a strain on the missionary department. We have had as many as twenty-two students at one and the same time in our American schools from Africa, supported by the Church. . . . Secondly, it is not good policy to educate students in one Church for work in another, and hence the objection to depending on workers for the A.M.E. Church who are trained elsewhere.[25]

The opening of Bethel Institute no doubt made education a little more accessible to blacks, but the $80 (£16) fee for tuition and board was too high for most prospective students. The AME church was aware of this limitation and accordingly awarded some scholarships and appealed to home churches for donations. In October, 1902, the *Voice of Missions* reported that "already, St. John's Church, at Norfolk, Virginia, has led off in the good work, and is paying fifty dollars a year toward the education of a native student." Financial difficulties notwithstanding, Bethel's physical plant as well as its enrollment increased within a year. In September, 1903, the school reportedly had a printing press and also planned to acquire two hundred acres of land. Inspired by Booker T. Washington's Tuskegee model, the institute would expand the curriculum to include agriculture, carpentry, mechanical engineering, brickmaking, tanning, leather dressing, harness- and bootmaking, tailoring, dairying, poultry raising, and laundry work. The reporter noted that Bethel had an enrollment of 376 boys and girls, among them a sprinkling of English, Afrikaners, Jews, Moslems (presumably the Cape Malays), and Chinese, and that the teaching staff had increased from three to ten. While Bethel Institute was the church's most ambitious project in size as well as in the level of training (or standards), there were modest experiments in education made in the Transvaal, Lesotho, Swaziland, and Rhodesia. In Lesotho, Con. A. A. Rideout reported in 1903 that Chief Lerothodi was agreeable to having the AME church open a school and that the chief had set aside £4,000 for that purpose. Rideout also visited Barotseland, where he was well received by King Lebusi Lewanika. When he reported that Chief Kgama of the Ngwato was receptive to the AME church, the chief wrote an angry

25. L. J. Coppin, "The Progress of Our Work in South Africa," *VOM*, November 1, 1902; L. J. Coppin, "The Dedicatory Service of Bethel Institute, Cape Town, South Africa," *ibid.*, February 1, 1902; L. J. Coppin, "Our South African School," *ibid.*, October 1, 1902.

letter to the *Christian Express* in which he repudiated Rideout's claims. Kgama challenged Rideout to produce documentary evidence, but to no avail.[26]

If the missionaries of the AME church were helped by their African ancestry, it was also the case that this racial component of their ministry disturbed the white rulers of southern Africa, who in turn sought to undermine the church's effectiveness. And as in so many instances when white administrators and missionaries criticized their ministry, AME church missionaries gave themselves away in the *Voice of Missions*, a publication readily available to missionaries and government officials in southern Africa. For example, in 1903, Reverend C. M. Tanner reported from South Africa that the Afro-Americans' color made their work a little easier. "The persons are much surprised to find that our Church in America is chartered under the name 'African.'. . . As soon as the native hears of a church called 'African' and having Black men as ministers, he feels a kinship and interest; is instinctively drawn toward it. The words 'African Church' catch his attention at once. He feels that here is a church especially for him. . . . The name 'African' is a passport to our people; it secures for the Church a welcome to and rapid progress among them. It is the oil of the machinery, the bait on the hook."[27] For their part, white missionaries and government officials were determined to neutralize this incipient black solidarity.

In Matebeleland, Reverend Makgatho experienced some difficulty in trying to obtain land for the fledgling AME church mission. The reason was that Rhodesian authorities and representatives of white missionary societies, all of whom followed the activities of the Ethiopians with concern, were opposed to the AME church on the grounds that its agents might politicize Rhodesian blacks. Consequently, when Reverend Makgatho applied to the Bulawayo municipality for a plot of land on which to build a school, white Protestant missionaries influenced the municipal council to reject the application. On February 11, 1903, the chief native commissioner for Matebeleland, Herbert Taylor, wrote to

26. "The Bethel African Methodist Episcopal Institute," *VOM*, September 1, 1903; Con. A. Rideout, "African Kings Won to the Gospel," *ibid.*, April 1, 1903; Coppin, "The Dedicatory Service of Bethel Institute"; "A Letter from Khama," August 13, 1902, in *CE*, September 1, 1902.

27. C. M. Tanner, "South African Notes," *VOM*, April 1, 1903.

the bishop of Mashonaland, asking for his opinion on the standing of the AME church, which, after failing to acquire a plot in Bulawayo, was now seeking land elsewhere in Matebeleland. Taylor gave the bishop the information he had on the church: "As far as I am able to gather, I am given to understand that this particular sect is entirely supported by the Negro Race; I have noticed in the Natal papers that there appears to be some objection towards encouraging the work of this particular denomination among the natives there, in fact, I believe the Government of that colony have made strong representations to the Home Government to this effect." In reply, the bishop said he was equally disturbed by the likely political consequences, pointing out that the church's officials drew parallels between the plight of Rhodesian blacks and Afro-Americans and insisted "on the autonomy of the Black race, need for unity, and so forth." The bishop proceeded to raise several objections, most of which were political. His letter reveals the close connection between church and state in dealing with the colonized people of southern Africa.

> If I may be allowed to say it as a citizen, and speaking generally but definitely, I should object to the intrusion of any sort of political propaganda over which the Government could have little or no control *when run by citizens of a foreign State, however friendly that State might be.*
>
> I am partly well acquainted with the common talk of educated natives in the Cape Colony, Basutoland and elsewhere and am not likely to deprecate any legitimate aspirations. But there is distinct danger, to my mind, that aspirations may be manufactured for political, social, or even religious reasons, and a *manufactured* political cry on the part of the natives of this country is bound to become *Racial Cry* to an even more dangerous extent than the manufactured political cry of the Dutch. We have seen what an "Afrikander Bond" can produce in Africa in the way of trouble; "A Native Bond" would produce an Armageddon from Cape Town to anywhere.[28]

The equation of Ethiopianism with Afrikaner nationalism indicates the extent to which the English-speaking clergy and laity feared the prospect of a black revolution. By the beginning of the twentieth century, the Afrikaner Bond, a quasi-cultural and po-

28. Chief Native Commissioner Herbert Taylor to the Bishop of Mashonaland, February 11, 1903, Bishop of Mashonaland to Taylor, February 25, 1903, both in item no. A/11/2/18/3, NAZ.

litical group, had effectively challenged British hegemony politi-
cally as well as militarily, the most serious confrontation being the
war that lasted from 1899 to 1902. Unlike the reality of the Afrikaner
threat, however, black nationalism in its political and religious
manifestations did not present a coherent challenge to white dominance. While sporadic incidents of armed conflict had occurred in
Rhodesia and South Africa, the white man still did not know "the
native" well enough to be able to predict and control his behavior.
That there was a quest to understand the African personality is
revealed in the publication of several articles in the early 1900s in
which whites tried to figure out, among other issues, the origins
of the African and the nature of "the native mind." The answer to
this essentially white problem was partially provided by a British
commission of inquiry—the South African Native Affairs Commission—which met between 1903 and 1905 and investigated several aspects of African responses to the European presence in southern Africa.[29] Not surprisingly, the commission, which in many
respects resembled a witch hunt, dealt with the issue of Ethiopianism and the role the AME church played in the development of that
movement.

Witnesses who appeared before the SANAC represented a whole
spectrum of southern African society: tribal chiefs, government
officers, missionary agents, Ethiopians, farmers, businessmen,
plain urban folk, and village peasants. Right from the start of the
hearings, it was quite clear that the commissioners were preoccupied with the Ethiopian phenomenon. While some questions
were asked about the formation of the Fourteenth District of the
AME church, the commissioners were more interested in the substantive matters pertaining to race and church independency. One
of the issues the SANAC tried to resolve had to do with a definition
of *Ethiopianism*. In this respect, white witnesses ascribed to it a
variety of attributes, the more perceptive ones pointing out that
the movement was not just religious but was geared to affect
several facets of African life. According to Reverend James Stewart,
principal of Lovedale, church control was the basis of Ethiopian-

29. See, for example, J. F. van Oordt, "An Open Letter to the Rev. E. Jacottet,"
in "Origin of the Bantu," *CE*, June 1, 1908; "The Native Mind—II," *ibid.*, December
1, 1908. The exasperating aspects of British colonial commissions of inquiry are
subtly dealt with in a parable by Jomo Kenyatta in *Facing Mount Kenya* (New York,
1962), 47–51.

ism: "The Ethiopian question, or movement rather is a revolt on the part of a certain number of native ministers of various missions or denominations against white control ecclesiastically. . . . It has arisen solely from a desire to have control of their own ecclesiastical affairs." Reverend J. J. McClure viewed Ethiopians more as political agitators than religious persons: "I suppose their main object is to establish a South African native State, or a country purely for South African natives." A more comprehensive characterization was provided by Sir James Liege Hulett, himself a former secretary of native affairs in Natal: "The Ethiopian Church is a term now used to generalise, rather than particularise. It is an influence that has caused a feeling of unrest by making a demand for recognition [by whites]. . . . The tendency is not only to influence the Christian Natives, but to stir up discontent amongst the raw Kafirs." Sir James seems to have grasped the pervasive influence of the Ethiopian movement.[30]

African chiefs were almost unanimous in their disapproval of independent black churches, but that reaction may have been caused by the more extroverted Ethiopians whom the chiefs saw as a threat to their already fast-declining power under white rule. Some were no doubt reluctant to show publicly their sympathy for Ethiopianism, fearing that colonial administrators could depose them. Typical of this sort of witness was the Zulu chief Johannes Khumalo, who, in spite of brisk Ethiopian activity in Natal, said he had merely heard about secessionists. George T. Moshweshwe, a Sotho chief, was opposed to Ethiopianism because the movement's doctrine was similar to that of the Trappists and the French Protestants who ran schools in Basutoland. He conceded, though, that one of his sons was in favor of allowing Ethiopians to open stations in his chiefdom. It was with difficulty that Moshweshwe persuaded his son to accept his point of view. Chief Jonathan, another Sotho chief, confirmed part of Rideout's report in the *Voice of Missions*: there was, he said, one Ethiopian church in Basutoland.[31]

African officers and followers of the Ethiopian movement gave

30. Testimony of James Stewart, in *SANAC*, IV, 905; testimony of J. J. McClure, in *SANAC*, II, 174; testimony of James Hulett, in *SANAC*, III, 165.
31. Testimony of Chief Khumalo, in *SANAC*, III, 486–88; testimony of Chief Moshweshwe, in *SANAC*, IV, 392; testimony of Chief Jonathan, in *SANAC*, II, 1234. See Rideout "African Kings"; Coppin," The Dedicatory Service of Bethel Institute."

the reasons why they had converted to Ethiopianism and also indicated the growth of the movement since the 1890s. There were also some witnesses who had broken with the AME church to form their own sects. Reverend Mangena Mokone and Reverend J. Z. Tantsi stressed that the purpose of the AME church was to evangelize, educate, and encourage their African followers in the habits of hard work. They denied that their church was hostile toward whites. "It is not right that our church should be credited with feelings of hostility towards the Europeans. . . . There are men of all colours in our church. A white man may enter our Church. We have a White Minister in Cape Town. We ordained him. He has all the privileges of our Church." Micah Makgatho, who, together with Reverend A. A. Louw, planted the Dutch Reformed church in Rhodesia in 1893, showed how his white colleague humiliated him even in the presence of church members. He testified before the SANAC: "The Rev. Mr. Louw was not civil to me, so I left the Dutch Reformed Church. . . . I joined it [AME church] because the Rev. Louw kept me out from my work. . . . He was always against me, and tried to find something against me. A few years later he almost beat me in the Church. . . . Owing to personal differences between myself and Mr. Louw I changed my church." The commissioners were not satisfied with Makgatho's testimony, which clearly blamed a white minister for his resignation from the Dutch Reformed church. They seemed relieved when he confessed a racial affinity with the AME church leadership: "I joined the Church because I understood it was a Church for Africans, I being an African too."[32] This confession would become one of the most treasured pieces of evidence the commission extracted from a black witness, for linking the AME church with racism was part of what the witch hunt was all about.

Some African witnesses expressed disapproval of Ethiopianism and all kindred black organizations. M. S. Radebe, an editor of a paper and a store owner, said he had no sympathy for Ethiopianism because Africans were not yet ready to "take responsible positions, like looking after the welfare of the people." Here Radebe was advancing a view that was consonant with white sentiment on the issue; it was also reminiscent of statements by some black students in a debate at Blythswood in 1898. Radebe was also critical

32. Testimony of Rev. Mokone and Rev. Tantsi, in *SANAC*, IV, 474–75; testimony of Rev. Makgatho, *ibid.*, 199, 202.

of the racial stand taken by some Ethiopian leaders. He cited the case of a bishop who implored a congregation to seek the spiritual guidance of black priests, asserting that only black intermediaries were acceptable to God. Another critic of the Ethiopian Church was F. Z. S. Peregrino, a Ghanaian who went to live in South Africa shortly after the Pan-African Conference held in London in 1900. Peregrino launched a paper of his own, the *South African Specta-tor*, in December, 1900, and for a time he supported the Ethiopian cause. He turned against the church when he found out that some of the leaders believed that South Africa belonged to indigenous blacks, a view that excluded whites as well as the Ghanaian him-self. Solomon Plaatje, an editor of the Tswana paper *Koranta ea Becoana*, (published in Mafeking) and a leading black intellectual, said he had nothing against the Ethiopian Church as such, but he was critical of some of its leaders, allegedly for their unexemplary ways of life.[33]

Even before the SANAC had completed its probe of AME church activities, the Fourteenth District suffered another setback. Seven ministers, led by Reverend Jacobus Brander, the son of a Sotho man and an Afro-American mother, left the church in May, 1904, to form their own independent "Ethiopian Catholic Church in Zion." When four of the ministers appeared before the SANAC in October, 1904, they declared that their new church had more than six hun-dred followers and gave their reasons for leaving the AME church. Reverend Brander said that the mother church in America had refused to help South Africans on three occasions and that he himself had not been paid during his six years as an AME minister, and yet all money collected in South African churches of the Fourteenth District was sent to America. Brander was disappointed to find that the much-publicized AME church school, Bethel In-stitute in Cape Town, turned away orphans who could not afford the fees. He summed up his group's disillusionment: "In joining the American Church we thought, that as they were our own colour, they would help us up but we found they helped us down, and they took all the best positions without telling us a word, sending men from America, and putting them into those positions,

---

33. Testimony of M. S. Radebe, in *SANAC*, III, 530–31; testimony of F. Z. S. Peregrino, in *SANAC*, II, 317–18; testimony of Solomon Plaatje, in *SANAC*, IV, 265–68.

and taking us away, without giving us any notice."[34] Brander's testimony suggests that the Ethiopians were as much concerned with the equitable distribution of power among themselves as they were with wresting leadership from white ministers. This is an aspect of church independency that tends to be overlooked by some students of Ethiopianism.

White missionaries and laymen took great pains to link Ethiopianism with racism; most of them concluded that black consciousness bred political revolution, which in turn could drive whites away from southern Africa. W. J. Clarke, who was chief inspector in the Criminal Investigation Department in Natal, testified that his secret agents had informed him that Ethiopians instilled in their followers the notion that they were "quite capable of running the country without the aid of the white man." D. A. Hunter, A Free Church of Scotland minister, said the Ethiopian movement politicized blacks. He proceeded to recite part of a speech that was supposedly given by an African: "This is our country; these are our farms, and our mines, why are we not working them for ourselves and for our own benefit instead of working them for the white people and giving them all the benefit?" According to Reverend Hunter, this kind of agitation was dangerous because blacks, who outnumbered whites, could well upset the status quo and rule the country.[35]

Many other white witnesses sought to blame Afro-American missionaries for the political consequences of Ethiopianism. Several people alleged that the creation of the Fourteenth District had fostered pride and vanity in South African blacks, characteristics they had supposedly lacked. A Free Church of Scotland missionary in Natal spoke about his fears of Afro-American influence: "I would like to say that there is a danger of a great deal of evil happening through these blacks from America coming in and mixing with the natives of South Africa. These men from America for generations suffered oppression, and they have naturally something to object to in the white man and a grievance against the white man. These men from America come in and make our

34. Testimony of Rev. Brander, in *SANAC*, IV, 522–23. On Brander's Afro-American mother, see G. Z. Lethoba, "The African Methodist Episcopal Church in South Africa" (MS in University of Cape Town Libraries), 12.

35. Testimony of W. J. Clarke, in *SANAC*, III, 615; testimony of Rev. Hunter, in *SANAC*, II, 685.

natives imagine they have grievances when there are no grievances.'' Reverend Scott suggested that Afro-Americans be declared
prohibited immigrants on account of their liberal political views.
Reverend James Stewart advanced similar objections to Afro-
American missionaries, but some SANAC members challenged the
principal's assertion that an overseas education bred Ethiopianism. They pointed out that Reverend Mzimba, who had only visited Scotland briefly in 1893, led a revolt against the Free Church
of Scotland at Stewart's own school in 1898.[36]

Nevertheless, the view that the AME church politicized Africans persisted and was reinforced by some disgruntled former
members of that Church, including Reverend James Dwane. In
1903, Dwane, leader of the Order of Ethiopia, confirmed that view:
''In the printed doctrines and teaching and all that you would not
find much that is objectionable; but in the practical teaching and
training the tendency is to set the black race against the white
race.''[37] This comment was certainly welcome fodder for a commission that was striving mightily to establish the subversive
activities of an array of organizations generally called the Ethiopian movement.

Having built a prima facie case against the AME church, members of the SANAC were naturally eager to interrogate Afro-
American missionaries themselves. At the 1903 hearings, the
church was represented by two erudite Afro-American officers,
Reverend Levi Jenkins Coppin and Reverend A. Henry Attaway.
Coppin attended the Protestant Episcopal Divinity School in Philadelphia and worked for many years before being assigned to South
Africa; Attaway was trained as a teacher and taught school for
twelve years before he took charge of Bethel Institute in 1901.
Attaway's testimony dealt with the mechanics of running the
Fourteenth District and the educational philosophy in AME church
schools, which, he showed, leaned heavily toward industrial training. Coppin put the case in universal terms: ''I think no people
have ever become strong and self-supporting who did not give
attention to industry.'' Attaway denied the existence of plans to
bring Afro-American settlers to South Africa. In this respect, he
was probably advancing his own views rather than those of the

36. Testimony of Rev. Scott, in *SANAC*, III, 375; testimony of Rev. Stewart and
rebuttal, both in *SANAC*, IV, 905–907.
37. Testimony of Rev. Dwane, in *SANAC*, II, 710.

Missionary Department, which evidently had always stressed the importance of sending black entrepreneurs, technicians, and missionaries to settle in Africa. Both Attaway and Coppin stated that candidates for the ministry should be of good character and should receive sound religious training. They thus seemed to refute the more exaggerated stories that appeared in white missionary magazines alleging that the AME church was hastily ordaining an unschooled clergy. In fact a Sotho candidate for the AME ministry had, in 1898, shown that the selection process for prospective clergy was not as haphazard as had been surmised: "I tried the examination in the [African] Methodist Episcopal Church. We were thirty who entered for this examination: fifteen failed, and the rest passed. I was fourth top. Arithmetic was pretty hard; we had ten questions in it; I missed six. This was the only subject the other students beat me in. Many subjects were put down for us. Bishop Turner and the Reverends Dwane and Xaba were examiners. After all was done Bishop Turner said to me I must try to go to America after two years to advance my education there." Some commissioners suggested that Afro-American missionaries abandon the South African field and devote more time to improving living conditions of blacks in America. In response, Attaway said that the universal nature of Christianity compelled the AME church to spread the faith to all mankind. He also pointed out that their presence in South Africa went a long way toward correcting the stereotypes Americans had of life in Africa. "We came from motives of humanity. We are not so exclusive as to limit our exertions among our own people. I am personally desirous of helping every man whom I think desires help."[38]

Even before the SANAC had completed evidence on the relationship between Ethiopianism and the AME church, another group was debating the impact of Ethiopianism on South African life. The South African Missionary Conference, representing several Protestant churches, met in Johannesburg in July, 1904. The AME church, having already known the hostility of some white missionaries toward its work, sought to avoid further criticism by sending a cable to the conference. The telegram expressed fraternal solidarity with that largely white organization and commended Reverend Edward Jacottet, a French missionary in Lesotho, for his

38. Testimony of Rev. Coppin and Rev. Attaway, both in *SANAC*, II, 216–19, 227, 252–57, 258; "Race and Religion," excerpt of the text in English translation.

sympathetic review of Ethiopianism at the Johannesburg conference. Further, the AME church was loyal to the British government
and disavowed any intention of recruiting members from established churches. White missionaries should sympathize with the
church on account of the harassment it was being subjected to. At
the same time, the special AME church conference in Pretoria
passed a number of resolutions reasserting their determination to
exist as a church and refuting several charges leveled against the
Ethiopian movement by the South African Missionary Conference. One resolution stated that all Protestant members of the
missionary conference had no right to challenge church secession
per se when the churches in question had left parent churches:
"We are at a loss to know what schism and discipline are since the
Missionary Conference in question was composed of schismatic
fragments of dissenters with conflicting doctrines and disciplines."
Another resolution pointed out that just as the exigencies of creating a black clergy had compelled the Wesleyan Methodists to
appoint poorly qualified ministers, so the AME church had broadened its requirements to enable itself to establish an indigenous
ministry.[39]

The AME church's tactical maneuver did not achieve the desired goal. The missionary conference sent a courteous telegram in
which they alleged that the activities of AME church agents belied
the ostensible brotherhood of the Pretoria conference. Until such
time as the Ethiopian Church stopped interfering with established
churches, the missionary conference would continue to regard its
members with suspicion. Reverend Jacottet took exception to the
AME church's commendation, and in his long reply he said that
his criticism of white missionary societies did not in any way
condone some of the activities of the Ethiopian movement. Reverend Jacottet proceeded to enumerate the familiar allegations
against the independent churches, which ranged from the so-called
low caliber of missionaries to lax discipline in the black churches.[40]
But the AME church was not cowed by these denunciations. It

39. "Ethiopianism: Interesting Correspondence, Comprehensive Resolution,"
VOM, December 1, 1904; "The AME Church and the Missionary Conference," *CE*,
December 1, 1904.
40. "Ethiopianism"; Rev. E. Jacottet, "The Ethiopian Church and the Mis-
sionary Conference of Johannesburg," *CE*, December 1, 1904. *Cf.* E. Jacottet, *The
Native Churches and Their Organization* (Morija, Basutoland, 1905).

seems as though the resilience of its officers grew in proportion to the intensity of the criticism. No sooner had Reverend Jacottet sent his note to the AME church than another bishop was sent to replace Reverend Coppin. Bishop Charles Spencer Smith was appointed resident bishop in South Africa. Before he left New York City, Bishop Smith gave a farewell address in which he reiterated the virtues of his church's mission to southern Africa, thus reinforcing most of the resolutions passed by the AME church at the Pretoria meeting in August, 1904. However, Bishop Smith described Bishop Turner's activities in South Africa in 1898 as bordering on recklessness. This presaged Smith's characterization of Turner when he appeared before the SANAC late in 1904. At that meeting he read the declaration by AME bishops that their South African mission was pursuing proper evangelical goals. When Smith was needled about the political activities of AME ministers, he said that the clergy was supposed to eschew politics, but the church could not guarantee that all ministers observed that injunction. "Of course, you will understand that we do not claim to have a mortgage on the political opinions of our ministers." Smith was asked to explain the content of some articles that appeared in the *Voice of Missions*, but he was obliged to disavow them and to repudiate the views of the paper's editor, Bishop Turner. "We do not take many things that he says about Africa seriously; his scheme for wholesale emigration to Africa, his principle of 'Africa for the Africans,' and all that kind of thing, none of us take seriously. He is a free lance; he is a man well advanced in years; and is quite a national character. He says just what he pleases, and we cannot control him. But we do not stand for many of his utterances in regard to Africa."[41]

However much the AME church may have actually politicized South African blacks, its officers were so consistent in denying the charge that SANAC members resolved at the conclusion of the hearings that the Ethiopian movement ought not to be banned. It

41. "Bishop H. M. Turner's Tribute to His Colleague," *VOM*, October, 1904; "Bishop Smith's Response," *ibid.*; testimony of Bishop Smith, in *SANAC*, IV, 962, 964. Apparently SANAC members overlooked or were unaware of the political import of a meeting of twenty-five chiefs from all over southern Africa held in Cape Town on August 20, 1901, and addressed by Bishop Coppin, F. Z. S. Peregrino, and Harry Dean. Coppin taught the chiefs his poem on Africa (see Appendix G). See "Bishop Coppin, D. D., Pleads with Chiefs and Leaders of Various Tribes in South Africa," *VOM*, November 1, 1901.

was merely an "outcome of a desire on the part of natives for ecclesiastical self-support and self-control," and in the commission's view, that was not necessarily a political act. The witch hunt had failed to uncover what had all along haunted whites, namely, that Ethiopianism was the harbinger of political revolution in South Africa. In that sense, the conclusion of the SANAC proceedings in 1905 was a turning point in the history of the Ethiopian movement. From that date onward, white opponents retreated from their overtly militant stand against black churches and regarded those institutions as nuisances. An indication of this new relationship between black and white churches could be observed in the pages of the *Christian Express*, which tempered its criticism of Ethiopianism. In 1906 the paper could declare:

> It may be that the missionary churches have been slow to recognize that the Native Church is quickly leaving its childhood behind, and is able to take upon itself an increased measure of self-control. It is conscious of new powers and is impatient of dictation. Because the parent has been slow to observe the development which was bound to come, and has not been quick to recognize the need of directing these new energies to work on useful and absorbing enterprises, the native church has in these separatist movements wrested from the parent's hand what it regards as its rights, and has asserted its ability to manage its own affairs. . . . It is no use railing at Ethiopianism, as if it were utterly bad.[42]

If this slight change of attitude toward Ethiopianism was salutary, white society in South Africa continued to believe that the United States fostered political discontent among black South Africans that in time could well lead to a revolt against white rule. This fear of a black revolution was variously called the "black peril" and the "black giant." Since it persisted, one way to allay it, so white opinion went, was to stem the flow of African students to America by opening a black college in South Africa.[43] Thus it appears that, largely because of political considerations, 1905 saw the beginning of the search for a Tuskegee in South Africa.

42. *Report of South African Native Affairs Commission*, LVDC22399 (Cape Town, 1905), 64; "Schism in the Native Church," *CE*, June 1, 1906.

43. SANAC members were not interested in white students the AME church sent to America. Hence when Reverend Attaway pointed out that the church had sent two Afrikaners to America, Commissioner Samuelson interrupted: "I would like you to confine yourself to aboriginals" (*SANAC*, II, 256). *Report of South African Native Affairs Commission*, 64.

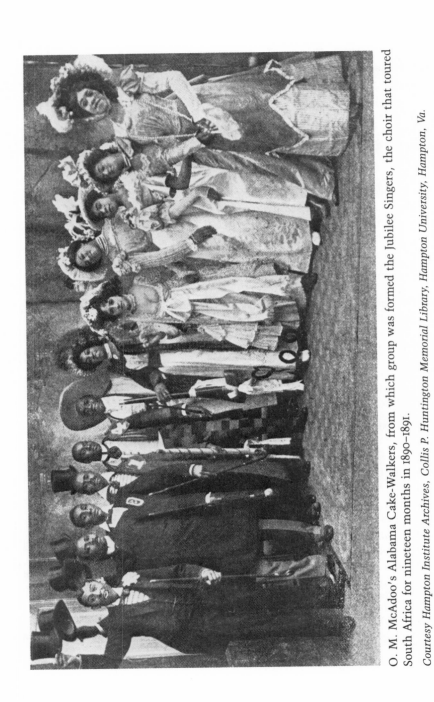

O. M. McAdoo's Alabama Cake-Walkers, from which group was formed the Jubilee Singers, the choir that toured South Africa for nineteen months in 1890–1891.

Courtesy Hampton Institute Archives, Collis P. Huntington Memorial Library, Hampton University, Hampton, Va.

John L. Dube, first president of the African National Congress
of South Africa (founded in 1912). Reverend Dube studied at
Oberlin College and went on to start a self-help industrial
school at Ohlange in Natal in 1901.

Courtesy Oberlin College Archives, Oberlin, Ohio

Chief Kgama III (*ca.* 1835–1923), ruler of the Ngwato tribe of Bechuanaland. He opposed the rise of independent churches.

Courtesy National Archives of Zimbabwe. Original on loan from the National Museum

Thomas C. Katiya as an undergraduate at Lincoln University in Pennsylvania. He enrolled in 1896, having been a member of the South African choir that toured the U.S. in the 1890s.

Courtesy Lincoln University

Reverend Thomas Chalmers Katiya in 1954 when he attended Lincoln University's centennial

Courtesy Lincoln University

Reverend Livingstone N. Mzimba in 1954 at Lincoln University's centennial

Courtesy Lincoln University

Simbini Mamba Nkomo in 1917

Courtesy Greenville College

John Tengo Jabavu
(1859–1921), owner and
editor of *Imvo
Zabantsundu.* He was a
leading politician and
critic of the Ethiopian
movement.

Courtesy Brian Willan

5/From Tuskegee to Fort Hare

The report of the South African Native Affairs Commission disappointed some whites because it failed to prescribe sure remedies for dealing with the African majority, the so-called black peril. But the SANAC made at least one suggestion that united an array of strange bedfellows, and this had to do with higher education for Africans. Church secessionists, African parents, white missionaries and laymen, and editors of the African press had previously followed their own different paths in prescribing the proper course for African education and development. Now, the search for an African institution of higher learning brought them together. The SANAC spelled out the case in its final report:

> The Commission has received much evidence pointing to the necessity for some improvement in the facilities for the methods of higher education for Natives, who themselves are strongly desirous of such advanced instruction, and setting forth the view that it is the duty and should be the policy, of the South African States to provide such opportunities. The evidence of education officers is to the effect that the supply of Native teachers is far from equal to the demand, and that many of those whose services are available are of inferior attainments. The Commission is impressed with the advisability of establishing some central institution or Native college which might have the advantage of the financial support of the different colonies and possessions, and which would receive Native students from them all. The immediate advantages of such a scheme appear to be, the creation of adequate means for the efficient and uniform training of an increased number of Native teachers, and the provision of a course of study in this country for such Native students as may desire to present themselves for the higher school and university examinations.

It is evident that SANAC members were agreed that higher education should be provided for Africans, but they were not clear about the level of training that ought to be offered. Was it going to be a technical college, a teacher-training institution, or a degree-granting university college? In this respect, SANAC members were as confused as Afro-Americans, who could not agree about their supposed South African showpiece, Bethel Institute. From its inception in 1897, Bethel was variously described as a "Kaffir University," the "South African College," a Bible seminary, and a teacher-training school.[1] But the AME church institution, which opened in 1902, was in fact a modest undertaking that was designed to provide Africans and members of other races some rudimentary training in the crafts as well as some instruction in the Scriptures. Indeed, the journey from Tuskegee as a model to the new college at Fort Hare was a circuitous one: more than ten years went by before the first students were admitted. Nevertheless, those years fostered a measure of esprit de corps as former antagonists joined hands in what was popularly known as the native college movement.

Even before the SANAC issued its final report, South African blacks and whites had aired their views on the kind of higher education that ought to be available to African youths. One of the most comprehensive statements was made by Peter Kawa, a Church of England minister who was superintendent of schools in a district in the Cape. Reverend Kawa no doubt had in mind technical and university education that ought to be provided by a nonsectarian community of scholars. In 1902 he said:

> The South African Native must be educated, if he be expected to take his place among the nations of this land. And from the first I must say I am in entire antagonism to the system of education which has been introduced into this country, and carried on with such apparent indifference by the missionary bodies. We want State not denominational education. We want that system of education which recognizes the fact that "there is dignity in labour," and we detest that system, where all the educated natives are expected to be either missionaries or school masters. We want practical schools rather than these too many Normal Institutions. We prefer Agricultural Schools, where our Native youths would be led to follow the agricultural pursuits. I am not

1. "Inter-Colonial Native College Approved by the Native Affairs Commission," *Imvo*, November 7, 1905; C. T. Loram, *The Education of the South African Native* (London, 1917), 296–312. See, for example, Parks, "Kaffir University"; "The Queenstown College."

averse to literary education, and am strongly of [the] opinion that these native lads who are able, should be taught the higher branches of study; for minds are not all alike. There are giant intellects fitted to grapple with the most intricate problems of the universe. If in our educational processes we overlook this important fact in the mental constitution of different individuals we are certain to do much injury. Let giant intellects have by all means what is generally termed "Higher Education," but let the masses be taught to make bricks, tables, dishes, wagons, shoes, and above all let them be thorough with their spade and ploughs.

Reverend Kawa elaborated on his views when he appeared before the SANAC in November, 1903. On that occasion, he said he favored accessibility of education on the ground that "the more educated they [Africans] are the more useful they are to the State." Reverend Kawa even advanced universal reasons for educating the youths of South Africa: "I say that because I see in other nations that the more the people are educated, the more useful they are to the State, and the little education that these people get seems to be doing them no good." He then addressed himself to vocational training: "It is useless to teach a boy mere book knowledge up to the fourth or fifth standard [sixth or seventh grade] and then have him to go into the country and fish for himself; he should be taught something in the line of the trade of a carpenter, or of a tinsmith, or something similar, which would be of some use to him." Girls should be taught sewing and dressmaking. Reverend Kawa's views were reinforced by John Tengo Jabavu, who deplored half measures in educating Africans: "The partly educated native is almost good for nothing in my opinion."[2]

In Botswana, some parents expressed their disapproval of mission education by keeping their children out of LMS schools or, for the few who could afford it, by sending them to Cape or Basutoland schools. In their notions of higher education, there was a premium on the practical use of education. Repeated pleas for useful education went unheeded until the LMS opened Tiger Kloof industrial school at Vryburg in the Cape. At the official ceremony in January, 1905, a Tswana chief praised the new institution and, in so doing,

2. Peter Kawa, "Native Education," Alice *Times*, n.d., enclosed in Rev. John Brown to Thompson, November 17, 1902, LMS Archives; testimony of Rev. Kawa, in *SANAC*, II, 611, 612–13; testimony of Jabavu, *ibid.*, 726.

spelled out the Tswana ideal of an efficient, practical school. Chief Bathoen said:

> You speak words today that we have long had in our thoughts. Because you came and taught only from the books, we have had some doubt in our hearts; if we are taught only from books, and are not taught wisdom, how shall we live. . . . The book learning is no help to give to the people to live; the books told us some of the things which we may expect when we come to die. Today we have heard words which I am very glad to hear. . . . Now we find what is to be done and what the books mean; a new prospect is now opened up before us.[3]

To be sure, white missionaries and government officials were not wholly unconcerned about the development of higher education for Africans. Part of the reason for what in retrospect was an apparently inept system of education stemmed from Victorian attitudes to education and life generally. The *summum bonum* in nineteenth-century Britain and in Europe seems to have been man's endless search for celestial bliss. In consequence, missionaries emphasized the teaching of the Scriptures. Chief Bathoen, in his criticism of "book learning," had grasped the limitations of this perennial theme in mission education. Yet some missionaries had since the 1880s begun questioning the usefulness of training evangelists rather than people in other vocations. In 1888 and 1891, Reverend John Smith Moffat argued that evangelism ought to include the teaching of industrial subjects. In commending this shift in educational emphasis to LMS directors, he displayed a familiarity with demographic and economic developments in southern Africa: "It seems to me that the preaching of the gospel in a broad sense includes this higher education. . . . These people will have to fight for their own lands some of these days; perhaps very soon, with the gold fever on in Southern Africa and reaching to the Zambezi; and if we do not give them something more in education than we have done, we do not give them a fair chance."[4] This view was shared by some missionaries, but the LMS typically attributed their failure to diversify the school curriculum to lack of money.

3. Rev. W. C. Willoughby "Historic Gathering at Tiger Kloof," *LMS Chronicle,* January, 1905, pp. 312–13; Chirenje, *A History of Northern Botswana,* esp. Chap. 5.
4. Rev. J. S. Moffat to Thompson, March 21, 1888, in Box 45, Jacket C, Folder Three, LMS Archives; Moffat to Thompson, September, 1891, in Box 49, Jacket C, Folder One, *ibid.*

Between 1903 and 1905, missionaries of other societies operating in southern Africa informed SANAC members that there ought to be built in South Africa a college for blacks, but they voiced that opinion less for academic than political reasons. Reverend James Stewart, who toured some black colleges in America in the early 1900s, felt that a local college could "remove the sense of injustice which they [black students] feel and which leads to their going to America and bringing back wrong ideas, political and social. At Booker Washington's place, Tuskegee, I found several who had been at Lovedale. . . . On my asking what brought them to America, the reply was, 'oh, Mr. Mzimba brought us here.' " Reverend Stewart's plea was echoed by other missionaries and was reinforced by the *Christian Express*. In 1905 the paper published an article in which the syllabus for students entering high school was criticized for ignoring the African student's special background. It was proposed that African schools offer the physical sciences, not so much to prepare students for jobs in industry as to stamp out superstition.

The exact nature of what should be provided is a matter that experts will no doubt have to settle but, speaking from a fairly long experience in Lovedale, we may be allowed to indicate some of the directions in which we think advance can wisely be made. For example, there is one important feature in native life that the present system of education to a great extent fails to deal with, and that is the belief in witchcraft. It is disappointing to find students who have been years at an Institution, still possessing unimpaired their belief in witchcraft, and allowing that belief to sway their conduct. . . . Many of our normal students, for example, when they go out to be teachers, are quite unable to discuss rationally the subject of witchcraft with their heathen or christian neighbours.

Christian teaching, in its struggle with superstition, ought to receive more effective support than it does at present from general education. Contact with the realities of nature is the best antidote to superstition. In this place and no doubt at other institutions there is a class of physics. But an earnest effort in this direction would mean far more than one class. It would mean that included in any higher curriculum, there should be a systematic course in natural science, during which the student in the laboratory and in the field would become so familiar with laws and processes of nature, that superstition would become for him unthinkable.

The educators at Lovedale, apart from wanting to design a curriculum that would enable the students to understand some of the laws of the universe, were also trying to make the native mind conform to Christian conceptions of the universe. In contrast to the *Christian Express*'s concern with superstition, a stance that amounted to cultural chauvinism, an *Imvo Zabantsundu* editorial was one of the most perceptive statements on the purpose of education: "The end of all education is the same for all peoples. It enables them to select and fulfill the duties of their spheres better than if they were uneducated. To our mind it is not so much to enable one to put in practice the subjects he was taught at college, as to train the faculties by the presentation of difficult problems for solution; and thus train one to being equal to the surmounting of any difficulties in after life." [5]

The secular press in the white community expressed divergent views on the issue of higher education for Africans. The Fort Beaufort *Advocate*, while sympathizing with blacks who wished to get university training, maintained that there was no demand for black graduates: "It is true that for a long time to come there will be no demand for university graduates of colour or for coloured men as lawyers or physicians. A few editors and a large number of school teachers and evangelists are all that this country needs just now." This position, which had been eloquently refuted by Reverend Kawa in 1902 and 1903, was taken up by the Bloemfontein *Post*. In December, 1906, the paper ridiculed the idea of a "Kaffir University" and proposed a system of "compulsory apprenticeship," by which African youths would be forced to learn a menial trade and in the process be dissuaded from emulating the white man's aspirations toward university education.

Both the Bloemfontein *Post* and the Fort Beaufort *Advocate* were criticized in editorials that appeared in *Imvo Zabantsundu*, which had from the beginning supported the idea of university education for blacks. In November, 1905, an editorial refuted the *Advocate*'s claim: "Our friend . . . takes up the astounding ground that there is 'no demand for university graduates of colour' which

5. Testimony of Rev. Stewart, in *SANAC*, IV, 905; "Native Higher Education, the Need for an Advance," *Imvo*, October 10, 1905 (excerpt from *CE*); "Native Higher Education," editorial, *ibid*.

in effect means that what is sauce for the white goose is not sauce for the native gander; which we cannot accept. The writer apparently does not realize that the civilization of a people comes from above, that a few hundred well-equipped natives are indispensable as leaders and interpreters of thought of the sable millions of their country.'' The editorial went on to assert that an educated black elite was an asset to the black community and to whites as well. Only through the cooperative efforts of both groups could a viable multiracial society be forged.[6]

The demand for higher education among Africans compelled John Tengo Jabavu to support the idea of a separate college for blacks, even though he had stood for multiracial schools and had criticized the Ethiopian movement for its racial exclusiveness. His advocacy was severely shaken when Dale College, a high school in King Williamstown, rejected in 1903 his son's application solely for racial reasons. Jabavu had subsequently sent Davidson Don to "England, where no obstacles are [placed in the way of] well-conducted students of colour.'' In consequence, Jabavu's *Imvo* commended Reverend Mzimba's efforts to send students to American colleges. Yet *Imvo*'s gesture was criticized by the *Cape Times*, which thought the whole scheme was imbued with Ethiopianism. ''We sincerely trust that this is not another symptom of the American Ethiopic Church movement which has lately established itself in the native districts of South Africa with disquieting results. It is a little difficult to understand what educational facilities a Cape Native can enjoy in the United States which he cannot equally as well avail himself of in this country.'' The paper contended that there were ample opportunities for higher education in South Africa for Africans which *Imvo* had overlooked in its criticism of South African education policies.[7]

In asserting that the educational needs of African students

6. "The Proposed Native College: Opinions of the Press," *Imvo*, November 28, 1905 (excerpt from Fort Beaufort *Advocate*); the Bloemfontein *Post*, December 6, 1906, excerpted in "Native Central College: Opinions of the Press," *ibid*., December 12, 1906; "Again the Native College," editorial, *ibid*., November 28, 1905.

7. "Native Education," editorial, *Imvo*, May 6, 1905; "Proposed Native College, a Mission to the Transvaal: Mr. J. Tengo Jabavu Interviewed," *ibid*., December 28, 1905 (excerpt from the *Transvaal Leader*); *Cape Times* quoted in "Native Education," editorial. For Reverend Mzimba's role in sending students to America, see Horace Mann Bond, *Education for Freedom: A History of Lincoln University, Pennsylvania* (Lincoln University, Pa., 1976), 512, 521–22, 526.

could be met at home, the *Cape Times* was tacitly passing judgment on the quality of education in American universities in general and black colleges in particular. The bias against American degrees was essentially a European reaction against its North Atlantic sister state. This attitude can be found in several letters from LMS agents based in South Africa, some of whom were derisively referring to Dr. John Philip as the "trans-Atlantic doctor" for the honorary doctor of divinity degree he was awarded by King's College (now Columbia University) in 1819.[8] Opinion had not changed much by the beginning of the twentieth century and was in some respects exacerbated by political considerations. In 1901 the *Christian Express* published an article in which American higher education was criticized and black colleges belittled:

> American universities, with a few notable exceptions, are not specially remarkable for their thoroughness even when they are organized by and for white people; and when negroes take to founding and managing universities and conferring degrees upon each other we have superficiality carried rather to an extreme. They are of course fully persuaded that their "educated men" are equal or superior to any class of men in the world, and a good many of our native friends here honestly believe that one of themselves who goes to America and studies for a few years at a negro university comes back with a knowledge of science quite equal to that of the Astronomer Royal, and that it is only our miserable ignorance and prejudice which keep us from recognizing the fact.

Reverend James Stewart was impressed by the industry and resourcefulness of several black colleges in America. Yet he informed the SANAC that South African blacks at Tuskegee could well have stayed on at Lovedale for their training: "The classes they were attending and the subjects taught did not seem higher or much in advance of those they had left."[9]

The bias against American degrees was dramatized by the Fort Beaufort *Advocate*, which equated the black South African search for higher education with a quest for gaudy fashions:

8. John C. Graham, Assistant Secretary of Columbia University, to the author March 7, 1971, states that John Philip received the honorary degree, in absentia, on June 5, 1819.

9. "The Native Church Movement," *CE*, December 1, 1901; testimony of Stewart, in *SANAC*, IV, 905.

The Bantu tribes have been dazzled by the audacious brilliancy of the American negro. He comes, this American Episcopal Minister or Bishop with clustering Academical Degrees appended to his name, and tells of 300 full fledged universities in the Great Western Republic, some for blacks, all of which grant diplomas and prepare for the professions. The aspiring Kaffir or Fingo is thus led to go or send his sons to America for college training, whence he returns full of the arrogant idea of Africa for the Africans. The American Colleges say to the Bantu [African], "We will make you B.A.'s, D.D.'s and qualify you for the practice of Law, Divinity, Engineering and Medicine, come then." They go and return, and from our point of view are practically ruined. They resume life here to propagate sedition and incipient rebellion. But give them at home the training they desire and no such blight may come upon them.

The statements by the *Christian Express* and the *Advocate* were issued ostensibly to discredit American universities. They are conspicuous by what they do not say, namely, the method or criteria for judging American degrees. Yet this stance is quite in keeping with the nature of prejudice, and the repeated discrediting of American degrees had its effects on some black elites. For example, Jabavu, who had belatedly endorsed Reverend Mzimba's scheme to send students to America, had reservations about American education and its influence on African students. A December, 1905, report was attributed to Jabavu: "He did not regard the influence of the native in America as entirely beneficial, and preferred that the future leaders of the native races should receive their education under British jurisdiction. As showing his preference for British principles and associations, Mr. Jabavu mentioned that his son was being educated at the University College at Bangor, Wales."[10] Some South African elites did not succumb to British cultural chauvinism but chose to avail themselves of educational opportunities in the United States. Mzimba, for one, sent several students to Lincoln University and Tuskegee Institute between 1901 and 1911.[11] Then there were some white missionaries and govern-

10. "The Proposed Native College, November 28, 1905; "Proposed Native College . . . Jabavu Interviewed." For Jabavu's vacillation, see Leonard Ngcongco, in C. C. Saunders (ed.), *Black Leaders in Southern African History* (London, 1979), 142–55; Solomon T. Plaatje, *Native Life in South Africa* (London, 1916), 165–70.

11. See, for example, P. J. Mzimba to Principal/President Rendall of Lincoln University, April 20, 1910, in "Letter from South Africa," *Lincoln University Her-*

ment officials, as well as some African elites, who sought to stem the flow of students to America by banding together to build the South African interstate native college. Significantly, AME missionaries were conspicuous by their absence from the steering committees that were set up throughout South Africa. Their indifference may have been premeditated, as Afro-American missionaries no doubt realized that the proposed interstate college was potentially a more viable undertaking than was the AME's Bethel Institute. In addition, completing the college would require that white missionaries take part. This combined effort would belie the *Voice of Missions'* oft-repeated ridicule of white missionary societies' inability to provide a college for black South Africans. The AME church's comment came from Bishop Charles Spencer Smith, who was unwilling to concede that the initiative had been taken away from the church. He informed a meeting in Washington, D.C., in August, 1906, that his church's activities in South Africa had spurred the movement to found a black college there: "A movement is now on foot to found an intercolonial and interdenominational college for the higher education of native youth, which will obviate the necessity of them going either to Europe or America for a classical training. In all probability this institution will embrace a course in medicine. This movement is precipitated by the knowledge of the fact that a large number of South African native youth were being educated in the schools of the A.M.E. Church of America." Having given evidence before the SANAC and having followed its proceedings closely, Bishop Smith was able to correlate the college movement and his society because witnesses had repeatedly disapproved of the AME church's sending black students to America.[12]

Concerned South Africans were quick to set up committees throughout southern Africa to effect the birth of a black college. Public opinion in South Africa favored full missionary support if the college scheme was to succeed at all. *Imvo* once more devoted an editorial to the college movement and commended the Edinburgh-based paper the *Scotsman* for giving "the most com-

---

ald, June, 1910, p. 4, Lincoln University Archives; Louis R. Harlan and Raymond W. Smock (eds.), *The Booker T. Washington Papers* (Urbana, 1977), VI, 64.

12. Bishop C. S. Smith, "The Relation of the British Government to the Negroes of South Africa," *VOM*, September, 1906.

plete outline of the policy that should be followed in realising the recommendation of the South African Native Affairs Commission on the subject of Native education." *Imvo* pointed out that committee meetings in support of the college had been held in King Williamstown and it urged blacks and whites to contribute generously. The support of missionary bodies was indispensable to the success of the college. The college scheme received a boost from a popular missionary figure, Reverend Stewart of Lovedale. A few weeks before he passed away, he addressed a letter to missionaries on November 16, 1905, urging their support:

> The recommendation of the recent Inter-Colonial Native Affairs Commission with regard to the establishment of a Central Native College aided by the various States for training native teachers and in order to afford opportunities for higher education to native students, has no doubt, occupied your thoughts. As, the proposal is being discussed by natives all over the country, and in view of any action the Government may take to give practical effect to the recommendation, it seems well that expression should be given to the opinion of missionaries and especially to those directly connected with the education of the more advanced native students.
>
> I therefore write to you and to our European missionaries to ask you to assist in carrying out this scheme for the advancement of Native education throughout South Africa that [through] cooperation with one another and cooperation with the Governments, [we] may ensure the missionary and inter-denominational character of the proposed college.
>
> Owing to my ill health, I fear very much I could not attend any meeting which might be convened for the purpose of discussing the matter and of uniting in some one line of policy, but my views on the subject can be condensed into a short written statement and a member of my staff would represent me.[13]

South African blacks expressed their support for the proposed college at a convention held at Lovedale in December, 1905. Jabavu had addressed several public meetings in the Cape and the Transvaal, imploring whites and blacks to support the plan. The Lovedale convention was attended by members of different denominations from all over southern Africa, including Ethiopians. The meeting displayed a measure of ecumenism and nonracialism,

13. "The Native College Movement," editorial, *Imvo*, November 7, 1905; Stewart to the editor, November 16, 1905, *ibid.*, December 23, 1905.

but African delegates were overly deferential to whites in trying to get their support. This was dramatized by Reverend S. P. Sihlali (the first black to obtain a high school diploma), who, in proposing that a white lay missionary, Mr. Weir, chair the convention, declared him to be a "black man." Mr. Weir was elected unanimously. Significantly, the Ethiopian movement had an active delegation. Reverend James Mata Dwane of the Order of Ethiopia and Reverend D. Msikinya of the AME church took part in the deliberations and both were elected to the college's eleven-member Executive Committee. The committee was empowered to negotiate for the buildings and the farm that were to serve as the nucleus of the college, and it was to solicit money from the various governments in southern Africa.[14]

Once the Lovedale convention had endorsed the proposal, the Executive Committee and supporters of the college went about canvassing and soliciting funds. It appears also that Reverend Stewart's appeal to missionaries became more significant after his death on December 21, 1905. Thereafter, missionaries and laymen alike looked upon the completion of the college as a tribute to Reverend Stewart and a monument to his service to the African people. In March, 1906, it was reported that LMS agents in Botswana and Matebeleland had resolved to support the construction of the college. By 1908 the South African Missionary Conference gave its formal endorsement, and its respective metropolitan headquarters donated substantial sums. African chiefdoms and states as well as individual blacks and whites gave a good account of themselves in the search for a Tuskegee in southern Africa and in the process forged a measure of cooperation. That new spirit was typified by W. P. Schreiner, a former prime minister of the Cape colony (from October, 1898, to June, 1900). On February 11, 1906, Schreiner wrote Jabavu, the organizing secretary of the College Committee:

I wish success to the Native College Scheme, and will be pleased to contribute £5 5s to the Guarantee Fund.

It is very necessary that the natural aspirations of the select youth of your people for a higher education should not be driven abroad for outlet.

I hope, all the same, that the support which such an institu-

14. "Inter-Colonial Native College Approved"; "Convention at Lovedale," *Imvo*, January 5, 1906.

tion requires may in considerable measure be contributed by the Native people themselves, for then the real *need* of it will stand demonstrated.[15]

In the event, the native contributed his tithe. An indication of the efforts of individual Africans occurred at Guba Location in the Cape, where residents pledged to donate 2s. 6d. each and were said to have raised £50. Wodehouse residents were reported to have given a total of £12 17s. At King Williamstown, the civil commissioner reported that in January, 1908, contributions amounted to £118 10s. 4d. In February, 1907, the Transkei General Council voted £10,000 to the college fund. Lesotho pledged £6,000 but apparently did not fulfill its promise—there were matters of protocol and questions about the choice of Lovedale as the site for the proposed college. Nevertheless, by August, 1907, the fund had pledges of over £43,000.[16] There was a lull in contributions until 1911, when it was reported that the English press had published favorable articles and that Lord Selborne and Lord Milner, former governor and high commissioner, respectively, at the Cape, had lent their support to the scheme. *Imvo Zabantsundu*, whose editor and proprietor had by now almost despaired of promoting multiracialism because blacks still suffered harassment by whites, welcomed the British gesture. Quite untypically, however, Jabavu asserted that such donations amounted to reparations for British entrepreneurs' improper exploitation of South African wealth. The appeal was likely to "be liberally responded to by many wealthy people in the Mother Country who are simply dying to do the Native people some good. There are also in England millionaires, made such by the mineral and commercial wealth of South Africa, who would only be too glad to disburse some of their great fortunes for such a taking cause." Furthermore, prospective donors would soon atone for their greedy accumulation of South African wealth by giving some of it to the fund. It is not clear if British philanthropists gave

15. Rev. David Carnegie and Rev. J. Tom Brown, in "L.M.S. Support," *Imvo*, March 13, 1906; "The Native College," editorial, *ibid.*, February 11, 1908; Schreiner to Tengo Jabavu, February 11, 1906, *ibid.*, February 25, 1906. See Appendix I.

16. "The Native College Scheme: Notes in Circulation," *Imvo*, February 27, 1906; "The Inter-State Native College," *ibid.*, April 2, 1907; "£10,000 for the College," editorial, *ibid.*, February 6, 1907; "The Inter-State Native College Scheme," *ibid.*, May 26, 1909 (excerpt from the *Basutoland Star*); "The Native College," *ibid.*, August 10,1907. See also "The Native College," *ibid.*, January 14, 1908. Individual contributions amounted to £68 10s. 4d.

generously, but a 1916 report showed that the Lord Bishop of Oxford and others had contributed £208. Nevertheless, by 1914 the fund had reached the £50,000 mark.[17] This sum spurred the Executive Committee to proceed with plans to build on land donated by the Free Church of Scotland at Fort Hare.

That decision made the birth of the college imminent. Another lively debate began, this time on such substantive issues as the curriculum and the preparation prospective undergraduates ought to have before matriculation. In the ensuing discussion of what type of education ought to be offered, none of the AME church colleges in America was apparently used as a model for the new college for blacks in South Africa. Instead, the choice was the nonsectarian Tuskegee Institute in Alabama. Its principal, Booker T. Washington, became the subject of favorable comment in missionary circles as well as in Jabavu's *Imvo Zabantsundu* from 1903 onward. In June, 1906, the paper carried an editorial in which Washington's character was praised and his philosophy of a practical education commended to the new institution at Fort Hare.[18] The editorial endorsed a report in the *Rand Mail* (Johannesburg) that Washington had been invited by the British government to visit South Africa and give advice on industrial education for Africans. The invitation was reportedly turned down because President Roosevelt thought that "Mr. Washington's time and talents would be far more usefully devoted to the education of American Negroes." *Imvo* went on to say:

> We are truly grateful to the British authorities for the steps taken in the direction of getting Mr. Washington out. It is an earnest of the sincerity of some of these officials to really help the Natives of South Africa on the paths of civilisation and Christianity. . . . Mr. Booker Washington, of all Negroes, is one whom all right thinking persons would be glad to see in South Africa. In America he is solely devoted to the gigantic task of smoothing the relations between the whites and his race. This he is doing by turning the thoughts of his people into

17. "Again the College," *Imvo*, January 24, 1911; "Again the College," editorial, and "The Native College" (excerpt from the *Cape Times*), *ibid.*, October 6, 1914; "S.A Native College," *ibid.*, December 5, 1916.

18. "Booker and South Africa," *Imvo*, June 24, 1906. Washington has been the subject of two excellent biographies by Louis Harlan: *Booker T. Washington: The Making of a Black Leader, 1856–1901* (New York, 1972) and *Booker T. Washington: The Wizard of Tuskegee, 1902–1915* (New York, 1983).

practical channels, urging them on to excel in everything that they handle to command merit, as all, be they white or be they black, are only too ready to recognize merit.[19]

Washington's efforts to reconcile blacks and whites were especially attractive to *Imvo*, and in this respect his moderate moves on politics contrasted sharply with those of Bishop Turner, whom the editorial reviewed unfavorably, ascribing racial tension to "firebrands of the Bishop Turner type who constantly preach to their people to oppose violence with violence." The editorial opined that someone should take Washington's place, but to no avail. Two years later, white American missionaries in Natal suggested that Washington give thought to coming to South Africa to apply his educational methods. Their letter implied that Washington could be a more creditable advocate of curriculum changes than were AME missionaries. Washington was again unable to go to southern Africa.

> I have tried to keep in touch as much as I could with the public opinion of South Africa and to learn as much as possible of the condition, the homes and aspirations of the natives of that country. I still have a dream of visiting South Africa before many years.
> I am still sorry that it was not possible for me to accept the invitation some time ago, which came from Lord Grey. I have since talked with Lord Grey who is now as you may know the representative of the English Government in Canada and he again expressed the wish that I should make a visit to South Africa at some time in the future.[20]

Even though no substitute for Washington was found, the quest for a practical education and a local black college went on unabated and proved to be a much more long-drawn-out undertaking than the SANAC and the Executive Committee had anticipated. And in the search for a type of education that would suit South African blacks, the Tuskegee model was brought up from time to time. On some occasions, Washington's works on education and his often optimistic prognosis for race relations in America were published in South Africa. In August, 1908, the *Christian Express* carried an article by Washington in which he discussed his philosophy of

19. "Booker and South Africa." See also Louis R. Harlan, "Booker T. Washington and the White Man's Burden," *American Historical Review*, LXXI (1966), 448.

20. "Booker and South Africa"; Rev. A. E. Le Roy to Washington, March 27, 1908, Washington to Le Roy, April 20, 1908, both in Box 818, Washington Papers.

industrial education as well as his faith in the ability of Negroes to advance in America. To emphasize what appeared to him to be a universal attribute of mankind, Washington drew parallels between western European progress and Negro advancement.

> If one had asked Caesar when he first discovered your forefathers in the condition that has been described, if in two thousand years they could be transformed into the condition in which they are now found in America, the answer doubtless would have been an emphatic "No." If one had asked Livingstone, when he first saw my forefathers in Africa, if, in the fifty years that have elapsed since then, or even in the two hundred and fifty years that have passed since the first African was brought to this country, a young Negro would be the class orator at Harvard University, the answer doubtless would have been a "No"— as emphatic as Caesar's.

Washington must have been referring to the Afro-American scholar Alain Locke, who graduated from Harvard in 1907 and went to Oxford University the same year as a Rhodes scholar, the first black to do so. To the doyen of Tuskegee, Locke's achievement and that of other blacks augured well for race relations in America. In another article published in September, 1908, Washington espoused, in the tradition of Bishop Turner in 1898, mutual coexistence of all races and the need to care for the weak in society. "When measured by the standard of eternal, or even present, justice that race is greatest that has learned to exhibit the greatest patience, the greatest self-control, the greatest forbearance, the greatest interest in the poor, in the unfortunate—that has been able to live up in a high and pure atmosphere, and to dwell above hatred and acts of cruelty. He who would be the greatest among us must become the least."[21]

Washington's philosophy of education was apparently rooted in humility, in humanism. By 1912, Washington's popular leadership had been widely acclaimed. In that year, for example, a South African reviewer of his newly published book, *My Larger Education*, informed readers of *Imvo*:

> His [Washington's] great problem has been how to reconcile and unite the antagonistic forces of public opinion, racial and sectional, so as to

21. Dr. Booker T. Washington, "The Educational and Industrial Emancipation of Negro—II," *CE*, August 1, 1908; Washington, "The Educational and Industrial Emancipation of the Negro—III," *ibid.*, September 1, 1908. See also "Black, but Chosen," *Imvo*, April 2, 1907, for commentary on Alain Locke.

inspire, uplift, and regenerate the Negro masses. Believing in education as the solvent influence, he set to work in "building a school
around the problem.". . . . No American of our time has so long and
steadily amid all cross-currents, pursued an undeviating aim at an
ideal of national importance, or has become more widely influential
than he. . . . Whenever Dr. Washington's line has been followed he
finds hostility transformed into cooperation.

This charitable assessment was to be corrected by Davidson Don
Jabavu's eulogy in 1915, when he pointed out that W. E. B. Du Bois
and others criticized Washington's moderate stand on political
issues.[22]

While South African elites were heaping praise on Tuskegee and
its principal, the problems surrounding the creation of a Tuskegee
in South Africa remained unsolved. Fort Hare University College
underwent a long period of gestation, which in retrospect was
salutary because it brought to the fore the complexities associated
with developing institutions of higher learning, especially degree-
granting ones. The intervening years enabled professional educators, government officials, missionaries, and Africans who held
widely differing opinions to participate in the debate over higher
education and to help bring the idea to fruition.

One of the issues proponents had to deal with was the entrance
qualification. In February, 1907, a Cape Colony government publication, the *Education Gazette*, reported that no African candidates had passed the matriculation examination that year and that
the situation was unlikely to improve in the foreseeable future.
The *Gazette* blamed Africans for the poor results and suggested
that if Lovedale could not prepare students for that examination,
African parents ought to build their own high school and hire
competent teachers so that its graduates could enter the proposed
interstate African college. This suggestion elicited a response from
Imvo. The paper agreed that an efficient high school ought to be
built, but it deplored the *Gazette*'s failure to appreciate the fact
that inadequate educational facilities, not students per se or indeed
their race, were to blame for the poor examination results. Further,
the practice of blaming the victim of unfortunate circumstances
was tantamount to "shutting one in a dark chamber and kicking
him for not seeing." *Imvo* went on to say that Africans longed "for

22. "Booker T. Washington: His New Book," *Imvo*, March 12, 1912; D. D. T.
Jabavu, "Booker T. Washington: A Character Sketch," *ibid.*, November 30, 1915.

the day when that [Education] Department of State will be so reformed as to be in sympathy with their feelings and aspirations."[23]

Education officials at the Cape did not treat the question with any urgency. Four months after the *Education Gazette* article appeared, Dr. Muir, the superintendent-general of education, was lamenting the shortage of black high school graduates and suggesting that a less rigorous curriculum be introduced to enable African students to enter the university college. Muir proposed that the college offer the high school diploma first, before it embarked on a university-level curriculum. *Imvo* supported Muir's proposal but went further, suggesting that during the first few years of its existence, the college should offer one program leading to the high school diploma and the other for degree candidates. The paper maintained that there was already a handful of matriculants who could take the degree courses. Nevertheless, the colonial machine was slow in bringing about change, and the new "University Senior School Leaving Certificate Examination" was introduced in 1910, barely six years before Fort Hare was opened.[24]

In the meantime, South African society mounted its campaign against American degrees. Some whites viewed this campaign as intellectual preparation for the opening of Fort Hare, the majority no doubt arguing that, by stigmatizing American degrees, prospective university students would vouch for a local black college. Not the most ingenious of schemes, the campaign had little effect on Africans for four main reasons: first, Africans were supposed to give preference to a college that had yet to be built; second, graduates of American universities, some of whom went on to take degrees at British universities, were returning to South Africa and were inspiring the youths with the high quality of their work; third, criticism of American higher education was inconsistent, the best example being the wholesale condemnation of American degrees and the perennial praise of Tuskegee and its principal; fourth, the AME church and Mzimba's Presbyterian Church of

23. "Department and College," editorial, "Proposed Inter-State Native College" (excerpt from the *Education Gazette*), *Imvo*, February 12, 1907. *Cf.* Charles H. Lyons, *To Wash an Aethiop White: British Ideas About Black African Educability, 1530–1960* (New York, 1975), 86–121.

24. "The Inter-State College," editorial, *Imvo*, June 25, 1907; "Report on University Senior School Leaving Certificate," *ibid.*, April 19, 1910.

Africa were impervious to South African criticism of any sort and continued to send students to America. An indication of Mzimba's satisfaction with American-trained graduates is to be found in a letter he sent to the principal of the predominantly black Lincoln University in 1910, thanking him for training seven members of the Presbyterian Church of Africa who graduated from Lincoln in 1909: "It is with the greatest pleasure that I convey to you, as Principal of Lincoln University, the thankfulness of our people and gratitude for educating our African students. They have returned to us a great success. Six of them are ministers. . . . We have been so much encouraged that we desire to send another group, and I would be very glad to know if they would be received as the others were." Nor was Mzimba alone in supporting an overseas education. Another African, having seen the flaws in the campaign against American education, came out in support of sending students to America and elsewhere for their education. In May, 1910, W. Yako wrote a letter to the editor of *Imvo*, criticizing an article that said students might get Ethiopian ideas in Afro-American colleges. Yako observed that Ethiopian ideas were more prevalent in South Africa than in America, and he asserted that black South Africans ought to be free to study wherever they liked. Yako cited a historical precedent in support of his argument: "Christianity, education and civilization are harbingers of more intellectual, more moral and more civil freedom to any race. So I cannot understand the meaning of those who urge that the native African is spoiled and made unfit for his native country after acquiring his education abroad as if the universal freedom was never intended for him. What is wrong is in the man himself be he black or white, whether educated at home or abroad. If there was anything wrong in getting education abroad the founder of Wesleyan Methodism [John Wesley] might never have gone to Germany to complete his studies."[25] Yako's views were reinforced by success stories *Imvo* published about black South Africans studying abroad.

In July, 1910, *Imvo* reported that two black South Africans had qualified as barristers at the Inns of Court in London: D. G. Montshiwa, a Motswana from Mafeking, and Pixley Ka Isaka Seme of Natal, who graduated with a B.A. from Columbia University. They joined the ranks of advocate Alfred Mangena, who had qual-

25. Mzimba to Principal Rendall, April 20, 1910, in "Letter from South Africa," 4; W. Yako to editor, May 11, 1910, in "A Native College," *Imvo*, June 7, 1910.

ified a few years earlier and was practicing law in the Transvaal, and other graduates who had returned to South Africa after completing their studies abroad. An *Imvo* reporter understandably praised their achievement:

> All our countrymen have reason to be proud over this advance in what may be termed Higher Education. Suppose we had a hundred more of such men working at the law and as many again of others qualified here (in preference to America) in medicine, arts, science, engineering, what a different atmosphere would they create for South Africa. Their presence alone would compel respect and justice for the multitudes to say nothing of demanding it. One has only to look at West Africa to appreciate the value of education to nations in the stage of semi-civilization, a stage that renders such nations easy victims for plunderers.
>
> Sierra Leone and Lagos teem with able [Negro] lawyers, merchants and doctors. . . . These have seen to it that their less privileged fellowmen shall receive just treatment at the hands of European settlers and traders by means of the book and not the assegai.[26]

At about the same time, Davidson Jabavu graduated with a B.A. from the University of London and enrolled at Birmingham University in the Midlands for the postgraduate teacher's diploma course, which he completed in June, 1914.[27]

Before he began his studies at Birmingham, Davidson undertook a journey to America, ostensibly to learn some of the workings of Tuskegee and to confer with its principal. As was the case with so much the editor's son did, his activities were well covered in his father's paper. In July, 1913, *Imvo* reported that Davidson was to "visit Mr. Booker Washington's Institution at Tuskegee, to study the methods that the world-famed Negro Educationist has adopted with so much advantage to his people." When the minister of native affairs in the newly formed (1910) Union of South

26. "Two South African Natives Created Barristers-at-Law," *Imvo*, July 12, 1910. That the editor should have cited West African examples and not a South African precedent is a little surprising, because Henry Sylvester Williams, a black from Trinidad who qualified as a lawyer in London, worked as an advocate in Cape Town from 1903 to 1904, when he left for London. See J. R. Hooker, *Henry Sylvester Williams: Imperial Pan-Africanist* (London, 1975), 64–82. See also Sylvester Williams, "Colour and Politics: Address by Advocate Williams," *South African News*, June 10, 1904.

27. "Mr. D. Tengo Jabavu," *Imvo*, July 8, 1913; "Academic Success," *ibid.*, July 28, 1914.

Africa learned of Davidson's visit, he asked Tuskegee administrators if the South African was competent to evaluate the Tuskegee education. After their favorable reply, the minister invited Jabavu to prepare a report on the applicability of Tuskegee's education system to South Africa.[28] Davidson spent six weeks at Tuskegee, during which time he met Washington and conversed with students and faculty to learn something about their school. He also charmed Tuskegeeans with his violin recitals. The *Tuskegee Student* reported that Davidson was "pleased with his visit and at finding much here that will be of help to him in his future efforts" to educate South African blacks. Washington himself was so impressed that he wished the South African could stay on at Tuskegee. Davidson Jabavu subsequently prepared a report in which he displayed mature judgment on several aspects of education in America and its application to the African situation. Jabavu made several cogent suggestions, especially in regard to agriculture. The Union government was advised either to employ Tuskegee graduates to train African students or to send some South African students to Tuskegee. The report was to have been published as a Blue Book by the government but, as the author indicates, the outbreak of World War I made that impossible.[29]

Failure to implement Jabavu's recommendations meant that the Tuskegee model was being dangled before the African community—thanks to *Imvo*'s relentless efforts—without ever being reduced to reality. This clearly whetted the appetite of youths for American education, with the result that the trickle of South African students to America was sustained. It is easy to exaggerate the number of southern African students studying at American universities at the turn of the century, but it is significant that the few (probably thirty by 1910) who succeeded in going there dis-

28. "Mr. D. Tengo Jabavu"; Minister of Native Affairs to Washington, telegram, September 2, 1913, Jabavu to E. J. Scott (secretary of Tuskegee), September 5, 29, 1913, all in Box 927, Washington Papers. See Appendix I for the text of the September 5 letter.

29. J. T. Jabavu "Musical Recital," August 13, 1913, in Carnegie Library, Tuskegee; Jabavu to Scott, September 4, 1913, in Box 927, Washington Papers; "Booker T. Washington's Methods," *Imvo*, August 26, 1913; "A Native South African in America," *ibid.*, September 2, 1913; "A South African Abroad," *ibid.*, November 18, 1913. The report was published as "Booker T. Washington's Methods Applied to South Africa," in D. D. T. Jabavu, *The Black Problem* (Cape Town, 1920; rpr. New York, 1969), 22–70.

played considerable initiative and determination. A case in point is that of the Zimbabwean student Simbini Mamba Nkomo, who came from Chipinge. Nkomo had great difficulty persuading his father to let him go to Adams Seminary in Natal. But getting that grudging approval was only part of the long and difficult road to America, as his own account shows:

> I had great desire and determination to go to school, and therefore, I went to a small town to seek employment. I obtained a position for two months at Two Dollars and Fifty cents a month. From there, I went to Salisbury, Rhodesia, and it was while I was in Rhodesia that I heard of an opportunity to get a position in a gold mine, where I could earn big wages. The trip to this mine cost $2.50, but I only had $1.00 in my pocket. In order to get there, I sold my two shirts and a pair of trousers, which were given to me by my brother, at a very small price. Then I bought my ticket and took the train to the mine, and there I worked hard for six months, and received enough money to enter Adams Seminary, which I did in the fall of 1905.

Nkomo's narrative then describes how he got to America and the hardships he faced. "For a period of two years, after the completion of my course in Adams Seminary, I taught school and made enough money to buy my ticket to America—I landed in America (in 1910) with little money to help me to go through school, but I managed to work my way through high school and college." Nkomo eventually entered Greenville College in Illinois and graduated in 1917.[30]

Meanwhile, the performance of returning graduates in their respective professions, as well as in those activities likely to ameliorate the condition of urban and rural dwellers, provided more fodder for the mystique of an overseas education. The returning students included members of Mzimba's church, the Presbyterian Church of Africa. The graduates kept their American sponsors and administrators of their universities informed about the work they were doing in Africa. They expressed their gratitude to the church for having paid their expenses and to university officials for having educated them.[31]

30. Simbini Mamba Nkomo, *How I Found Christ in the Jungles of Africa: The Story of My Conversion* (Greenville, Ill. 1917), 8–9. See Appendixes H and J.
31. Lincoln University graduates wrote regularly to the principal of that institution. See, for example, Katiya, "Letter from South Africa"; J. B. Zokufa to Principal of Lincoln University, in "A Word from Africa," *Lincoln University Herald*, February, 1909.

Among the men and women who gave a good account of themselves were Reverend J. Y. Tantsi, a bachelor of divinity graduate of Payne Theological Seminary at Wilberforce University, who succeeded Charlotte Manye, the founding principal of the Wilberforce Lillian Derrick Institute at Evaton, Transvaal. In 1908, Reverend Tantsi was appointed pastor of Bloemfontein; his former post was filled by Reverend Marshall M. Maxeke, a B.A. graduate of Wilberforce University. In 1909, Reverend H. N. Tantsi became principal of the Wilberforce Institute when Reverend Maxeke took charge of the Klerksdorp pastorate. In 1910, Reverend H. N. Tantsi reported on his work: ''The number of children registered this session is 99, the highest figure in the history of the school. The grounds are being cultivated, trees planted, the campus will soon be fenced in. The principal, assistant and male students make bricks, build and plaster in the afternoons. Our little knowledge of carpentry has helped us very much in this work. Every missionary to Africa ought to know something about this trade.'' [32]

The American Zulu Mission had perhaps the most resourceful minister of all agents educated abroad, Reverend John L. Dube, the son of Reverend James Dube, himself the first ordained minister of the American Zulu Mission. Dube was the first South African student sent to America. He arrived in 1887, and between then and 1914 he returned to the United States several times. He came under the influence of Tuskegee's self-help philosophy of several white sympathizers. Initially, Dube had been advised by Reverend W. C. Wilcox to attend Hampton Institute in Virginia, but he preferred the missionary's own alma mater, Oberlin College in Ohio. Upon arriving in the United States in 1887, Dube had exhausted his funds and relied on odd jobs to raise money to see him through college. Reverend Wilcox, who had initially aroused Dube's interest in further education and brought the young man with him to America, guided the young Zulu through his early days in Ohio. Reverend Wilcox gives an indication of the odds Dube had to face:

> When we reached Oberlin, there was only fifty cents left of the money that his mother put into my hands. I gave it to the young man and told him that now he would have to work or starve. His first job was on the road with a shovel, but one day of that work laid him on his back and he wished himself back in Africa. Afterward he tried various other

32. H. N. Tantsi, ''The Wilberforce Lillian Derrick Institute,'' *VOM*, September, 1910.

occupations. . . . He did not stick to anything very long, for he seemed to be too ambitious to make a rapid rise. . . . Nevertheless, all these experiences were a good school for the young Zulu. He never went into bad company, and when he had earned and saved a little money he went to school.[33]

Dube returned to Natal early in 1893 and in February took a teaching job in one of the American Zulu Mission schools. Dube must have become disenchanted, just as several other Africans had, with the education provided in the mission schools. He conceived of building an industrial school that would teach the Zulu some trades so they could fend for themselves in a South Africa that was fast becoming industrialized. With his wife, Nokutela, Dube went back to America for further training and raising funds for the construction of the Zulu Christian Industrial School. The Dubes were opposed in their new endeavor by their mentor, Reverend Wilcox, who thought the Zulu incapable of attaining self-determination in education:

We soon heard that they were raising money for a college among the Zulus, and the home [Boston] secretary wrote asking me what I thought about it. . . . From my knowledge of the Zulus in general, and some visionary ideas which I knew to be among them about a college which was to be run entirely by themselves, I had no faith in the scheme, and wrote my doubts frankly. That letter was used to oppose Mr. Dube's scheme. . . . When Mr. and Mrs. Dube came back to Natal with the money to start the Christian Industrial School, I was most happily disappointed. I had never before witnessed in him such evidence of humility. His Builder testified that Mr. Dube had wheeled stone and mixed up mortar with his own hands for the work on the building. When I saw all this, my heart smote me and I felt that I had done him a wrong, which I ought to undo so far as possible. I confess[ed] my mistake not only to John but I wrote a letter to the Natal *Mercury* and acknowledged my mistake publicly and told how Mr. Dube's conduct had disappointed my fears.[34]

33. Rev. W. C. Wilcox, "John L. Dube, the Booker Washington of the Zulus," *Missionary Review of the World*, December, 1909, pp. 917–19; W. C. Wilcox, "The Booker Washington of South Africa," *Oberlin Alumni Magazine*, March, 1927, article in John L. Dube Papers, Oberlin College Archives, Oberlin, Ohio.

34. "General Letter of the Zulu Mission, 1893," in American Zulu Mission, 1890–1899, Vol. I, Documents; Rev. John L. Dube, "A Native View of Christianity in South Africa," *Missionary Review of the World*, June, 1901, pp. 421–26; questionnaire, sent to Oberlin alumni for information to be published in *General Catalogue of Former Students*, in Dube Papers; Wilcox, "John L. Dube," 918.

In the final analysis, Dube's initiative was more decisive than missionaries' chicanery. Before he left America, Dube set up a committee to solicit funds and equipment for his school; he also recruited a West Indian builder at Tuskegee, Reynolds Scott, who constructed some of Ohlange School's facilities. Thus the school, which had its beginnings in 1898, was able to open its doors to sixty-three students on August 20, 1901. The Dubes were then assisted by two teachers. From 1904 onward, Reverend Dube was also assisted by his brother, Charles Dube, a graduate of Wilberforce University. Right from the start Ohlange stressed industrial education: agriculture, carpentry, and dressmaking. Reverend Dube, like Booker T. Washington, from whom he sought advice and material assistance for his school, wanted to prepare African youths for those categories of employment in which they would not compete with whites. Dube expressed his philosophy perhaps a little more diffidently than did the Tuskegeean: "We wish to be trained and be intelligent 'unskilled labourers,' in the house, store, workshop and farm—useful servants and assistants, small jobbers and peasant farmers."[35]

Reverend Dube's pioneering efforts in industrial education were commended by *Imvo* in 1909: "That it is an interesting experiment there can be no question. Conceived by a Native for Natives, it will be watched with the closest attention. To be sure, it is not the first institution of its kind in South Africa. Its chief interest however is in the fact that it is started spontaneously by a Native, and on the spontaneity of the moment may rest the seeds of its success." The editorial went on to state that Dube's African roots would enable him to empathize with the students and educate them more effectively than a white teacher could. Dube seems to have relished his stewardship of Ohlange and the satisfaction of watching his former students succeed in life. In 1914 he said:

35. American Committee, Statement No. 2, November, 1900, Statement No. 3, November, 1901, Annual Statement No. 4, November, 1902, all in Box 261, Washington Papers. Dube to Washington, November 30, December 3, 1907, both in Box 346, *ibid.*; Dube quoted in W. Manning Marable, "A Black School in South Africa," *Negro History Bulletin*, XXXVII (June-July, 1974), 258–61. See also Shula Marks, "The Ambiguities of Dependence: John L. Dube of Natal," *Journal of South African Studies*, I (April, 1975), 162–80; and R. Hunt Davis, "John L. Dube: A South African Exponent of Booker T. Washington," *Journal of African Studies*, II (Winter, 1975), 497–528.

We are pleased to see the transformation in the lives of our pupils, not only in the intellectual development and in the use of tools, but in their spiritual progress. This is our chief concern; we want to make them true leaders of the masses of our people who are still sitting in darkness.

It is refreshing to meet my former pupils holding important positions in various parts of South Africa. Some are carpenters, farmers, teachers of schools, missionaries, printers, overseers in native compounds on the mines, storemen, etc. We have nine teachers on our staff. . . . We have passed several boys in matriculation of the Cape of Good Hope University.

Perhaps the most favorable review came from a missionary in Natal, Reverend Wilcox, himself a former critic of Dube:

The popularity of the enterprise is phenomenal. More work has been obtained of the pupils than in any other school I know of in this land. I stood on the top of the long hill, and looked down to where the water had to be brought from in buckets, not only for all cooking and washing purposes, but for mixing mortar for the buildings, and I said if we should attempt to make our boys carry water up a hill like that, there would be a rebellion. They were at work daylight, their principal working with them, and they were still at it till dark at night. But how about the results? Well, I see what we so often fail [to achieve] in our schools, that much of the work seemed to be productive. Some of the boys gathered thatch grass on the place, which sells for a good price to the natives. Others quarried stone, which is used in the buildings and sold for building purposes—As in Booker Washington's College, so here, no money is expended for outside labour which the pupils can be made to do for themselves.[36]

On the other front in the search for higher education, Fort Hare University College opened in 1916. The event seemed to have a cathartic effect on the various groups that had labored so hard since 1905. But the part Fort Hare was destined to play in fulfilling its founders' conflicting expectations was yet to unfold.

36. "Mr. Dube's Work," editorial, *Imvo*, January 5, 1909; John L. Dube to Friends Overseas, April 30, 1914, in "News from Zul[u]Land," *VOM*, August, 1914; American Committee, *The Zulu Christian Industrial School* (Brooklyn, 1904), pamphlet in Hampton Institute Archives; W. C. Wilcox, "John L. Dube, the Booker Washington of the Zulus," *Missionary Review of the World*, December, 1909, pp. 917–19.

6/Ethiopianism in Action Again

Ethiopianism entered the twentieth century shrouded in uncertainty, its continued existence threatened by the white rulers of southern Africa. But, as we have seen, the SANAC proved to be a boon to independent African churches. The Ethiopian movement was grudgingly absolved of subversive intent, though its operations were kept under surveillance. The Ethiopian movement at this time had a variety of activists. Some Ethiopians put a premium on independence and secession from churches led by whites; others broke away from churches led by fellow Africans for reasons stemming from doctrinal differences, personality clashes, and church governance.

In Botswana, a most persistent cell of Ethiopianism was centered at Kanye, the capital of the Ngwaketse. Its leader was Mothowagae Mohlogeboa, who in 1903 skillfully used tribal legal remedies to save himself from banishment. But that reprieve did not bring lasting peace between him and Chief Bathoen. Between 1903 and 1910, Mothowagae, whose church in Ngwaketseland had seven hundred members, clashed with Bathoen several times. The chief complained that the Ethiopian did not pay him due respect; Mothowagae protested that Bathoen was interfering with his freedom of worship. They appealed to the colonial British administration for redress, and the local resident commissioner wavered between respecting Mothowagae's religious freedom and sanctioning the chief's desire to banish the Ethiopian. On one occasion the resident commissioner warned Mothowagae: "So long as your teaching does not include politics it will not be interfered with, but if it does and induces the people to refuse to obey their Chief or to act seditiously or illegally it will be stopped by the government which will not hesitate to use force if necessary." Mothowagae did not heed the official's advice, or at least did not accept his definition of insubordination. As a result, he and his followers were banished to Lekgolobotlo, an undesirable part of the chiefdom, in August, 1910. Nor did banishment mellow Mothowagae. He asserted his right to worship without official interference and relied on legal remedies to restrain abrasive officials. Mothowagae's resilience paid off: the Ethiopian preserved his church and attracted a core of dedicated followers well into the 1920s. By 1921 he was still fighting the chief in court for interfering with his church. LMS missionaries and colonial authorities alike prayed that old age and death would soon overtake a man they considered a nuisance.[1]

If Mothowagae's brand of Ethiopianism was deliberate and executed with skill, several daring Ethiopians appeared in Botswana in the guise of messiahs. Nevertheless, the ecstatic Ethiopian had one thing in common with Mothowagae, namely, the replacement of all forms of wretchedness with a millennium of bliss. Some messianic Ethiopians were easily suppressed by Tswana chiefs and colonial officials, but others doggedly continued to exist. Sencho Legong, for example, appeared in Chief Bathoen's territory in March, 1908, and proclaimed that extraordinary relief was imminent. Reverend Howard Williams, an LMS agent among the Ngwaketse at Kanye, gives an indication of the range of Legong's claims and to some degree reveals his mastery of mass psychology:

> To be strictly accurate [Legong] did not claim to be the Messiah except at some moments of abnormal mental excitement. He seems to have been content with a much less honourable title, though at the same time making claim to supernatural powers almost co-existent with those of the true Messiah Himself. He was a prophet, so he declared, not hailing from some obscure and unknown part of the desert, but a mo [Tswana] born, bred, and still living about 25 miles northwest of the place [Kanye], situated in the Chief Sebele's country. . . . His particular form of madness is by no means exceptional. In my long experience as a Missionary I have met others similarly affected, but in this instance his quasi-religious propaganda was allied to a cunning and method quite out of the common. Indeed one's first impressions were that his madness was of too sane a type to warrant any other treatment than that hard [prison] labour. The year 1908 had opened

1. Chirenje, *A History of Northern Botswana,* Chap. 6; interview between Resident Commissioner and Mothowagae, August 9, 1910, in "Church Dispute at Kanye," 410, R. C. 7/8, BNA. See, for example, Gagoanwe a Gaseitsiwe to Resident Commissioner, June 27, 1921, Acting Chief Tshosa Sebego to Resident Commissioner, October 20, 1921, both *ibid.*

with every prospect of a plentiful harvest, and this too after a year of great scarcity. Then the rain ceased and by the end of March it was evident that the prospective harvest was practically doomed to failure. At this critical time the "prophet" made his appearance at the boundary of the Chief Bathoen's territory. He announced himself as the herald of coming wonders—rain would fall and almost cover the hill tops, for the future harvests would be triennial, and the natives, freed from the control of the white man, would be allowed to recover all their heathen customs and ceremonies.

It was a measure of the prophet's influence that Legong could be praised when it appeared that rain might come, but was absolved when the rain disappeared. Some members of the LMS church burned their Bibles; others offered Legong gifts, which he reluctantly accepted. In the end, he acquired 30 heifers, 129 sheep and goats, a gun, a span of 14 oxen, one wagon, several fowl, and some corn. However, Legong stepped into a hornet's nest when he went to the Ngwato capital, Serowe. Chief Kgama tried him for his prophetic pretensions, sentenced him to a caning, and confiscated all his gifts.[2] Legong went back south after his unhappy brush with Kgama's laws. But peace eluded him there also, as chiefs and colonial officials harried him on all sides until 1913, when he decided to take a job in one of the Johannesburg mines. It is not clear if he proselytized among the miners, but he returned to Botswana shortly afterward and seems to have led a quiet life thereafter.

In Barotseland (now Zambia), the Paris Evangelical Missionary Society (PEMS) experienced the ripples of church dissent in 1900, when evangelist W. J. Mokalapa, whom the society had recruited there, broke away. Edward Shillito may have exaggerated when he claimed that the Ethiopian's secession led to Reverend Francois Coillard's death, but there is little doubt that the French missionaries were irritated by the Sotho evangelist. Mokalapa's secession was supported by the Lozi king Lebusi Lewanika, who encouraged him to affiliate his breakaway group with the AME church's Fourteenth District in South Africa. The groundwork was done by C. A. A. Rideout, who visited Barotseland in 1902 and convinced

2. Rev. Howard Williams, "The Native Messiah," *CE*, October 1, 1909; Kanye Annual Report, December 31, 1908, Rev. R. H. Lewis, Molepolole Annual Report, 1908, both in Box 4, LMS Archives.

King Lewanika that the AME church could improve the educational system, with which the Lozi were dissatisfied.[3]

Mokalapa was not unknown to the Lozi royal house, having earlier advised Lewanika to be wary of missionary advice in his dealings with representatives of the British South Africa Company. "Do not listen to these white missionaries. They do not love you. It is only we who love you," he is reported to have said. Mokalapa's break with the PEMS in 1900 coincided with Lewanika's disillusionment with the largely religious instruction at the society's schools. In addition to improving school efficiency, Mokalapa wanted to offer courses in English, the mastery of which the Lozi and other southern African communities valued very much. Mokalapa also wanted to build secondary, industrial, and teacher-training schools, innovations that made his Ethiopianism even more attractive.[4]

In 1903, Mokalapa went to South Africa and affiliated his group with the AME church; Reverend Attaway appointed him presiding elder in Barotseland. Mokalapa returned with new teachers he had recruited in South Africa and his native Lesotho and in the process annoyed PEMS agents. Nevertheless, Mokalapa's innovations attracted Lewanika's children as well as the children of his *indunas* (councilors) and servants. In April, 1904, all evangelist trainees at the PEMS seminary threatened to withdraw and enroll in the AME church school, where English was taught. As Edward Shillito shows, they decided against that course of action when Reverend Coillard showed signs of failing to cope with the new wave of Ethiopianism and retreated into solitary spells of meditation in the woods. Coillard died later that year. Mokalapa and his fellow missionaries, in addition to providing Lewanika a relevant education, also did secretarial work for the royal family, a service that endeared them to the king. Lewanika gave them land and £100 for travel expenses. He was to render the AME church inestimable

3. Edward Shillito, *François Coillard: A Wayfaring Man* (London, 1923), 219; testimony of Stewart, in *SANAC*, IV, 906; Rideout, "African Kings"; Gerald L. Caplan, *The Elites of Barotseland, 1878–1969* (Berkeley, Calif., 1970), 80–81.

4. T. O. Ranger, "The 'Ethiopian' Episode in Barotseland, 1900–1905," *Rhodes-Livingstone Journal*, XXXVII (June, 1965), 26–41; Shillito, *François Coillard*, 206–27; Jacottet, "The Ethiopian Church." For the missionaries' role in colonizing Bulozi, see Robert I. Rotberg, *Christian Missionaries and the Creation of Northern Rhodesia, 1880–1924* (Princeton, 1965), 22ff.

service in 1904 when he dissuaded the British administration from deporting Mokalapa and his Sotho teachers on charges contrived by the British South Africa Company, which had been incensed by the church's influence on Lewanika.[5]

Mokalapa's school did not, however, run smoothly. For one thing, Lewanika did not fulfill his promise to pay the teachers' salaries. On a more serious level, Reverend Attaway imprudently advised Lewanika to invest £636 in a Cape Town firm (in which he was a partner). It went bankrupt, and the king lost all his money.[6] Faced with Attaway's unprofitable advice and the consequent failure to get financial help from Lewanika, Mokalapa sent an appeal to the mother church in America in 1905. He reviewed the plight of his mission in Barotseland and asked AME church members— and Christians of any denomination, for that matter—to support the fledgling undertaking. He painted an unfavorable picture of the state of Christianity in Bulozi and freely used emotive terms to support his plea for missionary assistance:

> Fathers, Brothers and Sisters of the African Methodist Episcopal Church at Home and Elsewhere:
> On behalf of the A.M.E. missionaries beyond the Zambezi River, I humbly beg to appeal to you for help.
> We, your sons, were sent to that heathen land to develop a new missionary work among those poor miserable benighted souls. This mission is totally amongst heathens; none of them have ever heard the Gospel of Christ up to date. They are still living in terrible darkness, worshipping graves of their ancestors, the sun and the moon, residing in dark, dense woods, in small huts, wearing skins.
> The Conference in South Africa has failed to support those labouring missionaries in that A.M.E. foreign field, who are suffering with their wives in that heathen land.
> Our foreign mission work among the heathens in the interior of Africa is bright, our future is brilliant, and our hopes are bright for the salvation of those benighted people. The A.M.E. Church has done excellent work by sending its missionaries among the heathens. But, now I am afraid those poor missionaries are going to die, since they are simply left to the hands of destitution and privations, with their poor wives, who sacrificed everything for the Redeemer and His Church's sake. They are without medicines to help themselves from terrible

5. Shillito, *François Coillard*, 206–27; Ranger, "The 'Ethiopian' Episode," 26–41.
6. Ranger, "The 'Ethiopian' Episode," 26–41; Caplan, *Elites*, 80.

fever of that country; they are without clothing; they shall soon be forced to wear skins.

We really thank Dr. A. H. Attaway for the box of medicines, books and a church bell he offered to these missionaries. We deeply thank our beloved Madame F. Gow, the President of the Mite Missionary Society in Cape Town, with her army, for the clothing and other things she offered to these missionaries. We also thank dear Mrs. Atkinson for the box of books she sent to this mission. God may bless His children for what they did for this mission work.

I am afraid this great foreign mission work is going to fall down, since there is a bad idea amongst the brethren that this mission work should be withdrawn, because the support is needed. Oh, what shall the Heaven say! What shall the earth say if the church withdraws the Zambezi mission work? Yes, our enemies shall glorify and say there is nothing that the A.M.E. Church can do.

I therefore humbly appeal to the fathers (Bishops) of the Church, to the ministers, to the sisters of the Mite Missionary Society and to the members of the Church of Christ in general, and to all friends who pray for the enlightenment and salvation of these poor benighted Africans.

Kindly help these poor labouring missionaries. Don't you think the church has done well by sending them to preach the Gospel among those poor and miserable benighted people?

Kindly help us and we shall be able to carry on this great mission work. God has opened every door for the A.M.E. Church among the heathens.

Fathers, brothers, sisters, pray for this great mission field. Help these missionaries in the dark country.

W. J. MOKALAPA, President of the Zambezi
AME Foreign Mission Field

Mokalapa's appeal came to nought. Unlike Reverend Dube, who traveled to America in person to solicit donations for his school and established an American committee to raise money for Ohlange, Mokalapa canvassed by the written word alone. The lack of response is therefore not surprising. Without money, the school could not function. By the beginning of 1906 all AME church teachers had left. Only Mokalapa remained in the kingdom to fan the embers of Ethiopianism well into the 1920s. The British South Africa Company sought to outflank the Ethiopians by founding in 1906 the Barotseland National School (BNS), which became the most efficient and popular school in colonial Northern Rhodesia.[7]

7. W. J. Mokalapa, "An Appeal for the Zambezi Foreign Mission Work in Central

In Southern Rhodesia, Reverend Micah Makgatho had more odds to overcome to sustain the AME church there than did the Sotho evangelist in Barotseland. Part of the reason for Makgatho's difficulties was that Rhodesian authorities had seen the kind of stiff resistance that well-organized blacks could mount in the Chimurenga war (1896–1897) and in Chief Kadungure Mapondera's daring challenge to white rule in the Mount Darwin area (1901–1902).[8] The government's vigilance in watching the AME church was not therefore surprising. As a corollary to this fear of Ethiopianism, authorities encouraged white missionary societies to plant stations all over the country with a view toward checking the spread of the Ethiopian movement. Although the government grants to societies were not as generous as they had been in the late 1890s, officials continued to offer land free of charge to various missionary groups and followed missionary progress reports with sympathy. Reports of the chief native commissioners are full of references to missionary activities. A 1903 report noted: "Mission work is being earnestly pursued throughout the Province. During the year several new Mission Stations have been opened, and I am informed by different missionaries that their work in this direction has been very encouraging."[9]

In spite of obstacles placed in his way, Makgatho succeeded in purchasing some land from the Riversdale Estate near Bulawayo on which he built a church and school; by 1907 the school had an enrollment of twelve students. Reports of chief native commissioners for Matebeleland complain of the political influence of Makgatho's church. In 1906, the commissioner reported:

Africa," *Christian Recorder*, May 25, 1905; Ranger, "The 'Ethiopian' Episiode"; Caplan, *Elites*, 80–81.

8. T. O. Ranger, *Revolt in Southern Rhodesia, 1896–1897* (London, 1967); Resident Commissioner (Salisbury) to High Commissioner in South Africa, telegram, September 28, 1901, Administrator to Army Commandant (Tete), October 7, 1901, both in Colonial Office, 879/76, Confidential Print, p. 216, PRO, London; Private Secretary to Resident Commissioner, February 27, 1902, Foreign Office to Colonial Office, September 5, 1902, both in Colonial Office, 879/78, Confidential Print, p. 163, *ibid.*

9. T. O. Ranger, "The Early History of Independency in Southern Rhodesia," in *Religion in Africa: Proceedings of a Seminar Held in the Centre of African Studies* (University of Edinburgh, 1964), 52–74; "Report of the Chief Native Commissioner, Matabeleland, for the year ended March 31, 1903," p. 6 (MS in Royal Commonwealth Society, London).

The influence of the Ethiopian movement which has in a small way been established here for four years, has not made itself felt. It would appear that the objective of this particular order in the first instance is to impress on the uncivilized and unenlightened native that the sect is conducted quite independently of any European control and is supported entirely by people of their own colour. The dissemination of such propaganda would convey to the native mind some political meaning. A close observance of this movement is kept.

By 1916 the refrain against the AME church was still being maintained. In that year the commissioner noted that missionary work under whites was to be encouraged, but that Ethiopian churches were dangerous to the country and therefore "meet with no sympathy or assistance" from the government. It is significant that he did not mention the AME church by name, but complained of "native propagandists." He must have known of Matthew Chigaga Zvimba's church, the Original Church of the White Bird (Shiri Chena), founded in 1915.[10]

Matthew was a disappointment to missionaries and the Native Affairs Department because he defied their attempts to cultivate a corps of docile chiefs. To accomplish this end, the new rulers bypassed legitimate traditional chiefs who appeared to advance nationalist causes, and in their stead appointed malleable loyalists. Chief Chigaga Zvimba was one such appointee, and his two sons, Mishak and Matthew, were educated at the Nenguwo (Waddilove) Methodist school with a view toward grooming them for future leadership. For some time the scheme appeared to have worked, and Matthew impressed a white observer as emulating European ways of life, He went on to start the first Methodist school in the Zvimba Reserve. However, Matthew's Methodist mentors did not recognize the deep resentment against Europeans harbored by blacks since the imposition of white rule in the late 1890s. Nor did the Methodist missionaries sympathize with African aspirations: some agents looked on the government's harassment of blacks as an impetus to conversion. It is little wonder that Chief Chigaga Zvimba, in spite of appearing to favor the Methodists, resented their presence in his chiefdom. In 1900, Reverend Avon Walton reported on Chief Zvimba's veiled resistance to the Methodist mission: "Z[v]imba the paramount chief, while pro-

10. "Reports of Chief Native Commissioner for 1906 and 1907," pp. 1, 4, 14, 16; "Report of Chief Native Commissioner for 1916," p. 3.

fessing friendliness is, I fear, opposed to us at heart." This prognosis did not, however, temper missionary high-handedness: Chief Zvimba and his subjects were moved from their land and settled twenty miles away. The Methodists appropriated the chief's land for themselves.[11]

The trauma of eviction, and white intransigence generally, must have weighed heavily on Matthew. Then in 1907, Matthew was transferred by the church to Gatooma. Like Mothowagae who faced the same dilemma in 1901, Matthew refused the new appointment and in consequence was dismissed as teacher and catechist. But Matthew was not cowed: he denounced white ministers and laymen while preparing himself for the task of launching his own church. His political awareness of the white man's injustice was reinforced by divine inspiration. Matthew should found a church to save his people. In this respect, he had something in common with messiahs in southern Africa. Matthew berated whites for suppressing black aspirations, and when he launched Shiri Chena in 1915, the fallen Zvimba Shona patriots in the 1896–1897 war were revered as saints and martyrs of the new Ethiopian church. Matthew persistently dismissed his white critics as detractors who wished to deprive the people of Zvimba of the true gospel of Christ.[12]

Matthew clearly mixed politics with religion. Rhodesian authorities therefore kept an eye on both Zvimba brothers. One government officer reported: "I have—arranged with a trusty local native—to keep these two men watched, particularly with reference to anything they may say, whether in their private conversation, or in public utterance, that may be of an unsettling nature. I hope later on to be able to procure some small reward for this native's work, particularly as he does not relish it becoming known that he is assisting us." Reverend J. H. Loveless, a Wesleyan missionary in the Zvimba Reserve, together with an African teacher called J. Msanje also kept Matthew's church under surveillance and informed Rhodesian authorities about the Ethiopians' activities.[13]

11. T. O. Ranger, *The African Voice in Southern Rhodesia, 1898–1930* (Evanston, Ill., 1970), 19–25; Rev. H. Oswald Brigg (at Kwenda) to Marshall Hartley, April 28, 1901, Avon Walton (in Bulawayo) to Hartley, December 28, 1900, Rev. John White (at Rudaka [Marondera]) to Hartley, August 27, 1902, all in WMMS.

12. Matthew Zvimba to Native Commissioner, November 22, 1915, in Item no. A3/6/9, NAZ; Ranger, *The African Voice in Southern Rhodesia*, 19–25.

13. J. Msanje to Rev. J. H. Loveless, October 9, 1915, in Item no. A3/6/9, NAZ.

A white trader in the Zvimba Reserve, Ruben Rubenstein, was also an informant for the native commissioner and had reason to dislike the Zvimba brothers. They organized a successful boycott of his store, which failed four months after it was opened. Rubenstein later reported that the Zvimba brothers were in the habit of saying the white settlers would shortly be driven out of Rhodesia by Africans. He then gave an account of how his business collapsed. "Several of the natives have told me that they have been advised by Matthew and Mishak not to patronise my store and not to sell me anything, saying if they refused to sell me foodstuffs I would starve and would soon leave their district—The result of this was that I was unable to purchase a fowl at any price and I could not buy eggs under five shillings per dozen—The women of the district were afraid to come to my store—I was boycotted and had to close down my store."[14]

The leader of Shiri Chena opposed the white man's rule and religion throughout his life, and officers of the Native Affairs Department, who did not grasp Matthew's resilience, were apt to dismiss him as insane. But the Methodist church was evidently adversely affected by Matthew's activities. In 1921 a white missionary reported that an African minister they posted to Zvimba was unable "to win the confidence of the people. It can only be said that the work in this Zvimba Reserve is very difficult, and we must either pursue a more vigorous policy . . . or withdraw from the work altogether."[15]

If Shiri Chena was confined to Zvimba, its message of self-determination reached other parts of Southern Rhodesia, where the Ethiopian movement was making headway in the guise of the AME church. Rhodesian authorities, true to their pledges in the early 1900s, had officers of the Native Affairs Department keep them apprised of Ethiopian activities. By 1917, the AME church had opened branches in southern Mashonaland, Gwelo, Mashaba, and Fort Victoria. Southern Mashonaland had had an independent church since about 1910, when Isaiah Charles Chidembo planted the First Ethiopian Church. Chidembo had converted during the early 1890s when he worked as a cook in the Transvaal; by the time he returned to Rhodesia, he had become a bishop. The First Ethi-

14. Ruben Rubenstein statement, October 7, 1915, *ibid.*
15. Testimony of Mr. X of Zvimba, personal communication, October, 1973; S. D. Gray "Report of the Rhodesia District, 1921," in WMMS.

opian Church does not seem to have attracted a large following right away, but by 1938 it had about one thousand members.[16]

Before 1920, there were minor secessions from white churches within Rhodesia itself, though government officials tended to be preoccupied with AME church activities. A case in point is a report of 1917: "Instances have occurred where native evangelists have seceded from religious bodies under the supervision of Europeans and adopted Ethiopian tendencies. This is sometimes due to friction between the native evangelist and the white missionary. The real significance of Ethiopianism is in its racial character. From a political point of view, the administration have considered it desirable to keep under careful observation any movement of this nature." Nevertheless, the villain in government eyes continued to be Micah Makgatho of the AME church. In 1919 a municipal officer in Fort Victoria's African township wrote: "It appears that he [Makgatho] has baptized some 40 natives at Mashaba and has gone back to Bulawayo. The native, whose certificate of baptism I enclose states that this man told them that their church was one purely for the natives and quite independent of Europeans—rather a mischievous thing in a country like this."[17] He also advised that Makgatho be forbidden to enter African reserves. In consequence Makgatho could not open a station at Ndaba Ezinduna in 1920, but the elusive Ethiopian, who had started the Dutch Reformed church mission in Rhodesia in 1893 before breaking with that church in 1900, was able to wriggle his way through official surveillance. He opened some stations in other reserves, including Chief Segwala's reserve in Lower Gwelo. In 1925 the chief native commissioner could report: "The A.M.E. or Ethiopian Church is reported to be showing renewed vigour, after a long period of somnolence."[18] This report indicates that however much whites detested its political activities, the AME church had weathered the storm of

16. "Report of the Chief Native Commissioner for the Year 1917," p. 6; for Bishop Chidembo, see M. L. Daneel, *Old and New in Southern Shona Independent Churches* (The Hague, 1971), 369–74.

17. "Report of the Chief Native Commissioner for the Year 1917," p. 4; W. E. Thomas (Superintendent of Natives, Fort Victoria) to Chief Native Commissioner (Salisbury), July 4, 1919, in CNC.

18. 82/1919, NAZ. "Report of Chief Native Commissioner, 1925," pp. 3–4. See also reports for 1921, 1922, 1926, and 1931. Chief Native Commissioner (Salisbury) to Superintendent of Natives (Fort Victoria), September 29, 1919, in No. Z. 3137/3930, NAZ; "A.M.E. Missionaries Penetrate Wild Africa," *VOM*, December, 1917.

criticism directed against it since the early 1900s and that its survival was now more or less assured.

Makgatho's counterparts in South Africa seem to have consolidated their position after 1906. Secular and religious authorities looked on Ethiopian churches more as nuisances than a serious challenge to white hegemony. Some officials who spied on Ethiopians were convinced that some groups did engage in political activities, but the individuals were easily apprehended and dealt with according to colonial law. As a result of this cautious vigilance, Ethiopian churches were able to sustain themselves while new sects proliferated. One example was Reverend Mzimba's Presbyterian Church of Africa, which took advantage of the post-SANAC spirit of tolerance and consolidated itself. The church also benefited from a dispute within the white-dominated Presbyterian churches of Scotland. It was decided in 1900 to merge the Free Church of Scotland and the United Presbyterian church into one, the United Free Church of Scotland. Some members of the Free Church, a minority at that, opposed the union and claimed the entire church heritage. This group, variously referred to as "Wee Frees" and "Legal Free Church," stunned the Scottish religious community by successfully suing for possession of the church heritage, which the House of Lords awarded them in August, 1904. However, the Legal Free Church's glee was short-lived, as a royal commission reversed that decision in April, 1905, and restored the property and heritage to the United Free Church of Scotland.[19]

While those claims and counterclaims were sapping the vitality of the church, the South African Presbyterians (*i.e.*, of the Synod of Kaffraria) lost one of their prominent elders when Reverend James Stewart died in 1905. In February, 1906, a Lovedale missionary reported that Mzimbaites were going to take over at Lovedale: "I have been assured by several natives that the Mzimbaites are quite convinced that since Dr. Stewart's death, it is certain that Lovedale will pass into their hands, and that Mzimba will yet be Principal of Lovedale." In addition, Mzimbaites were joined by local headman Bovani Mabandla in their opposition to giving the Lovedale farm to the interstate African college. In the meantime, Mzimba was organizing a petition to affiliate the Presbyterian

19. J. R. Fleming, *A History of the Church in Scotland, 1875–1929* (Edinburgh, 1933), 56–81.

Church of Africa with the Legal Free Church of Scotland, even though the fortune of that group was lost in April, 1905. The Legal Church's short-lived possession of Presbyterian property had apparently impressed Mzimba, who saw in the Wee Frees' situation much that resembled his fight with Lovedale missionaries. By June, 1907, Mzimba had mustered 35,000 petitioners for affiliation with the Wee Frees, and among his supporters was headman Menziwa Luzipo of the Transkei. Although the petitioners represented the entire membership of the Presbyterian Church of Africa (7,000 full members and 28,000 adherents), Mzimba had influenced African Presbyterians against the United Free Church of Scotland. At least one observer, Professor M'Culloch, who, early in 1907, visited South Africa under the auspices of a learned society called the British Association, reported that African Christians preferred the Free Church. Although M'Culloch's observation was challenged by Lovedale missionaries, Reverend Mzimba's influence was acknowledged by *Imvo*. Although the paper opposed Ethiopianism, it suggested that the United Free Church of Scotland come to terms with Mzimba. However, reconciliation was not achieved, since neither side would compromise.[20]

Reverend Mzimba died on June 25, 1911, and was succeeded by Reverend J. S. Mazwi the same year. A plethora of eulogies offered conflicting assessments of Mzimba's impact upon South African society. Perhaps the most sympathetic tribute to Mzimba's work was given by Dr. M. Robert Mahlangeni, who wrote from Ireland in 1912:

> When I heard of the founding of the Presbyterian Church of Africa, I felt that a new era had dawned upon South Africa, and that the spirit of unity which has been for so long the bane of our race was making its presence felt amongst us. Not only those who are truly concerned in the moral and religious upliftment of our country, but even the spiritual sceptics will admit that such a church will serve the double purpose of keeping ablaze the fire of Christianity in Africa, and at the

20. Rev. John Lennox to Dr. Smith, February 17, 1906, No. 7801, in Free Church of Scotland Archives; Rev. E. Makiwane to the editor, April 22, 1907, in "The Free Church in South Africa," *Scotsman*, May 20, 1907; Rev. Mzimba to Free Church of Scotland, telegram, July, 1907, Lennox to Smith, March 5, October 5, 1906, June 10, 1907, all in No. 7801, Free Church of Scotland Archives; "Free Church Members in South Africa," *Scotsman*, March 7, 1907; Rev. Lennox to the editor, April 8, 1907, in "The Free Church in South Africa," *Scotsman*, undated clipping; "Facts and Comments. Mr. Mzimba," *Imvo*, August 10, 1907.

same time maintaining and strengthening our national spirit and patriotism. . . . Though I am of another denomination I am sufficiently broadminded as to realize that there are many roads to truth, purity and goodness, and that any church, no matter its denomination cannot but be an important factor in moral, social and religious advancement of South Africa. For this reason, if for no other, I wish the Presbyterian Church of Africa all prosperity and success.

Mahlangeni went on to suggest that Mzimba's followers guard against petty jealousies and greed and that they "substitute altruism for egoism so that the world may be able to realize that Africans also possess the spirit of patriotism, communion and christianity."[21]

Mzimba's contemporary, Reverend James Dwane, was plodding on since his Order of Ethiopia had become affiliated with the Anglican church in 1900. He was discovering that his white spiritual partners were less enthusiastic about his group than he had hitherto imagined. In 1907 the Anglican bishop of Cape Town implied that Dwane's group was unreasonable in insisting on a distinct identity within the Anglican church. He also reported that only 50 to 60 of the 1,400 members had been confirmed in the Anglican church. In 1908 the Order of Ethiopia was reported to have 1,346 confirmed members and 3,410 adherents. A church commission investigating relations with the Order reported that "never for a moment had they [Dwane's group] lost sight of the original motives of Ethiopianism." For that reason, the commission said, most of the Anglican clergy were unable to cooperate with the Dwaneites. This tarnished relationship with the Anglicans must have bewildered Dwane, whose quest for recognition and honor partly led to his break with the AME church. Nor was Dwane to relinquish his search for honor. He sought to make his group more respectable by taking an active role in civic affairs. For example, he supported the native college movement. In 1911, Dwane used his group's tenuous links with the Anglican church to communicate with the king of England. He and the acting Anglican bishop of Cape Town sent a cable to the king, on behalf of the Order of Ethiopia, in which they asked "to be permitted to offer our humble

21. Dr. M. Robert Mahlangeni to the editor, May 25, 1912, in "Presbyterian Church of Africa," *Imvo*, July 30, 1912. For eulogies, see, for example, "The Late Rev. Jeremiah Mzimba"; "Rev. E. Makiwane's Appreciation," *Imvo*, October 3, 1911.

congratulations on your Majesty's Accession to the Throne and approaching Coronation, and to give the assurance of our constant prayers that your Majesty may be long preserved in health and wealth, and may be ever guided by heavenly wisdom in the discharge of the difficult duties of the exalted position to which your Majesty has been called."[22] The cable was sent through the Cape governor, and Dwane was trying to curry favor with colonial officials to save his church. In fact, the Order of Ethiopia survived Dwane, who died on February 9, 1916.

Among the more charismatic leaders who emerged early in the twentieth century was Isaiah Shembe who was transformed from a womanizer (isoka) to a champion of Zulu religious regeneration. Shembe was born in 1896, and his early life is obscure. From 1906 to 1911 he was a member of William Mathebule Leshega's African Native Baptist Church in The Rand. Leshega had broken with the National Baptist Convention and had founded his own church in 1905. Change came to Shembe after he had experienced a trance in which a voice told him to go to a mountain in Zululand called Inhlangakazi. After he got there, he prayed. In a dream he saw a skeleton of a white evangelist that said that God was going to give him power to heal; the two angels at the mountain gave him some sacrament. Shembe called his church Isonto Lama Nazaretha (Church of the Nazarites), and its headquarters was at Ekuphakameni near Ohlange, north of Durban. In due course, Shembe gained much fame as a healer and his church observed two important annual festivals, the January feast held at Inhlangakazi mountain and the July celebration at Ekuphakameni. Sundkler has shown that Shembe's healing power won him support among some Zulu and their chiefs.[23]

Nevertheless, some Zula chiefs and their subjects remained traditionalists and frowned upon Ethiopianism and the white man's medicine. In 1912, Reverend Frederick Bridgman of the American Zulu Mission reported on a Zulu chief's contempt for Western medicine:

22. "The Order of Ethiopia of the Church of the Province of South Africa," CE, December 1, 1909; "Order of Ethiopia," Imvo, June 13, 1911.

23. Absalom Vilakazi, "Isonto Lama Nazaretha (The Church of the Nazarites)" (M.A. thesis, Kennedy School of Missions, Hartford Seminary Foundation, 1954), 31; Esther L. Roberts, "Shembe: The Man and His Work" (M.A. thesis, University

Oh, the white doctors! Yes, I have consulted several of them at different times. The wonder is that they all agree in their nonsense. They
tell me that my trouble is due to beer and that I won't get well unless
I give it up! What foolishness! We Zulus have drunk this beer for
generations. Up and down these hills and valleys people are drinking
beer, some of them men as old as I am, but not one of them has such
[swollen] feet. If it were due to beer, surely others would have the same
disease. The whites are very clever, but there are some of our native
diseases which they cannot understand.[24]

If the Zulu chief's statement is a poignant restatement of African
traditions, 1912 was also a high-water mark in the African initiative
to achieve self-determination and to restore human dignity. A
number of secular and religious leaders banded together to form the
South African Native Congress (SANC). The South African Native
Congress was renamed the African National Congress (ANC) in the
1920s. Nor was the birth of a political party altogether unexpected;
in many respects it was complementary to the religious ferment
in the African community. The SANC, like the Ethiopian movement, sought to promote the political and social well-being of the
irredentist masses. The ten years preceding the formation of the
SANC had seen a hardening of white attitudes toward Africans as
whites sought to consolidate their respective states into the Union
of South Africa. Africans were called the "black peril" and the
"black giant," the names indicating the whites' perennial fear of
an African revolt. And in this fear-ridden atmosphere, whites sought
to entrench themselves by discriminating against blacks, some
whites actually resorting to summary measures to punish Africans. In some cases, Africans were alleged to have committed sex
offenses. In 1908 a correspondent wrote to a church paper, expressing fears that anti-African feeling might well lead to senseless
killings: "It has seemed to me as I have watched the papers for the
last four years, that there is a steady and continuous effort to rouse
the white population to lynch the Natives. . . . Lately I have noticed
. . . in the *South African News* attitude towards what it calls the

---

of South Africa, 1936), 26–34; Bengt G. Sundkler, *Zulu Zion and Some Swazi
Zionists* (London, 1976), 161–72.

24. Frederick B. Bridgman, "Notes from Natal," April 18, 1912, in 722, South
Africa Mission, Zulu Branch, 1910–1919, Vol. I, Documents, Houghton Library,
Harvard University.

'Black Peril.' It is awful to contemplate the possibility of such scenes being witnessed in this land as have so often been seen in America.''[25] If the correspondent's fears were exaggerated, racial discrimination did exist. And some Africans, including the mission-educated elite, were lynched.

J. B. Luti was a victim of discrimination. As we have seen, he had in 1898 opposed Ethiopianism and favored continued white control in church affairs. Luti subsequently completed his studies at Blythswood and was appointed to teach there. In 1907 the manager of the Standard Bank at Butterworth in the Transkei rejected Luti's application for a checking account because of his race. *Imvo* deplored the manager's judgment and implied that a boycott might be justifiable: "Why was a [bank] branch opened at Butterworth? It was opened in view of the resources of the country. Any business to stand in the Transkei must be supported by the Natives. . . . We are always against boycotting. . . . We believe in *Fair-Play*, but when one starts a stone rolling down a hill we are not responsible for its consequences." It is not clear if this threat was carried out, but the wave of discrimination seems to have affected several aspects of African life. Not the least of these areas was travel on trains, where Africans were subjected to indignities, prompting *Imvo* to criticize the railway management. African resentment was succinctly stated by a correspondent in 1912: "The writer of this letter travels some 8000 miles per year on the lines within the Cape Province. Allow me therefore to commence with Blaney Junction Coffee Stall where Natives are made to wait until nearly all Europeans have been served which is hardly ever before the train starts moving." The letter listed the stations at which blacks were subjected to discriminatory treatment. Perhaps forming "a society for the protection of the Native travelling public" would bring redress. Nor were canteens the only places where blacks were

25. "Fair Play" to the editor, October 14, 1908, in "The Black Peril," *CE,* November 1, 1908. For summary measures taken by white settlers, see, for example, "Killed in Cold Blood. Sensational Tragedy at Bulawayo. His Own Judge, an Angry Father's Retribution," *South African News,* May 18, 1911. See "White Women in Danger," London *Daily Express,* June 30, 1911, "South Africa's Black Peril," London *Daily Telegraph,* June 6, 1911, "Natives and White Women," *Transvaal Leader,* June 6, 1911, all in MSS. Brit. Emp. S22, G.200, Rhodes House, Oxford. See also Solomon T. Plaatje, *The Mote and the Beam: An Epic on Sex-Relationship 'Twixt White and Black in British South Africa* (New York, 1921), in which he ridicules official attitudes toward sexual relations between blacks and whites.

inconvenienced. There is evidence to show that considerable harassment occurred on trains, as Reverend John L. Dube found out in 1913 when he was arrested for traveling without a pass. *Imvo* angrily reported: "Rev. J. L. Dube was taken out of the train by policemen at Van Reenen on the border of the Free State . . . for being without a pass; an episode which is a disgrace to the Union [of South Africa] which permits such laws to continue within its borders."[26]

The indignities perpetrated on blacks were abhorred by neighboring chiefs before and after the formation of the Union of South Africa. If Sotho chiefs had inherited a dislike of their white neighbors from their nineteenth-century nation builder Moshweshwe, Tswana chiefs had an equally unhappy record of relations with whites. Chief Kgama III of the Ngwato had, as far back as the 1870s, characterized Afrikaner settlers as unchristian because they violated Ngwato territory; other Tswana chiefs had their share of troubles with Afrikaners. As a result, Tswana chiefs opposed suggestions that they join the Union of South Africa and cited injustices suffered by Africans in the white republics as the main reason they would remain under a British protectorate. Chief Kgama was emphatic in his rejection and reassured Lord Selborne, the Cape Colony governor, that the decision of Tswana chiefs to seek British protection in 1895 was irrevocable.

> As regards the present question of Union of South Africa, I am very distressed. My "Union" was made with England a long time ago, when at that time [1895] the Chartered Company tried to take us under their control, I fled to England, passing by the Cape Colony, Transvaal, and the Free State, colonies that were then existent as now, when I arrived I saw the Great Ruler, Mr. Chamberlain and said, "I do not wish to be under the control of the Chartered Company, but under the control of England," and Mr. Chamberlain said, "All right, there is no one who will compel you to do what you do not want to do.". . . And I repeat, I belong to the Government of England, and I do not wish to go under the administration mentioned of the Union of South Africa.

Kgama's views were reinforced by several Tswana chiefs. The Tswana disapproval of white rule was again voiced in 1912, when the LMS proposed a union of all its Congregational churches in

26. Story in untitled paragraph, *Imvo*, March 19, 1907; "Native Traveller" to the editor, in "Native Travelling," *ibid.*, October 15, 1912; "Native College Convention," editorial, *ibid.*, February 4, 1913.

southern Africa. Tswana Christians and chiefs (some of whom were non-Christian) opposed the move because it would impose a political link with two undesirable states, the Union of South Africa and Southern Rhodesia.[27]

In the Union of South Africa proper, pervasive racial discrimination led Africans to form an all-embracing political organization, the South African Native Congress. The High Commission territories—Basutoland, Bechuanaland, and Swaziland—were represented at the inaugural conference as well as in the executive committee elected at that meeting. Reverend John L. Dube was elected president of the SANC; elected to the executive committee were some members of the AME church, the Reverend Henry R. Ngcayiya being the most outstanding. Between 1912 and 1916 the SANC opposed several measures introduced by the Union government to undermine the political and economic well-being of blacks, but to very little effect. The white rulers were more determined than ever to complete their domination of blacks. In the welter of frustration that greeted incipient African nationalism, the only ray of hope lay in the progress made in building a new African college. At long last, in 1916, Fort Hare University College opened its doors to students.[28]

27. Chirenje, *A History of Northern Botswana*, pp. 81ff.; "Meeting of Lord Selborne. The Protectorate Chiefs," *Imvo*, April 19, 1910; "Copy of Minutes of the Magistrate's Court, Serowe, January 9, 1912," in Jennings to F. H. Hawkins, January 19, 1912, LMS Archives.

28. Peter Walshe, *The Rise of African Nationalism in South Africa* (Berkeley and Los Angeles, 1971), 30–42ff.; F. Z. S. Peregrino, "Native National Congress, What It Is," *Imvo*, March 26, 1912; Bridgman, "The Black Giant Aroused," in "Notes from Natal"; "S.A. Native College. The Opening of Classes," *Imvo*, March 7, 1916; "Prof[essor] Kerr's Inaugural," *ibid.*, March 21, 1916.

7/A Consummation of Sorts

During the first thirty years of its existence in southern Africa, Ethiopianism was dominated by the church secessionists who were dissatisfied with their subordinate position. They wrested leadership from white missionaries in moves that were often carefully calculated. The Ethiopian's quest for black leadership was supplemented by the "prophet" or "messiah" who relied mainly on the contemplative and the transcendental aspects of his vision for redressing ills afflicting African communities. The important point is that all these African-led religious groups were alienated from domineering white missionaries and laymen. They were desperately improvising a modicum of African dignity and survival in a ruthless colonial milieu. Soon after their conversion, the black Christians, who had forsaken their traditional religion with all the sociopolitical security it guaranteed, tested Christian teaching—love and the universal brotherhood of man—in practice and found it wanting, riddled at every turn with contradictions.

Yet, when Africans sought to partake of meaningful religious experience through church independency, they found the road to fulfillment marred by many hurdles of the white man's making. The white groups correctly surmised that church independency enhanced the African's self-esteem, which in turn was bound to spur blacks to challenge white rule. In consequence, religious and secular white authorities did everything in their power to discredit church independency and to render it ineffective. To achieve this end, the whites resorted to colonial laws to harass nascent Ethiopians while at the same time carrying out smear campaigns in which church secessionists were depicted as advocates, for example, of polygamy and beer drinking. While some Ethiopians incorporated some of these indigenous practices to make Christianity compatible with African traditions, the whites chose to highlight these innovations and to underplay the more compelling reasons behind Ethiopianism. The whites softened their opposition to Ethiopianism only when they were satisfied that the Ethiopian movement did not have the capacity to upset white political power.

For their part, African church secessionists, Mokone's Ethiopian Church of South Africa in particular, quickly realized that their assertion of independence would come to nought unless their movement was led by skilled agents. They invited qualified Afro-Americans to come to their aid as missionaries and they sent African students to black colleges in America. In the process, Africans and Afro-Americans exchanged views on the need for the latter group to come to South Africa. These exchanges contain some of the most profound statements ever made on black solidarity and touched on two main lines of pan-American thought. On the one hand, Afro-Americans revealed that they had over the years achieved a metaphysical transcendence of the slave experience and construed their bondage to have been a divinely inspired apprenticeship for service in Africa.[1] On the other, black South Africans displayed corresponding historical empathy with Africans of the diaspora by describing themselves as "those who escaped transportation to America."[2] They confirmed the Afro-American prophetic vision of his role in black history by inviting him to come and minister in southern Africa. The convergence of both schools of thought established a link between southern Africa and the United States that has over the years survived the vagaries of politics.

The advent of the AME church in southern Africa opened a new chapter in relations between Africans of the diaspora and the continent. Hitherto Afro-Americans had proselytized among West Africans, whom they regarded as their natural progenitors. Now they chose to work in a region that afforded them a unique experience. By 1916, the South African Conference of the AME church (the

1. See, for example, Tule to AME Church, November 12, 1895, in "Letter from South Africa"; Majeke, The Role of the Missionaries in Conquest, 25ff.; Rev. Mokone to President Councill"; Turner, "Speech"; J. Mutero Chirenje, "The Afro-American Factor in Southern African Ethiopianism, 1890–1906," in David Chanaiwa (ed.) Profiles of Self-Determination: African Responses to European Colonialism in Southern Africa, 1652 to the Present (Northridge, Calif., 1976), Chap. 7.

2. See "The Jubilee Singers," editorial, Imvo, October 16, 1890.

Fourteenth District) had 108 ordained ministers and 216 preachers and lay helpers, more than 18,000 full members and 2,065 probationers, and more than 1,000 day students in the primary and lower primary schools. Bethel Institute, Lillian Derrick Institute, and Chatsworth Institute all had between them more than 500 students in postprimary courses. It is difficult to get accurate figures for all independent African churches, but the fact that Reverend Mzimba's Presbyterian Church of Africa by 1910 had 13,335 members, 30,000 adherents, and 27 ordained ministers suggests that church independency attracted considerable following.[3] Significantly, some teachers the AME church employed in its postprimary schools had received university training in America on AME church scholarships. The African students who studied in America and the Afro-American missionaries assigned to Africa learned to appreciate each other's culture and to inform their countrymen about their observations.[4] Most of the black missionaries were impressed by African humanism, which they contrasted with racially stratified American society, in which, as Bishop Turner complained, men's worth was judged on the basis of the "colour of their skin and the texture of their hair." The Afro-American performances in the mission field as well as his empathy for African aspirations enhanced the African's image of himself as much as it promoted a cordial working relationship between the two groups.[5] This is an aspect of the Afro-American missionary enterprise in which the agents contributed far more than did their white coun-

3. F. M. Gow, "The Seventh Annual Session of the South African Conference," *VOM*, May, 1916; Wright *et al.* (eds.), *Encyclopaedia*, 321; Mzimba to J. B. Rendall, April 20, 1910, in "Letter from South Africa," 4; Lennox to Smith, June 10, 1907, in No. 7801, Free Church of Scotland Archives. By 1932, the Presbyterian Church of Africa, now headed by Mzimba's son, Livingstone, had eighty thousand members and adherents and forty ministers, some of them graduates of Lincoln University. See *Lincoln University Herald*, September, 1932.

4. See, for example, Thomas B. Khalane, "Journey from South Africa to the United States," *VOM*, April, 1916; I. G. Sishuba and H. R. Ngcayiya, "Kind Words," *ibid.*, November, 1904; and Simbini M. Nkomo, "The Call of Africa: The Tribal Life of the People of South Africa" (Oration delivered at college commencement, Greenville, Ill. in June, 1917), in Moorland-Spingarn Research Collection, Howard University.

5. Turner, "My Trip to South Africa," 809–13; Fanny Jackson Coppin, "My Visit to South Africa," in her *Reminiscences of School Life and Hints on Teaching* (Philadelphia, 1913), 122–31; James Walter Doughty, "What Foreign Mission Has Done for the Negro," *VOM*, April, 1905.

terparts; in a very real sense it represents the high-water mark in the Afro-American presence in southern Africa.

If the missionary movement enabled Afro-Americans to prove their worth before a largely skeptical white world, it also afforded them ample ground to appreciate the limits of their evangelism. From 1905 onward, AME agents made more restrained statements in regard to their church's capabilities in the mission field. Some promoted ecumenism and cooperation with other Christian bodies.[6] The new sense of realism was expressed by Bishop Charles Spencer Smith, who succeeded Reverend Coppin as resident bishop in South Africa in 1904. In 1905, Bishop Smith said:

> I now take occasion to repeat what I said when I first spoke from this rostrum; that the coloured people of America cannot fight your battles; they cannot furnish you your leaders. All that the church, of which I am a humble, and perhaps unworthy, representative can do for you is to give you such advice, encouragement and moral support as occasion may require; and such as is consistent with that growing international comity . . . such as is in harmony with that ever-increasing inter-denominational comity and fraternal spirit that now most happily characterizes the present movement of the present religious bodies throughout Christendom. . . . I want to dispel a delusion that I find exists in the minds of some of our adherents in these regions that their connection with the African Methodist Episcopal [church] will insure them help from America in case they should get in trouble.[7]

While this rethinking on mission work reflects a new tolerance of other denominations, the AME church was at the same time unwittingly aligning itself with white missionaries in checking the spread of Islam, which they described in more or less the same unfavorable terms that Bishop Turner had used to discredit white missionaries.[8] Islam, though of little consequence in South Africa, thus became a part of the international bogeyman that AME church members, like other Christian missionaries, sought to overcome.

6. Claude M. Severance, "Why Protestant Christian Negroes of America Should be Most Interested in the Evangelization of Africa," *VOM*, February, 1907; John A. Johnson, "Africa's Appeal to the American Negro," *ibid.*, January, 1910.

7. Charles Spencer Smith, "African Methodist Episcopal Church in South Africa. Extracts from a Sermon Delivered by Bishop C. S. Smith, in the Chapel of Bethel Institute, Cape Town, South Africa, Sunday, May 21, 1905," MS in Box 307, Washington Papers.

8. See, for example, "Africa for Christ or Mahommed?" *VOM*, April, 1910; "Shall Africa be Mahommedan or Christian?" *ibid.*, September, 1910. *Cf.* "Islam

The advent of the AME church in southern Africa was also apt to undercut the Ethiopian spirit of self-reliance. Once the Ethiopian Church was absorbed into the AME church, South African members quickly came to expect black Americans to provide money for building and operating schools. In a word, The Afro-American was expected to perpetuate more generously and efficiently the role of the discredited white missionary. However, some assertive African members of the AME church were dissatisfied with the material support the mother church in America was willing to provide. More important, others questioned the propriety of having the affairs of the Fourteenth District directed from America, which in their view smacked of the same tyranny the Ethiopians had rebelled against in white-dominated Protestant churches. In consequence, Reverend James Mata Dwane broke with the AME church in 1899; Reverend Jacobus Brander in 1904 formed the Ethiopian Catholic Church in Zion. Dwane, however, compromised himself by joining the Anglican church, where he worked under several white clerical leaders. Brander's group was more consistent in founding a church in which they enjoyed unfettered clerical independence, because self-determination was the hallmark of Ethiopianism. The Ethiopian Catholic Church in Zion thus demonstrated that the Ethiopian movement, far from wanting merely church leaders of their own color, cherished a higher principle, namely, an accessible leadership that resided within the church parishes and was accountable to the members. In this respect, the Ethiopian Catholic Church in Zion was conforming to a universal Protestant practice that started with the Reformation.

At about the time Ethiopian churches were taking root, there arose a need to build a university college for blacks. The college scheme brought together diverse white and black groups. Whites imagined that the emergence of a local college might well stem the flow of students to America, whose influence they disliked. On the other hand, blacks welcomed the college scheme: a university education was the surest way to enhance African political aspirations. This correlation of education and politics, while not wholly fallacious, was certainly more optimistic than South African geo-

---

in Government means absolute despotism, wholly unrestricted and only slightly tempered by the fear of assassination'' (James Stewart, *Dawn to the Dark Continent of Africa and Its Missions* [London, 1903], 65).

politics warranted. In the event, white hegemony prevailed long after Fort Hare University College sent out its first two graduates in 1924. The reason was that whites were able to control the curriculum, the enrollment, and the tone of campus life, making the college less revolutionary than conformist. A Tuskegee made to measure in South Africa was certainly no harbinger of revolution.

The pervasiveness of white power, which this study has shown to have dogged every aspect of African life during the period under review, persisted even in the wake of the first organized black political party, the African National Congress. When it was formed in 1912, delegates elected an executive committee composed mostly of educators and ministers of religion, the majority of whom eschewed radical politics. The president Reverend John L. Dube, who was principal of Ohlange in Natal, typified the moderate mold of the ANC leadership. In 1912, Dube informed an American supporter of his school that in his new capacity as president of the ANC, he regarded it as his duty to "keep in check" those members of his organization that might agitate for radical political change.[9] The inescapable conclusion to be drawn from Dube's stricture is that, far from envisaging African self-rule, he merely wanted his people to be ruled well by whites.

Writing about church independency and the political ramifications of that movement from the perspective of the 1980s has its limitations, chief among them being the hindsight that is affected by the African revolutions of the 1960s and 1970s. Having been a witness to these revolutionary experiences tends to impose on the historian a Whig interpretation that pits unfavorably the Ethiopians of the early 1900s against the revolutionaries of the 1970s and 1980s. Yet, if the activities of the Ethiopian movement and allied organizations, such as the African National Congress and Matthew Zvimba's Original Church of the White Bird, are viewed in the context of their time, they will be seen to be no less acts of self-determination than are the armed struggles for national liberation now taking place throughout southern Africa. The case for church independency in its ideological and emotive dimensions was put succinctly by Reverend Mzimba of the Presbyterian Church

9. Harlan, "Booker T. Washington and the White Man's Burden," 460; Manning W. Marable, "Booker T. Washington and African Nationalism," *Phylon*, XXXV (March, 1974) 405.

of Africa. When in 1903 he was asked by a member of the South African Native Affairs Commission if his church's accomplishments justified his secession, Mzimba said: "I cannot say I am satisfied, but the idea that we are working for ourselves and that we are responsible for what we are doing stimulates us in making self-sacrifice in our work."[10] Reverend Mzimba's statement suggests that, regardless of how imperfectly church secessionists used it, *freedom* was what Ethiopianism was all about.

10. See testimony of Mzimba, in *SANAC*, II, 794.

Appendix A

The Free Church of Scotland Monthly
November 1, 1897

The First Kafir [African] Convert

We have received a copy of a remarkable little book, *Ntsikana: The Story of an African Hymn*, by John Knox Bokwe, the Kafir musician and man of business, who is Dr. James Stewart's right-hand man at Lovedale. He visited Scotland in 1892. Ntsikana was the first Kafir convert, having learned Christ from Dr. Vanderkemp in 1799, and like Krishna Pal, Carey's first Bengali convert in 1880, he wrote a hymn famous ever since among his countrymen. The chant to which the Kafir words are sung was published for the first time in the sol-fa notation at Lovedale, South Africa, in 1876, the music having been handed down only by tradition till then. The words had been committed to print by the early missionaries, and the hymn is in every Christian Kafir hymn book now in South Africa. The words and music were both composed by Ntsikana. It is a weird air, chanted to lines expressive of what the man took God and the gospel to be.

The First Kafir Hymn

It is the first Christian hymn composed and sung in Kafirland to real native music, and it is to Kafirs a precious legacy left by Ntsikana to his native fellow-Christians, and is highly valued and loved by them. The literal translation is:

> The Great God, He is in heaven.
> Thou art Thou, Shield of truth.
> Thou art Thou, Stronghold of truth.
> Thou art Thou, Thicket of truth.

Thou art Thou, who dwellest in the highest
Who created life (below) and created (life) above
The Creator who created, created heaven,
This Maker of the stars and the Pleiades
A star flashed forth, telling us
This Maker of the blind, does He not make them on
purpose?
The trumpet sounded, it has called us,
As for His hunting, He hunteth for souls
Who draweth together flocks opposed to each other,
The leader, He led us;
Whose great mantle, we put it on
Those hands of Thine, they are wounded.
Those feet of Thine, they are wounded.
Thy blood, why is it streaming?
Thy blood, it was shed for us.
This great price, have we called for it?
This home of Thine, have we called for it?

Appendix B

"Confidential Information Received from Young Chief Tsekelo
Moshesh," *Cape Argus*, January 22, 1863

Mabolele, 10th December 1862

To the Editor:

Sir,—My father has informed me that he has received a letter from
the acting President and another from the Landrost of Winberg,
Capt. van Brandis, concerning the boundary line, as they purposed
sending a commission this month, and requesting my father, the
Chief Moshesh, to send a deputation to arrange the matter with the
commissioners. My father informed me, however, that he has been
prevented from taking any steps on account of the severe drought;
his people are occupied in cultivating their gardens; that he cannot
do anything without the consent of his people and they are too
much engaged at present to attend a meeting. Moshesh is quite
willing to settle this matter, especially as he has been requested
to do so by his Excellency the Governor, Sir P. E. Wodehouse; for
it is well known that the Free State Government have asked the
Governor of the Cape Colony to interfere in this affair. To have it
settled as soon as possible the Governor wrote to Moshesh, who
in reply stated that it was not at his request he interfered, but at
the request of the Free State; and as the Free State Government
wished it, His Excellency could certainly do what he thought
proper for the Basuto Tribe, and he (Moshesh) sincerely hoped that
everything would be arranged peaceably. Moshesh doubts that this
can be brought to a satisfactory conclusion on account of the
absence of the President; but although his Honour is absent, I have

assured Moshesh that the matter can be settled with Government, especially as the British Government takes an interest in the affair; and I have done my best to inspire my father with confidence that he might keep intact the treaty between the Free State and the Basutos, and that he might lose the confidence of the white people. Further I Tsekelo, advise the Free State Government to treat Moshesh with respect, that there may be no misunderstanding, as I see the Free State authorities rely very much on the British Government. But I think if the affair cannot be settled with the Free State, the British Government can do but little. There is another circumstance that I wish to inform the inhabitants of the Free State. The great chief of all the Basutos, Moshesh, has made a proclamation this month in his great council concerning the Free State Police, that if they came into Basutoland in the day time they are to go to the first Chief and inform him of their intention after which they could proceed; but if they came in the night, they were to get a guide who would accompany them as far as they would go, until they were satisfied in their researches. The great Chief Moshesh proposed this plan on account of the many bad characters that are continually coming in his country, because these people also steal from him, they steal from the Free State, and then bring the stolen cattle into Basutoland, and his people get blamed for stealing. As he (Moshesh) does not wish his country to be a refuge for these bad characters. The Free State Police ought not to act like the colonial police for they are not strong enough, and there might be some misfortune between them and the Basutos for the Government are too weak, and that is the reason why the natives go to the Free State even without passes. But this could soon be put a stop to if the Government was powerful enough. We hope the Free State will increase the Police force. Again I see the white policemen are weak, and wish too much to make friends with natives, that if they run away they will find people who will help them to escape. And it is well known that they are always deserting.

If I speak in this way it is not that I praise myself. But I wish that the policemen were people who would take an interest in the country, and try to keep peace. And although I am Moshesh's son everybody knows that I will do my duty. If one of my people does wrong, I will not take his part. I have entered the service of my own will, for if I feel tired I could leave the service, as I have not joined by deceitfulness, and I also joined it with my father's sanction. He repeated it again in his last meeting, for he had told his people of my intention before I left. He is willing that I should remain in the service if I do my duty, and if I still like the employment, and he has no objection that I should live in the Free State if I like. My father has also desired that his communications should come to me that I might explain them, as there is no one in the Free State who can do it. The President was also agreeable to this arrangement, as he thought that if one who wishes the good of the country was there to explain matters there would be no misunderstanding. Also, the Z. H. Edele Staatpresident has promised to settle this affair when he comes back, and to arrange these matters. Also there is nothing I would hide either from the Basutoland or the Free State, for I am not a spy. If anyone of the Free State or Basutoland did wrong I would excuse neither, for if anything was not right it is to the Governor of the Cape colony that I would appeal, as the Free State Government always takes him as arbitrator in any difficulty. It is all I have to say for the present. If I have any more to say I will let you know another time.

Your obedient servant,
TSEKELO MOSHESH

Appendix C

To the Editor of the
Southern Workman, January, 1894

Perhaps after the amount of sympathy awakened here amongst the officers, teachers, and students by Dr. Stewart in his noble work of educating the head, heart, and hand of the South African native, a Hampton boy's impression of Lovedale will prove of a little interest to you.

While in South Africa recently I had the pleasure of visiting this African Hampton. Our company was in Grahamstown, when there came a letter from the officers of the Lovedale Institute to my brother, begging that we pay them a visit and sing our songs for them. The school is about sixty miles from Grahamstown, and there is no railroad. The regular mail coach was too small to carry our large party—so a long, covered "Dutch Wagon" was chartered. This was drawn by eighteen huge oxen in charge of the owner and a native boy.

We had to leave Grahamstown on Sunday night in order to get to Lovedale in season to sing on Wednesday. We arranged ourselves as comfortably as possible in our close quarters, and for the first few miles enjoyed it, but in a little while the constant jolting began to make us ache all over and we were indeed glad to welcome the sun. This was in the month of November, the beginning of summer in the Southern Hemisphere, and the heat was so intense that it was next to impossible to travel in the middle part of the day. After two days and three nights our sixty miles were accomplished, and were were in the beautiful little town of Alice, and just across the river, surrounded by the most beautiful tropical trees, and the ground enclosed by a splendid cactus hedge, was the school.

After a hurried dinner at our hotel we were escorted to the

school by two of the young men who were sent down for us. The many nice buildings, the boys at work on the lawns and in the workshops, the girls at their different labors, made me imagine that I was at Hampton. We were unshered into the Treasurer's office where we were introduced to several of the officers. Dr. Stewart was away in central Africa at this time but we met his "right hand man," a native who had finished his studies and was, if I remember aright, the treasurer. We were shown through the different apartments of work, which are conducted much on the same plan as Hampton. In the classrooms it was at once apparent that both girls and boys applied themselves earnestly to their studies, their answers and arguments being beautifully arranged and in the best English. From the classrooms we were taken for a look at the dining room and kitchen; here as elsewhere everything was scrupulously a model of ours here at Hampton, and had it been Tuesday instead of Wednesday I might have expected some Baked Beans in their pans.

We were soon shown into the Assembly Room where we were to sing, and the girls and boys came in much in the same way as do the students here. There were nearly five hundred of them, and their faces were a picture of interest and anticipation. We sang for them for nearly a couple of hours, and then they favored us with some of their songs, which we thoroughly enjoyed, for their voices were indeed good. In passing out many of them shook our hands and bade us goodby after thanking us for our singing.

This Institution at Lovedale is a great power for good, and in that town of Alice, where its influence is chiefly felt, we found a more respectable class of natives than in any other part of the country we visited. The graduates from there are mostly sincere in their work of assisting their less fortunate brothers, and we found them scattered over different parts of Africa engaged in teaching.

Dr. Stewart is surely the Gen. Armstrong of South Africa and for him and his great work we wish every success.

Respectfully yours,
EUGENE MCADOO

Appendix D

"Native Churches," *Imvo Zabantsundu*, November 14, 1898

To appreciate aright the observations under the heading it is, we think, proper to state that they are intended as an appeal to Native Christians, and represent what is passing in the minds of observant European missionaries, as the result of certain marked developments in missionary work among the Natives of the present time. The subject is one that some may, at first sight, consider as scarcely suitable for a secular paper, inasmuch as our people are not yet ripe for a purely religious journal, but it is not possible for *Imvo* altogether to ignore matters affecting Church life—in this country. But apart from this, papers of the standing of the *Spectator* and the *Speaker* in London do not hesitate to take in their purview matters relating to religious thought; and we are not far out in following their cue.

Sole Aim of Missions

The aim of all Christian Missions to heathen lands is, not only to carry the gospel into them, but to see the work of the Church so established among the Native people that they will in time be able to support and conduct themselves. In carrying out this great purpose, missionaries do not go about shouting it on the hill-tops, but reveal it in the work they do, in the results they effect. It may never occur to many amongst whom they labour that all they do is bringing the people nearer the realization of this end. By the action of many of these times it would seem that they do not wish to recognize this very important and real development of our mission work; and hasten to reap what others have sown by gathering the harvest into what are known as purely Native denominations.

Participation of Natives

However easily and safely this claim can be made for missionary effort the world over, the best and most incontestable proof of our opening assertion is to be found in the fact that the members of the various existing Mission Churches are admittable to all the offices of the church and are at this moment occupying these very offices. There may be unimportant exceptions to this statement arising out of particular systems of church government, but what we wish to emphasize is that in both the lay and ministerial divisions of the church's work the Native people are having a part and are thus being brought forward to increased capability and fitness for bearing upon their own shoulders the burden of the management of the Church of Christ in their land. When the work of the Church can be left entirely in their hands is a very different matter, and depends on how quickly the people are making themselves efficient and sufficient from the work laid upon the church by Christ, its glorious and exalted Head. It can be said that the wisest and most spiritually-minded members of our Native missions know and acknowledge that this stage has not yet been reached and that, for the consideration and advancement of Christ's kingdom among them, the presence, knowledge, influence, and efforts of the white missionaries are not only most desirable but most essential. It is only foolish pride and self-ambition that thinks and says the contrary.

Misguided Movements

The attempts at the present time to originate so-called "purely Native denominations" arise from a very short-sighted vision and imperfect conception of the mission, composition and work of the Church of Christ. We do not gather nations, races, or tribes as such into the fold of Christ: we gather sinful men; and when they are gathered they are members of the Church of Christ without distinction of race, tribe, or country, and, as members of that Church, they are all one; and work for highest good of all. The Church of Christ is a home of believers, a family of which God is the Father, Jesus Christ the Elder Brother, the Holy Spirit, the Power that cements the whole and guides to all that makes life blessed, fruitful and holy. This family has but one name and we dare not soil it with anything national, racial, earthly: it is universal. In plain language we do not have a place in that family as Kaffir, Fingoes, Basutos, English, Jews or Socts, but only and solely redeemed sinners of mankind. A church of Fingoes or Chinamen is an anomaly, a non-existent in the spiritual sphere. Convenience alone makes men link the church with the name of their native land, and no one ever thinks of excluding others from its pale on that account. There is, it is true, a Church of Scotland, but it is not a Church of Scots: it is Christ's church in Scotland, and any believer who lives there of whatever clime or race may partake of all its privileges and find a place in all its offices. Were any one to arise and declare he had a vision or revelation that there should be a Church of Scots, only for Scots, men would without hesitation or mistake easily discern where such a vision or revelation came from. The Church of Scotland admits all men of whatever class, colour or condition; and any church that cannot do that or rises into existence for any one section of humanity to the exclusion of another is not a church of Christ at all, for it opposes the genius and spirit of His religion which breaks down all barriers and opens the church to whomsoever will come into it. The men who are leading these exclusive movements among our Native people are going back to pre-Pharisaic Jews who made God the God of the Jews only and not of the Gentiles as well. Let us understand, then, that a vision or revelation that contradicts the teaching and tenor of God's word reveals its true source and carries with it its own condemnation. When revelations are held up for our acceptance they must be brought to the touchstone of God's Word. ''To the law and to the testimony: if they speak not according to this word, it is because there is no light in them.'' Isa. viii, 20.

True Aim of the Church

The white missionaries along with Native Christians have been doing for long what these new-lights are today proposing or trying to do. There is usually no one who believes that they come from over the sea to do anything else than bring into existence ''Native Churches'' and these churches that at present exist because of their efforts are as really native churches as those aimed at by the advocates of ''purely Native denominations.'' The efforts of these people, moreover, are exceedingly ill-timed; for the tendency of our times in all the spheres is towards union. Alike in the world and in the church this movement prevails. Doubtless it is thought an enviable thing to originate a new denomination; but the man who is ambitious for such fame must be living in a very small world and apart from the forces and influences of his generation. Besides a unity of spirit within believers there must be effort of external and visible unity, so that they may thus be stronger to fight the enemies of God and advance to win the world for Christ. Instead of this working and reaching out towards unity we are witnessing men in our midst doing their utmost to sunder and scatter the flock of Christ, leading the weak and unwary away from the rich dewy meadows of Zion into a bare and barren wilderness, wrenching the sons and daughters of Jerusalem from the mother who bore and reared them. Such men, deluding the people and making factions in the church, are guilty of the sin of schism, and there is but one course open to the church that gave them their rank and function, viz, to cast them out. They are then no longer ministers of the church or of Christ its Head; and those who acknowledge them as such set themselves against the church and against Christ. Christian men and women, know ye not that ye are Christ's? See, then, that no man take you out of Christ's hand. Be not deceived when another calls you with enticing words to leave His folds; for His voice you have known of old and a stranger's you will only obey to your discomfiture. This is not a question between men and men, it is a question between Christ and men. Christ by His church bids you to abide within the fold which is His. Others call you to leave it. Are you to obey Christ or man? "Let no man, then, glory in men." "He that glorieth, let him glory in the Lord."

Desideratum of the Time

At this juncture of the Church's life in South Africa there is a loud call to the faithful to buckle on the armour of truth and righteousness, and be valiant for the faith once delivered to the Saints. There is a loud call to a deeper spiritual life—a life that would have rendered recent regrettable and painful events in our churches impossible. There is a loud call to church members to purify themselves from heathen influences and practices which are sapping the spiritual life of many, and keeping them from going forward. There is a loud call to brotherly love and the sinking of all race feelings and strife so that we may meet as Christian brethren and rejoice in the common blessings of Christ's salvation. There is a loud call to prayer and work that Christ's Kingdom may come and His will be done among all men. If this call be obeyed and responded to, God's heritage will again rejoice and prosper, and glory shall dwell in the land.

Appendix E

"The Ethiopian Order," *Christian Express*, October 1, 1900

The following are the resolutions passed between the Bishops of the South African Synod of the Anglican Church and the Ethiopian Church as represented by the Rev. James M. Dwane, Superintendent, and approved at the Synod of Bishops held in Grahamstown on August 22nd:—

Resolved, that the Bishops of the Province assembled in Synod, welcome with gratitude to Almighty God the desire for unity with them in Catholic Faith and Order of the body of their fellow Christians designating themselves members of the Ethiopian Church.

The Order of Ethiopia

Whereas the Body hitherto called the Ethiopian Church *(Ibandla Lase Tiyopia)* has approached the Bishops of the Province, with the desire of being admitted into the full unity of the Catholic Church.

And, whereas at a conference of their committee, held at Queenstown, October 6, 1899, the following resolutions were passed, namely:—

1. That having regard to the great importance of Christian unity, and being convinced that the Scriptural and Historical safeguard of the same is the Catholic Episcopate, this Conference resolves to petition His Grace the Archbishop of Capetown and the other Bishops of the Church of the Province of South Africa to give to our body a valid Episcopate and Priesthood, and to make such arrangements as may be found possible to include our body within the fold of the Catholic Church, on the lines indicated in our Superintendent's letter to the Archbishop of Capetown.

2.   That this Conference accepts and embraces the Doctrine, Sacraments, and Discipline of Christ, as the same are contained and commanded in Holy Scripture according as the Church of England has set forth the same in its Standards of Faith and Doctrine.

And whereas, in the correspondence above referred to, a desire has been expressed that this community should retain, within the Church, its corporate character;

And whereas the whole subject has been a matter of constant prayer, of a long correspondence, and of a conference between chosen representatives of the Ethiopian community, and of the Church of the Province;

The Bishops of the Province, in Synod assembled, after earnest prayer to Almighty God, and careful deliberation, have drawn up the following scheme of an order to be formed within the Church, and to be called the Order of Ethiopia:

The Order of Ethiopia "Ibandla Lase Tiyopia" Hitherto Called

1.   Each Diocesan Bishop will appoint missioners to visit the existing Ethiopian Missions in his Diocese, to instruct, examine, and receive into the church members thereof.

2.   These Missioners shall present to the Diocesan Bishop those whom they deem fit for confirmation.

3.   The Missioners shall recommend such of those who are at present holding office in the Ethiopian Community as they may deem fit, to the Diocesan Bishop to be licenced as Readers, Catechists and Sub-Deacons, in accordance with the Canons of the Province, after consultation with the Provincial of the Order.

4.   Each Diocesan Bishop will forthwith make arrangements for the instruction, training, and examination of candidates for Holy Orders in accordance with the regulations of the Diocese and Province, and the Canons of the Church.

5.   The first members of the Order of Ethiopia shall be those who are licenced under the above provisions.

6.   The Visitor of the Order shall be the Metropolitan of the Province.

7.   The Provincial of the Order shall be appointed by the Bishops of the Province, but, after the first appointment, due consideration shall be given to the recommendation of the chapter of the Order.

8.   The ordinary term of office of the Provincial shall be five (5) years.

9.   The chapter shall consist of the Provincial and twelve (12) members, six (6) of whom shall be appointed by the Visitor, and six (6) by the Provincial; and it shall be the business of the chapter to superintend the affairs of the Order, including its finances.

10.   All proceedings of the chapter shall be subject to review by the Provincial Synod. A Diocesan Bishop may suspend the operation within his Diocese of any new regulation until such review.

11.   The Chapter shall have authority to frame the Constitution of the Order subject to the approval of the Visitor; such Constitution to be provisional until confirmed by the Bishops of the Province at their next Synod.

12.   Should a Bishop at any time be appointed or consecrated for the Order, the office of Provincial shall be thereupon declared vacant, and he shall be ex-officio Provincial, and he shall exercise Episcopal functions in each diocese only as an Assistant of the Bishop thereof, and at his request.

13.   The Provincial shall recommend clergymen for the charge of vacant Missions of the Order to the Diocesan Bishop, with whom the final appointment shall rest.

14.   No clergyman shall officiate without the licence or permission of the Diocesan Bishop.

15.   The Diocesan Bishop, at his discretion, either by himself or by the Archdeacon or other clergyman appointed by the Bishop as his representative to report to him, shall visit the Mission of the Order from time to time to examine candidates for Baptism and Confirmation.

16.   No new Mission work shall be begun by the Order within ten miles of any Mission Station or outstation of the Diocese, nor any new Mission work of the Diocese within ten miles of any Mission Station or outstation of the Order without the consent of the Diocesan Bishop.

17.   With regard to Missions already in existence, the difficulties arising from proximity shall be dealt with by the Diocesan Bishop before he issues any new licence.

18.   The Bishops of the Province undertake to draw up and submit to the Provincial Synod, a scheme securing representation for the mission of the Order in both Provincial and Diocesan Synods.

19.   All members of the Order and of its mission shall be eligi-

ble equally with others for Diocesan office (e.g., Chapter, Finance Board, Diocesan trustees, etc.).

20.   Discipline shall be exercised in all missions, as provided for in the Book of Common Prayer, and of Provincial Canons, and the Acts of the Diocese.

21.   Members of the Church, passing from one mission to another, whether of the Order or of the Diocese, shall be provided with proper letters of commendation (see Provincial Canons, p. 83).

22.   All property of the Order shall be conveyed to the Provincial Trustees, upon such trusts as are approved by the Visitor after consultation with the Provincial.

23.   All Churches shall be open to all people, without distinction of race or colour.

The New Provincial

The Rev. James Dwane, after being confirmed by the Archbishop of Capetown on 26th August, was vested with the authority to exercise the rights and privileges of Provincial of the Order of Ethiopia.

Appendix F

"*Bishop H. M. Turner,*" *Voice of Missions,* March 1, 1900

Firm as a rock amidst a storm,
  On some wild wave beat shore,
Who cares not for the thunder's crash,
  Nor heeds the billow's roar.

Serenely calm, sublimely great,
  Of earth nor hell afraid—
He stands amidst the storms of hate
  Undaunted, undismayed.

And in the face of deadly foes,
  And in the foreman's land,
Though howling mobs and hell oppose
  He dares to be a man.

He dares for justice and for law
  To plead in thunder tone,
When coward friends forsake his side
  He dares to plead alone.

The great apostle of mankind
  The prophet of his race—
His name shall stand for truth and right
  In every time and place.

And when the march of time shall cease,
  And warring foes contend no more,
His weary soul shall rest in peace,
  On that bright beautific shore.

Shall then receive his just reward;
  The victor's palm, the martyr's crown,

And dwell forever with the Lord
Where neither strife nor hate are found.
—Isadore Thomasson

Pine Bluff, Arkansas, Feb. 8, 1900

Appendix G

"Song of Africa," *AME Church Review*, October, 1902

Stretch forth thy hand; Jehovah bids thee come
And claim the promise; thou hast had thy doom.
If forth in sorrow, weeping, thou hast gone,
Rejoicing to thy God thou shalt return.

Stretch forth thy hand, no longer doubt, arise;
Look! see the "Signo" in the vaulted skies.
Greet the new century with faith sublime.
For God is calling now, this is thy time.

Stretch forth thy hand to god, the night is past;
The morning cometh, thou art free at last.
No brigands draw thee from thy peaceful home,
But messengers of love to greet thee come.

Stretch forth thy hand to kindred o'er the sea;
Our cause is one, and brothers still are we.
Bone of bone, one destiny we claim;
Flesh of our flesh, thy God and ours the same.

Stretch forth thy hand: "What tho' the heathen rage."
And friends of darkness all their wrath engage.
The hand of God still writes upon the wall.
"Thy days are numbered; all the proud shall fall."

Stretch forth thy hand, nor yet in terror flee:
Thick darkness but a swaddling band shall be
The waves and billows which thy way oppose
Shall in their bosom bury all thy foes.

Stretch forth thy hand to God, 'tis not for thee
To question aught, nor all His purpose see.
The hand that led thee through the dreary night

Does not thy counsel need when comes the light.

Stretch forth thy hand; stretch forth thy hand to God;
Nor falter thou, nor stumble at His word.
And if in service thou shalt faithful be,
His promise of salvation thou shalt see.

—L. J. Coppin

Appendix H

Voice of Missions, November 1, 1901

We present the readers of *Voice of Missions* with two remarkable letters from Mr. Charles Dube. They speak for themselves. Dube is a very excellent young man, honest, studious, industrious, ambitious. We regret exceedingly that the Department is unable to provide him $75 a year to meet his expenses at a medical college. He is one of the many African students that have come to us for help and no one is more deserving than Mr. Dube. Anyone who may be pleased to contribute anything toward helping this young man may send their contribution to 61 Bible House, New York City, care H. B. Parks, D.D., Missionary Secretary.

Wilberforce University, June 24, 1901

Rev. H. B. Parks, D.D., New York.

Dear Sir: I take pleasure in writing you these few lines. I am a native South African. I was born of Christian parents, Natal, Inanda Mission Station that is where my mother still makes her home. I came to this country on June 1896, seeking an education. I then made my way to Wilberforce, where I was very well cared for by Bishop Arnett, who succeeded in getting me under the care of the Missionary Department. I have now been attending school here for five years, and I have completed Freshman, Classical, and now I desire to go to a medical school, after which, if I be successful, I will return to my native land Africa. But I have no means whatever. My parents cannot support me; my father died when I was young, and I have a mother who does well to support herself. So I am here seeking whatever aid may be granted me, and I assure you whatever help you give me will be of benefit to me and to my race. I am going to work this summer in order to get whatever may help me through school. I am a young man of 23 years, born June 16, 1877. I belong to the Zulu race, raised in a Christian home, joined the A.M.E. Church in this country (which Church, was the first for me to join) and I am still a member of the said Church. Hoping to hear from you soon, and that God may help you to get me the means and help me to be very successful, I remain

Yours truly,
CHARLES DUBE

Wilberforce University, August 20, 1901

Dr. Parks, New York City.

Dear Sir: I take pleasure in writing to you these few lines. I hope you received my application letter, and have tried to get some one to help me. It is now coming to fall and schools take up next month. I will be very glad to hear from you and to get your advice in this undertaking. I feel like God will provide a way for me to go to a Medical School. Although I have no means I am trusting. I have been working all the summer and the time is short. A person cannot make money enough to clothe himself and take himself to school. I have written to Washington, D.C.; they promise to charge $40 tuition if I am received for missionary work. The hardest thing to contend with will be my board. I hope I will hear from you soon. Send my regards to your family.

Yours truly,
CHARLES L. DUBE

Apparently Dube was unsuccessful in procuring financial help and went back to South Africa to teach school.

Appendix I

The Institute [Tuskegee]
5th September 1913

E. J. Scott, Esq.

Dear Sir:

In regard to the question as to whether I am sufficiently qualified to make a "Commission Report" of this Institution, I desire to express myself as follows:

I am in total agreement with you that to discharge such a task one must, indispensably, be familiar with the Institute's working, not only during a vacation, but in full working time.

This familiarity I, of course, do not, at present, possess, because I came here in the beginning of July.

Nevertheless there are other considerations which I believe render this lack not so serious as at first it seems.

I had already been given the hint that I might be called upon by my Government in South Africa to give them my impressions as to the adaptability of your methods here to the conditions in my country. And I had been making my observations with this end in view so that I might print a little pamphlet and give it to our Government gratuitously.

Inasmuch as the reputation and prestige of your School is thus at stake, I must leave it to you as to how far you are prepared to allow me to represent your work and as to whether I am sufficiently informed on the matter.

I venture however to say that I think I know the kind of information our Education Department is seeking for.

Your work is quite unknown to them, and the various pamphlets, catalogs, and books (and those of the Principal) is the kind of thing they want, put in concise form, and supplemented, point by point, by my opinions and suggestions as to how far it is possible to apply these principles to our country.

In my country our Government supports Academic Education, and Industrial Training is only in its infancy. They want to know how they can correlate these two and to adjust our schools, or some of them, experimentally, on your model.

Now, I reckon myself to be already in a position to give them suggestions as to all the industries which I have seen at work during this vacation. The authority I am in need of is that of seeing all of these actually full working, as I have seen some of them and that only in partial working.

Inasmuch as the Government has gone thus far in this affair I am prepared to make the utmost sacrifices of my interests in England to supply them with this desideratum if in your judgment I am good enough for it.

In England I am engaged to start a Pedagogy course in the Birmingham University from October 6th and I intended to sail on the 25th inst. for that purpose.

I think I would be allowed to postpone my entrance by about two weeks (I could cable and ascertain) and probably longer.

This would allow of me to remain in Tuskegee until October 9th, to attain this qualification.

Anyway I prefer to leave the whole question to your judgment, whilst I shall be ready to act on and follow your advice and instructions all along the line.

Yours truly,
DAVIDSON JABAVU

Appendix J

"Journey from South Africa to the United States,"
Voice of Missions, April, 1916

While in Johannesburg, South Africa, I happened to see a paper which had an advertisement of Booker T. Washington's school. I had heard that the Tuskegee school was an important one for colored people and I, therefore, left Johannesburg to go to Cape-town, with a determination to make enough money to bring me to the United States of America for a better education.

God was with me. By 1905 I had saved enough money to pay my passage to the United States. In February of that year, I sailed for this country, without knowing one word of the English language. The captain of the steamship was very kind to me. He used to come to see me very often. While I was on the ocean, not one day was I sick. It seemed that the angels of the Almighty God were my guard.

Finally we reached London, England, at the end of twenty-five days. When we reached England, we found that the American boat was waiting for us, which made me glad. It was the most lucky thing I ever saw. I do not know what I should have done.

When the captain knew that I could not express myself in English, he immediately went to the American captain and told him that I was going to the United States, and that he should take care of me in the steamer. This he did as requested.

We left London at 9:00 a.m., Monday, on our way to the United States.

On reaching New York City I was sent to Dr. H. B. Parks. When I saw this man, I thought he was an African; because, after I left Africa, I never saw a colored man on the boat. But we found that neither of us could understand the other. However, I gave him a letter which was given to me by Rev. Gow in Capetown, South Africa, for introduction to him. When he opened the letter, he found that I was a man who did not know the English language, and that he was supposed to send me to Booker T. Washington's school.

Dr. H. B. Parks thought the school was not suited for me to enter. He told me about Wilberforce University, Wilberforce, Ohio, saying that it was the place for me. This word "Wilberforce" was the only English word I knew.

By the aid of the train conductor, who received instructions from Mrs. H. B. Parks, I was brought to Wilberforce College, where I remained till last year, lending myself to the American discipline and influence, that my mind and spirit might reach the Christian ideal.

I fould it difficult to acquire English, not having any African-to-English and English-to-African dictionary to assist me in my efforts. I had to study hard and to the best of my ability, that I might make myself understood to my teachers. They were very kind to me and helped me in many ways.

While at Wilberforce College, I was never called to the discipline committee concerning my character. President W. S. Scarborough was just like a father to me. Surely he had showed his love to me, and he gave me privileges before all the student body. Boys and girls were in my hand. After I had found out that I was a privileged character, I began to organize the religious societies. This part of my work was pleasing in the sight of President Scarborough and he made me head of all religious work in Wilberforce University.

In my first year in college class, I was made eligible to enter the rhetorical contest in which I became victor, at that educational school. I was also a member of the College Debating Society.

On May 2, 1910, I was promoted to become an officer in the military company by Lieutenant Green of the United States Army.

On June 17th, 1912, I was graduated from the printing office.

During my school life in Wilberforce, I was very successful in every line of my work.

I have written several times to my father and mother while at Wilberforce, but have received no reply. I wrote to the American Consul at the nearest city to my home, but he could give me no information concerning my relatives. I am praying that the Almighty God may give me strength to finish my work here and enable me to go back to my people, with education sufficient to bring them from darkness to the Christian light.

Therefore, I ask you to pray for me and my people that the missionaries, who go to them, may be men and women whose lives may always be spiritual.

T. B. KHALANE

Bibliography

Archival Resources

Africa

Botswana National Archives, Gaborone
   Archival Series: 410, R.C. 7/8, "Church Dispute at Kanye; No. 715, R.C. 10/11; S.1/2; No. 1331.S.42/3; No. J. 1288.S.41/2; No. J. 23.S.2/5; H.C. 5/12; No. 2384.S.179/1; H.C. 192; H.C. 5/12; No. T. 1024.S.32/5.
Killie Campbell Collection, University of Natal Library, Durban
   Papers on Ethiopianism.
Makokoba AME Church Archives, Bulawayo, Zimbabwe
National Archives of Zimbabwe, Harare
   Correspondence of the chief native commissioner, members of the Native Affairs Department, and the Anglican bishop of Mashonaland, Item No. A/11/2/18/3; Item No. A3/6/9; Item No. N3/5/2; No. B 4725/3930; No. Z. 3137/3930; No. Y. 2503/3930; CNC. 82/1919; correspondence on Zvimba's Original Church of the White Bird.
South African Library, Cape Town
   Back copies of several black and white South African newspapers.
University of Cape Town Libraries
   Rich Africana collection.

Great Britain

Free Church of Scotland Archives, National Library of Scotland, Edinburgh
   Incoming Letters from Missionaries in South Africa: Archival Series 4392, 7514, 7776, 7789, 7798, 7804.
London Missionary Society Archives, School of Oriental and African Studies, University of London

Missionary Letters, Incoming, 1816–1926; Annual Reports, 1820–1920; Letters from Directors, Outgoing, 1880–1920; Deputation reports, 1883–1884, 1892, 1893, 1913.
Rhodes House Library, Oxford
    Papers of the British Foreign Anti-Slavery Society and the Aborigines Protection Society, especially MSS. Brit. Emp. S.22, G.200, 1910–1912, South Africa (cuttings, Black Peril).
Royal Commonwealth Society, London
    Reports of the chief native commissioner, Southern Rhodesia, 1900–1930.
Selly Oak Colleges Library; Birmingham
    W. C. Willoughby Papers
Wesleyan Methodist Missionary Society Archives, London
    Missionary Letters: Incoming, South Africa, Box XVIII, 1868–1876; Box XVI, Queenstown, 1877–1885; Transvaal, 1881–1891; Clarkbury, 1881–1885; Box C, Mashonaland, 1891–1899.
    Deputation Report: A Summary Report by the Rev. John Kilner Deputation to the South African Mission Field, Confidential (London, February II, 1881).

United States

African Methodist Episcopal Church Archives, New York City
    Back issues of *Voice of Missions by Way of the Cross.*
American Board of Commissioners for Foreign Missions Archives (Zulu Mission), Houghton Library, Harvard University
    Folios: Africa 21/625, South Africa Mission, Zulu and Rhodesian Branches, 1900–1909, Vol. I, Documents; Africa 10.389, Zulu Mission, Vol. XXI, 1880–1890; ABC. 15.496, Vol. IV; Africa 22, No. 626, Vol. II, Documents; ABC. American Zulu Mission, 1890–1899, Vol. I, Documents; 722, South Africa Mission, Zulu Branch, 1910–1919, Vol. I, Documents.
DuSable Museum of African-American History, Chicago
    Harry Dean Diaries and Papers.
Hampton Institute Archives, Collis P. Huntington Memorial Library, Hampton, Va.
Library of Congress, Washington, D.C.
    Booker T. Washington Papers: Boxes 127, 129, 146, 197, 232, 261, 266, 307, 322, 332, 346, 373, 818, 927, 1022. Correspondence

with South Africans as well as with some white missionaries in South Africa.

National Archives, Washington, D.C.
United States Consular Despatches, Cape Town, Pretoria, and Johannesburg. General Records of the Department of State. Record Group 59, Microcopy T.191, rolls 15, 18.

Oberlin College Archives, Oberlin, Ohio
John L. Dube. Newspaper clippings.
Pamphlets by American supporters of Ohlange, Dube's school in Natal.

University of California at Los Angeles, Research Library
Imvo Zabantsundu (King Williamstown). Microfilm.

Wilberforce University Archives, Carnegie Library, Xenia, Ohio
Levi Jenkins Coppin Papers. Some correspondence about the AME church's South African mission.

Theses and Dissertations

Brock, Sheila M. "James Stewart and Lovedale: A Reappraisal of Missionary Attitudes and African Response in the Eastern Cape, South Africa, 1870–1905." Ph.D. dissertation, University of Edinburgh, 1974.

Coan, Josephus Roosevelt. "The Expansion of Missions of the African Methodist Episcopal Church in South Africa, 1896–1908." Ph.D. dissertation, Hartford Seminary Foundation, 1961.

Roberts, Esther L. "Shembe: The Man and His Work." M.A. thesis, University of South Africa, 1936.

Vilakazi, Absalom. "Isonto Lama Nazaretha (The Church of the Nazarites)." M.A. thesis, Kennedy School of Missions, Hartford Seminary Foundation, 1954.

Newspapers, Periodicals, and Journals

African Methodist Episcopal Church Review, New York City.
African Methodist Episcopal Zion Quarterly Review, New York City.
American Historical Review, Washington, D.C.
Botswana Notes and Records, Gaborone.
Cape Argus, Cape Town.
Cape Mercury, Cape Town.
Cape Monthly Magazine, Cape Town.

Christian Recorder, Philadelphia.
Christian Express, Lovedale, South Africa.
Free Church of Scotland Monthly, Edinburgh.
Grahamstown (South Africa) *Journal*.
Imvo Zabantsundu (Native Opinion) and its supplement, *Itole le'mvo*, King Williamstown, South Africa.
Journal of African History, London
Journal of Religion in Africa, Leiden.
Journal of the Royal Anthropological Institute, London.
Lincoln University Herald, Lincoln University, Pa.
London *Daily Telegraph* (clippings in Rhodes House Library).
Missionary Review of the World, London.
Negro History Bulletin, Washington, D.C.
New York Age, New York City.
Oberlin Alumni Magazine, Oberlin, Ohio.
Phylon, Atlanta, Ga.
Rhodes-Livingstone Journal, Livingstone, Zambia.
Scotsman, Edinburgh (clippings in the National Library of Scotland).
South African News (clippings in Rhodes House Library).
Southern Workman, Hampton, Va.
Tennessee Historical Quarterly, Nashville.
Voice of Missions by Way of the Cross, Atlanta and New York City.

Books and Pamphlets

Asiegbu, Johnson U. J. *Slavery and the Politics of Liberation, 1787–1861*. New York, 1969.
Baeta, C. G. *Christianity in Tropical Africa*. London, 1968.
Barkun, Michael. *Disaster and the Millennium*. New Haven, 1974.
Berry, Llewelyn L. *A Century of Missions of the African Methodist Episcopal Church, 1840–1940*. New York, 1942.
Bond, Horace Mann. *Education for Freedom: A History of Lincoln University, Pennsylvania*. Lincoln University, Pa., 1976.
Bowen, J. W. E., ed. *Africa and the American Negro: Addresses and Proceedings of the Congress of Africa Held under the Auspices of the Stewart Missionary Foundation for Africa*. Atlanta, 1895.
Broadbent, Samuel. *A Narrative of the First Introduction of Christianity Among the Barolong Tribe of Bechuanas, South Africa*. London, 1865.

Bundy, Colin. *The Rise and Fall of the South African Peasantry.* London, 1979.

Campbell, John. *Hottentot Children: With a Particular Account of Paul Dikkop, the Son of a Hottentot Chief, Who Died in England, September 14, 1824.* London, n.d.

———. *A Journey to Lattakkoo in South Africa.* London, 1835.

Caplan, Gerald L. *The Elites of Barotseland, 1878–1969.* Berkeley, Calif., 1970.

Cell, John W. *The Highest Stage of White Supremacy: The Origins of Segregation in South Africa and the American South.* Cambridge, England, 1982.

Center of African Studies. *Religion in Africa, Proceedings of a Seminar Held in the Center of African Studies, 10th–12th April 1964.* University of Edinburgh, 1964.

Chalmers, John A. *Tiyo Soga: A Page of South African Mission Work.* Edinburgh, 1878.

Chapman, James. *Travels in the Interior of South Africa.* Vol. I. London, 1868.

Chirenje, J. Mutero. *Chief Kgama and His Times, 1835–1923: The Story of a Southern African Ruler.* London, 1978.

———. *A History of Northern Botswana, 1850–1910.* Cranbury, N.J. 1977.

Cohn, Norman. *The Pursuit of the Millennium.* New York, 1970.

Coppin, Fanny Jackson. *Reminiscences of School Life and Hints on Teaching.* Philadelphia, 1913.

Coppin, L. J. *Observations of Persons and Things in South Africa, 1900–1904; Part Second, Letters from South Africa.* Philadelphia, 1905.

———. *Unwritten History.* Philadelphia, 1919.

Cousins, H. T. *Tiyo Soga: The Model Kaffir Missionary.* London, 1897.

Crummell, Alexander. *The Relations and Duties of Free Coloured Men in America to Africa.* Hartford, Conn., 1861.

Daneel, M. L. *Old and New in Southern Shona Independent Churches.* The Hague, 1971.

Davenport, T. R. H. *The Afrikaner Bond: The History of a South African Political Party, 1880–1911.* Cape Town, 1966.

Davis, Richard H. *Nineteenth Century African Education in the Cape Colony.* Ann Arbor, 1969.

Dean, Harry, with Sterling North. *The Pedro Gorino: The Adventures of a Negro Sea Captain in Africa and on the Seven Seas in His Attempt to Found an Ethiopian Empire.* Boston, 1929. The book was published in London under the title *Umbala.*

Du Bois, W. E. B. *The Souls of Black Folk.* 1903; Longmans edition, London, 1965.

Du Plessis, J. *A History of Christian Missions in South Africa.* London, 1911.

[Ecumenical Conference]. *Report of the Ecumenical Conference on Foreign Missions, Held in Carnegie Hall and Neighbouring Churches, April 1st to May 1st.* 2 vols. New York, 1900.

Elphick, Richard. *Kraal and Castle: Khoikhoi and the Founding of White South Africa.* New Haven, 1978.

Elphick, Richard, and Herman Giliomee, eds. *The Shaping of South African Society, 1652–1820.* London, 1979.

Etherington, Norman. *Preachers, Peasants and Politics in South East Africa, 1835–1880: African Communities in Natal, Pondoland and Zululand.* London, 1978.

Fleming, J. R. *A History of the Church in Scotland, 1875–1929.* Edinburgh, 1933.

Franklin, John Hope. *From Slavery to Freedom: A History of Negro Americans.* New York, 1980.

———. *George Washington Williams and Africa.* Washington, D.C., 1971.

Fredrickson, George M. *White Supremacy: A Comparative Study in American and South African History.* Oxford, 1981.

Freeman, J. J. *A Tour of South Africa.* London, 1851.

George, Carol V. R. *Segregated Sabbaths: Richard Allen and the Rise of Independent Black Churches.* New York, 1973.

Griffith, Cyril E. *The African Dream: Martin R. Delany and the Emergence of Pan-African Thought.* University Park, Pa., 1975.

Hahn, Theophilus. *Tsuni-Goam: The Supreme Being of the Khoikhoi.* London, 1881.

Haight, Mabel V. J. *European Powers and South-East Africa, 1796–1856.* London, 1967.

Haile, A. J. *A Brief Historical Survey of the London Missionary Society in Southern Africa.* Morija, Basutoland, 1951.

Haliburton, Gordon MacKay. *The Prophet Harris: A Study of an African Prophet and His Mass Movement in the Ivory Coast and the Gold Coast, 1913–1915.* New York, 1973.

Harlan, Louis R., and Raymond W. Smock, eds. *The Booker T. Washington Papers.* Vol. VI, *1901–1902.* Urbana, 1977.

Harris, Clara E. *History of the Women's Mite Missionary Society of the A.M.E. Church.* Baltimore, 1935.

Hinchliff, Peter. *The Church in South Africa.* London, 1968.

Holt, Basil. *Joseph Williams and the Pioneer Mission to the South-Eastern Bantu.* Lovedale, South Africa, 1954.

Holub, Emil. *Seven Years in South Africa: Travels, Researches and Hunting Adventures Between the Diamond Fields and the Zambezi.* Translated by Ellen E. Frewer. Vol. I. London, 1881.

Hooker, J. R. *Henry Sylvester Williams: Imperial Pan-Africanist.* London, 1975.

Huggins, Nathan I., *et al.*, eds. *Key Issues in the Afro-American Experience.* Vol. II, *Since 1865.* New York, 1971.

Jaarsveld, F. A. van. *The Afrikaner's Interpretation of South African History.* Pretoria, 1964.

Jabavu, Davidson Don T. *The Black Problem: Papers and Addresses on Various Native Problems.* 1920; rpr. New York, 1969.

―――. *The Life of John Tengo Jabavu, Editor of Imvo Zabantsundu, 1884–1921.* Lovedale, South Africa, 1922.

Jacottet, E. *The Native Churches and Their Organization.* Morija, Basutoland, 1905.

Johns, Sheridan W., III. *Protest and Hope, 1882–1934.* Stanford, Calif., 1972.

Jordan, Artishia Wilkerson. *The African Methodist-Episcopal Church in Africa.* Nashville, n.d.

Jordan, Lewis G. *Up the Ladder in Foreign Missions.* Nashville, 1901.

Kenyatta, Jomo. *Facing Mount Kenya.* New York, 1962.

Kerr, Alexander. *Fort Hare, 1915–48: The Evolution of an African College.* New York, 1968.

Kilson, Martin L., and Robert I. Rotberg, eds. *The African Diaspora: Interpretive Essays.* Cambridge, Mass., 1976.

King, Kenneth J. *Pan-Africanism and Education.* Oxford, 1971.

Kotze, D. J., ed. *Letters of the American Missionaries, 1835–1838.* Cape Town, 1950.

Livingstone, David. *Livingstone's Missionary Correspondence, 1814–1856.* Edited by Isaac Schapera. London, 1961.

―――. *Livingstone's Private Journals.* Edited by Isaac Schapera. London, 1960.

Loram, C. T. *The Education of the South African Native*. London, 1917.

Louis, W. Roger, ed. *Imperialism: The Robinson-Gallagher Controversy*. New York, 1978.

Lovett, Richard. *The History of the London Missionary Society*. 2 vols. London, 1899.

Lynch, Hollis R. *Edward Wilmot Blyden: Pan-Negro Patriot, 1832–1912*. London, 1967.

MacKenzie, John. *Austral Africa: Losing It or Gaining It*. Vol. I. London, 1886.

MacMillan, W. M. *The Cape Colour Question: A Historical Survey*. London, 1927.

Majeke, Nozipho. *The Role of the Missionaries in Conquest*. Johannesburg, 1952.

Marais, J. S. *The Cape Coloured People, 1652–1937*. London, 1939.

Marks, Shula. *Reluctant Rebellion: The 1906–8 Disturbances in Natal*. Oxford, 1970.

Marks, Shula, and A. Atmore, eds. *Economy and Society in Pre-Industrial South Africa*. London, 1980.

Martin, Marie-Louise. *Kimbangu: An African Prophet and His Church*. Translated by D. M. Moore. Oxford, 1957.

Matthews, Z. K. *Freedom For My People. The Autobiography of Z. K. Matthews: Southern Africa, 1901–1968*. London, 1981.

Miller, Floyd J. *The Search for a Black Nationality: Black Colonization and Emigration, 1787–1863*. Urbana, 1975.

Moffat, Robert. *Missionary Labours and Scenes in Southern Africa*. London, 1843; New York, 1850.

Mzimba, Livingstone Ntibane. *Ibali Lobomi Nomsebenzi Womfi Umfundisi Pambani Jeremiah Mzimba*. Lovedale, South Africa, 1923.

Newitt, M. D. D. *Portuguese Settlement on the Zambesi*. New York, 1973.

Nkomo, Simbini Mamba. *How I Found Christ in the Jungles of Africa: The Story of My Conversion*. Greenville, Ill. 1917.

Oosthuizen, G. C. *Post-Christianity in Africa: A Theological and Anthropolitical Study*. London, 1968.

Palmer, Colin. *Slaves of the White God: Blacks in Mexico, 1570–1650*. Cambridge, Mass., 1976.

Payne, Daniel A. *History of the African Methodist Episcopal Church*. Nashville, 1891; rpr., New York, 1969.

Philip, John. *Researches in South Africa Illustrating the Civil*,

Moral, and Religious Conditions of the Native Tribes. 2 vols. London, 1828.

Phillips, Clifton J. *Protestant America and the Pagan World: The First Half Century of the American Board of Commissioners for Foreign Missions, 1810–1860.* Cambridge, Mass., 1969.

Plaatje, Solomon T. *The Mote and the Beam: An Epic on Sex-Relationship 'Twixt White and Black in British South Africa.* New York, 1921.

———. *Native Life in South Africa.* London, 1916.

———. *Sechuana Proverbs and Literal Translations and Their European Equivalents.* London, 1916.

Ponton, M. M. *Life and Times of Henry M. Turner.* Atlanta, 1917; rpr. Westport, Conn., 1970.

Ranger, T. O. *The African Voice in Southern Rhodesia, 1898–1930.* Evanston, 1970.

———. *Revolt in Southern Rhodesia, 1896–1897.* London, 1967.

Redkey, Edwin S. *Black Exodus: Nationalist and Back-to-Africa Movements, 1890–1910.* New Haven, 1969.

Robinson, Ronald, and Jack Gallagher, *Africa and the Victorians' Official Mind of Imperialism.* London, 1961.

Rotberg, Robert I. *Christian Missionaries and the Creation of Northern Rhodesia, 1880–1924.* Princeton, 1965.

Roux, Edward. *Time Longer Than Rope.* Madison, Wis., 1966.

Saunders, C. C., ed. *Black Leaders in Southern African History.* London, 1979.

Schapera, Isaac. *A Handbook of Tswana Law and Custom.* 1938; rpr. London, 1970.

———. *The Tswana.* London, 1952.

———, ed. *The Early Cape Hottentots.* Cape Town, 1933.

Scott, C. C. *Emigration, Submission, or What.* Columbia, S.C., 1907.

Shepherd, Robert A. W. *Lovedale, South Africa: The Story of a Century, 1841–1941.* Lovedale, South Africa, 1941.

Shepperson, George, and Thomas Price. *Independent African.* Edinburgh, 1958.

Shillito, Edward. *François Coillard: A Wayfaring Man.* London, 1923.

Sillery, Anthony. *Founding a Protectorate.* London, 1965.

———. *John MacKenzie of Bechuanaland, 1835–1899.* Cape Town, 1971.

Skota, T. D. Mweli, ed. *The African Who's Who.* Johannesburg, 1967.

—, ed. *The African Yearly Register: Being an Illustrated National Biographical Dictionary (Who's Who) of Black Folks in Africa.* Johannesburg, 1930.

Smith, Charles Spencer. *A History of the African Methodist Episcopal Church: Being a Volume Supplemental to a History of the A.M.E. Church by Daniel A. Payne.* Philadelphia, 1922.

Snowden, Frank M., Jr. *Blacks in Antiquity: Ethiopians in the Greco-Roman Experience.* Cambridge, Mass., 1970.

South Africa. *Report of South African Native Affairs Commission, LVDC22399.* Cape Town, 1905.

—. *South African Native Affairs Commission: Minutes of Evidence.* 5 vols. Cape Town, 1903–1905.

Stewart, James. *Lovedale Past and Present.* Cape Town, 1879.

—. *Dawn to the Dark Continent of Africa and Its Missions.* London, 1903.

Sundkler, Bengt G. *Bantu Prophets in South Africa.* 1948. Rev. ed. London, 1961.

—. *Zulu Zion and Some Swazi Zionists.* London, 1976.

Taylor, J. Dexter, ed. *Christianity and the Natives of South Africa.* Lovedale, South Africa, 1928.

Walshe, Peter. *The Rise of African Nationalism in South Africa.* Berkeley and Los Angeles, 1971.

Webster, James Bertin. *The African Churches Among the Yoruba, 1888–1922.* Oxford, 1964.

Welbourn, F. B., and B. A. Ogot. *A Place to Feel at Home: A Study of Two Independent Churches in Western Kenya.* Nairobi, 1966.

Wells, James. *Stewart of Lovedale: The Life of James Stewart.* London, 1908.

Wilson, Monica, and Leonard M. Thompson, eds. *The Oxford History of South Africa.* 2 vols. Oxford, 1969, 1971.

Williams, Donovan. *Umfundisi: A Biography of Tiyo Soga, 1829–1871.* Lovedale, South Africa, 1978.

Williams, George Washington. *History of the Negro Race in America from 1619–1880.* 2 vols. Washington, D.C., 1883.

—. *The Negro as a Political Problem.* Boston, 1884.

Williams, Walter L. *Black Americans and the Evangelization of Africa, 1877–1900.* Madison, 1982.

Wright, R. R., *et al.*, eds. *The Encyclopaedia of the African Methodist Episcopal Church.* Philadelphia, 1947.

Articles

"Academic Success." *Imvo Zabantsundu,* July 28, 1914.

"Africa for Africans." *Voice of Missions,* October, 1904.

"Africa for Christ or Mahommed?" *Voice of Missions,* April, 1910.

"African Colonization, Bishop Turner and T. McCants Stewart Disagree. . . ." *New York Age,* October 3, 1891.

"Africans Abroad." *Cape Mercury,* March 18, 1884.

"Again the College." *Imvo Zabantsundu,* January 24, 1911.

"Again the Native College." *Imvo Zabantsundu,* November 28, 1905.

"The AME Church and the Missionary Conference." *Christian Express,* December 1, 1904.

"The AME Church Movement." *Christian Express,* June 1, 1900, pp. 88–89.

"The A.M.E. Conference at Queenstown." *Christian Express,* March 1, 1900.

"A.M.E. Missionaries Penetrate Wild Africa." *Voice of Missions,* December, 1917.

"An American Bishop at the Opera House." *Cape Argus,* April 25, 1898.

"Another Account of the Conference." *Christian Express,* March 1, 1900.

Attaway, A. Henry. "The Part the Twentieth Century Negro Will Play in the World's Civilization." *Voice of Missions,* February 1, 1901.

"Basutoland and the College." *Imvo Zabantsundu,* September 5, 1916.

"The Bethel African Methodist Episcopal Institute." *Voice of Missions,* September, 1, 1903.

"Black, but Chosen." *Imvo Zabantsundu,* April 2, 1907.

Bokwe, John Knox. "Classics for Natives." *Imvo Zabantsundu,* July 1, 1885.

"Booker T. Washington: His New Book." *Imvo Zabantsundu,* March 12, 1912.

"B[ooker] T. W[ashington] on Education." *Imvo Zabantsundu,* November 24, 1914.

"Booker T. Washington's Methods." *Imvo Zabantsundu*, August 26, 1913.

"Booker T. Washington's Methods Applied to South Africa." In D. D. T. Jabavu, *The Black Problem* (Cape Town, 1920; rpr. New York, 1969), 22–70.

Bridgman, F. B. "The Ethiopian Movement, I." *Christian Express*, October 1, 1903.

Brisbane, A. L. "Letter from A. L. Brisbane, Brewerville, Liberia, February 12, 1893." *Voice of Missions*, April, 1893.

Burger, John S. "Captain Harry Dean: Pan Negro Nationalist in South Africa." *International Journal of African Historical Studies*, IX (1979), 83–89.

Bush, Nannie. "Dwane Missionary Society." *Voice of Missions*, November, 1898.

"The Case of the Rev. P. J. Mzimba, II." *Christian Express*, March 7, 1899.

Cheeseman, President. "A Letter from President Cheeseman," *Voice of Missions*, September, 1894.

Chirenje, J. Mutero. "The Afro-American Factor in Southern African Ethiopianism, 1890–1906." In *Profiles of Self-Determination: African Responses to European Colonialism in Southern Africa, 1652 to the Present*, edited by David Chanaiwa. Northridge, Calif., 1976.

"Claims of the Thembus." *Cape Argus*, June 23, 1884.

"College Constitution." *Imvo Zabantsundu*, January 26, 1915.

"The College Principalship." *Imvo Zabantsundu*, May 18, 1915.

"The Colonial Native and the American Negro." *Christian Express*, September 6, 1897.

"Condition of Mission Schools." Editorial. *Imvo Zabantsundu*, September 22, 1886.

"Convention at Lovedale." *Imvo Zabantsundu*, January 5, 1906.

Coppin, Fanny J. "Mrs. F. J. Coppin's Great Missionary Appeal." *Voice of Missions*, December, 1908.

Coppin, L. J. "Bishop Coppin, D.D., Pleads with Chiefs and Leaders of Various Tribes in South Africa." *Voice of Missions*, November 1, 1901.

———. "Bishop L. J. Coppin's Interview upon South Africa." *Voice of Missions*, June, 1906.

———. "The Church and the School in South Africa." *Christian Recorder*, October 31, 1901.

———. "The Dedicatory Service of Bethel Institute, Cape Town, South Africa." *Voice of Missions*, February 1, 1902.

———. "Five Hundred Miles up [South Africa] Country." *Voice of Missions*, November 14, 1901.

———. "Our South African School." *Voice of Missions*, October 1, 1902.

———. "Our Work in South Africa: How It Can Be Strengthened." *Voice of Missions*, April 16, 1902.

———. "The Outlook in the 14th District." *African Methodist Episcopal Church Review*, January, 1904.

———. "The Progress of Our Work in South Africa." *Voice of Missions*, November, 1902.

———. "A Service with the Natives." *Christian Recorder*, April 25, 1901.

———. "Through Matebeleland." *Voice of Missions*, October 1, 1903.

Davis, Richard Hunt. "John L. Dube: A South African Exponent of Booker T. Washington." *Journal of African Studies*, II (Winter, 1975), 497–528.

———. "School Vs. Blanket and Settler: Elijah Makiwane and the Leadership of the Cape School Community." *African Affairs*, LXXVIII (January, 1979).

"Death of Dr. W. A. Soga." *Imvo Zabantsundu*, July 25, 1916.

"Death of Rev. J. M. Dwane." *Imvo Zabantsundu*, February 15, 1916.

"Death of William Anderson Soga, M.D." *Imvo Zabantsundu*, August 8, 1916.

"Department and College." *Imvo Zabantsundu*, February 12, 1907.

"Dr. Washington's Opinion." *Imvo Zabantsundu*, October 27, 1914.

Donahey, A. W. "Wilberforce University." *Voice of Missions*, August, 1914.

Doughty, James Walter. "What Foreign Mission Has Done for the Negro." *Voice of Missions*, April, 1905.

Douglass, Frederick. "Oration by the Hon. Frederick Douglass on the Occasion of the Second Annual Exposition of the Coloured People of North Carolina, Delivered on Friday, October 1, 1880." *African Methodist Episcopal Zion Quarterly Review*, V (July, 1895), 174–75.

Dube, John L. "Mr. Dube's Work." *Imvo Zabantsundu*, January 5, 1909.

―――. "A Native View of Christianity in South Africa." *Missionary Review of the World*, June, 1901, pp. 421–26.

―――. "Need of Industrial Education in Africa." *Southern Workman*, July, 1897, pp. 141–42.

―――. "News from Zul[u]Land." *Voice of Missions*, August, 1914.

DuPlessis, J. "The Dutch Reformed Church and Its Mission." *Christian Express*, December 1, 1909.

Dwane, James Mata. "Historic Epistle. Rev. James M. Dwane, Superintendent of Our South African Work to the Bishops. His Personal Experience Told from a Heathen Child to a Christian Divine." *Voice of Missions*, December, 1897.

―――. "Our South African Superintendent Writes." *Voice of Missions*, May 1, 1897.

―――. "Vicar Bishop Dwane of South Africa Visits This Country by Special Orders." *Voice of Missions*, December, 1898.

―――. "Vicar Bishop Dwane, the Connecting Link." *Voice of Missions*, March 15, 1899.

"Ecclesiastic Envoys from South Africa." *Voice of Missions*, July, 1896.

"Education Through Books." Editorial. *Imvo Zabantsundu*, August 29, September 5, 1889.

"The Episcopal Church of the Province of South Africa." *Christian Express*, October 1, 1900.

"Ethiopianism: Interesting Correspondence, Comprehensive Resolution." *Voice of Missions*, December 1, 1904.

"The Ethiopian Order." *Christian Express*, October 1, 1900.

"Facts and Comments. Mr. Mzimba." *Imvo Zabantsundu*, August 10, 1907.

"Fair Play" [pseud.]. "The Black Peril." *Christian Express*, November 1, 1908.

Feaster, William D. "Africa's Redemption Has Come." *Lincoln University Herald*, February, 1897.

"The First Kafir [African] Convert." *Free Church of Scotland Monthly*, November 1, 1891.

Fitzpatrick, I. N. "The Eloquent and Timely Address Before the South African Conference." *Voice of Missions*, May 1, 1900.

———. "Letter of Great Interest from Elder Fitzpatrick to the Church." *Voice of Missions*, April 1, 1900.

Flournoy, B. M. "The Relationship of the African Methodist Church to Its South African Members, 1896–1906." *Journal of African Studies*, II (Winter, 1979).

"Foreign Mission Notes by Secretary Jordan, 8th July 1898." *Voice of Missions*, August 1, 1898.

"The Future of Our Native Churches." *Christian Express*, August 1, September 1, 1898.

Gabashane, A. A. "Tour of Bishop J. H. Johnson, D.D., through Orange Free State, South Africa." *Voice of Missions*, August, 1911.

Gabashane, Marcus. "Letter from South Africa." *Voice of Missions*, July, 1897.

Gailey, Harry A. "John Philip's Role in Hottentot Emancipation." *Journal of African History*, III (1962), 419–33.

Gow, Francis. "Dreadful Letter from South Africa." *Christian Express*, February 1, 1900.

———"The Seventh Annual Session of the South African Conference." *Voice of Missions*, May, 1916.

"Hampton in Africa." *Southern Workman*, June, 1897, pp. 120–21.

Harlan, Louis R. "Booker T. Washington and the White Man's Burden." *American Historical Review*, LXXI (1966), 441–67.

Hayford, Casely. "Important Letter from Africa." *Voice of Missions*, October, 1893.

Hutchins, P. S. L. "About Rev. Jackson of Cape Town, South Africa." *Voice of Missions*, August 1, 1898.

"In Memory of Booker T. Washington." *Imvo Zabantsundu*, May 2, 1915.

"Inter-Colonial Native College Approved by the Native Affairs Commission." *Imvo Zabantsundu*, November, 1905.

"The Inter-State College." *Imvo Zabantsundu*, June 25, 1907.

"The Inter-State Native College." *Imvo Zabantsundu*, April 2, 1907.

"The Inter-State Native College Scheme." *Imvo Zabantsundu*, May 26, 1909.

Irvine, Cecilia. "The Birth of the Kimbanguist Movement in the Bas-Zaire, 1921." *Journal of Religion in Africa*, VI (1974), 23–76.

"Is the African Methodist Episcopal Church Loyal?" *Christian Express*, August 1, 1902.

Jabavu, D. D. T. "Booker T. Washington: A Character Sketch." *Imvo Zabantsundu*, November 30, 1915.

Jackson, R. A. "A Baptist Missionary in South Africa." *Voice of Missions*, November, 1899.

Jacottet, E. "The Ethiopian Church and the Missionary Conference of Johannesburg." *Christian Express*, December 1, 1904.

Jaques, A. "The Story of the French Mission in Basutoland," *Christian Express*, March 1, April 1, May 1, 1902.

Johnson, A. E. "Afro-American Literature." *New York Age*, January 30, 1892.

Johnson, John A. "Africa's Appeal to the American Negro." *Voice of Missions*, January, 1910.

Johnson, Walton R. "Afro-Americans and Southern Africa: A Reassessment of the Past." *Africa Today*, XIX (Summer, 1972), 9–10.

Jonas, E. "Cape Colony Conference, African Methodist Episcopal Church." *Voice of Missions*, January, 1906.

Jones, J. D. " 'Mahoko a Becwana'—The Second seTswana Newspaper." *Botswana Notes and Records*, IV (1972), 111–20.

"The Jubilee Singers." Editorial. *Imvo Zabantsundu*, October 16, 1890.

"Jubilee Singers' Concert." Castlemaine *Leader*, May 18, 1892.

Katiya, Thomas Chalmers. "Letter from South Africa." *Lincoln University Herald*, October, 1906.

Keto, Clement T. "Black American Involvement in South Africa's Race Issue," *Issue* (1973), 6–11.

Kgama III, Chief. "A Letter from Khama." *Christian Express*, September 1, 1902.

Khalane, Thomas B. "A Letter . . . to President W. S. Scarborough." *Voice of Missions*, September, 1915.

———. "Journey from South Africa to the United States." *Voice of Missions*, April, 1916.

"Khama's Mission." *Imvo*, December 19, 1895.

"Khama's Success." *Imvo*, November 21, 1895.

"Killed in Cold Blood. Sensational Tragedy at Bulawayo. His Own Judge, an Angry Father's Retribution." *South African News;* May 18, 1911.

Knox, Rev. T. E. "The Negro Is at Home Here." *Christian Recorder*, May 15, 1890.

"The Late Rev. Jeremiah Mzimba." *Imvo Zabantsundu*, July 4, 1911.

"The Launch." *Imvo Zabantsundu*, November 3, 1884.

"Launch of the College." *Imvo Zabantsundu*, January 12, 1915.

"Letters from Hampton Graduates." *Southern Workman*, April, 1887, p. 41.

"L. M. S. Support." *Imvo Zabantsundu*, March 13, 1906.

"Lord Ripon and the Native Choirs." *Imvo Zabantsundu*, February 9, 1893.

"The Lovedale Girls' School Report." Editorial. *Imvo Zabantsundu*, January 17, 1889.

"The Lovedale Native Congregation versus Mzimba and Others." *Supplement to The Christian Express*, March 7, 1899.

"Lovedalian's Reply. *Imvo Zabantsundu*, July 22, 1885.

McAdoo, Eugene. Letter to Editor. *Southern Workman*, January, 1894, p. 15.

McAdoo, Orpheus M. "A Letter from South Africa: Black Laws in the Orange Free State of Africa." *Southern Workman*, November, 1890, p. 120.

Mahlangeni, M. Robert. "Presbyterian Church of Africa." *Imvo Zabantsundu*, July 30, 1912.

Makiwane, Elijah. "The Free Church in South Africa." *Scotsman*, May 20, 1907.

———. "The Natives and Politics." *Imvo Zabantsundu*, February 2, 1887.

———. "Natives in Towns." *Imvo Zabantsundu*, July 19, 1888.

———. "Rev. E. Makiwane's Appreciation." *Imvo Zabantsundu*, October 3, 1911.

Marable, W. Manning. "A Black School in South Africa." *Negro History Bulletin*, XXXVII (June-July, 1974), 258–61.

———. "Booker T. Washington and African Nationalism." *Phylon*, XXXV (March, 1974), 398–406.

Marks, Shula. "The Ambiguities of Dependence: John L. Dube of Natal." *Journal of Southern African Studies*, I (April, 1975), 162–80.

———. "'Khoisan Resistance to the Dutch in the Seventeenth and Eighteenth Centuries." *Journal of African History*, XIII (1972), 55–80.

Maxeke, Marshall. "An Appeal from the Jungles of Africa." *Voice of Missions*, July 1, 1904.

Mazwi, J. S. "The Rev. E. Makiwane's Appreciation of the Late P. J. Mzimba." *Imvo Zabantsundu*, October 17, 1911.

"Meeting of Lord Selborne. The Protectorate Chiefs." *Imvo Zabantsundu*, April 19, 1910.

"Minutes of a Meeting Held at Kalk Bay." *Christian Express*, March 1, 1900.

"Mr. and Mrs. Makiwane." *Free Church of Scotland Monthly*, May 1, 1899.

"Mr. D. Tengo Jabavu." *Imvo Zabantsundu*, July 8, 1913.

"Mr. Mzimba's Advice." Editorial. *Imvo Zabantsundu*, February 2, 1887.

Mokalapa, W. J. "An Appeal for the Zambezi Foreign Mission Work in Central Africa." *Christian Recorder*, May 25, 1905.

Mokone, Mangena. "Grand Letter from South Africa." *Voice of Missions*, July 1, 1897.

———. "Pleading for a Free Hand and Help." *Voice of Missions*, September, 1910.

———. "Rev. Mokone of South Africa to President Councill." *Voice of Missions*, April, 1896.

Mokone, Mangena, and J. G. Xaba. "Ethiopian Mission." *Voice of Missions*, December, 1895.

Morris, Charles S. "South Africa and Her People." *Christian Express*, February 1, 1900.

———. "A Work for American Negroes." In *Report of the Ecumenical Conference*, I, 469–70.

"Native Central College: Opinions of the Press." *Imvo Zabantsundu*, December 12, 1905.

"Native Churches." *Imvo Zabantsundu*, November 14, 1898.

"The Native Church Movement." *Christian Express*, December 1, 1901.

"The Native College." *Imvo Zabantsundu*, January 14, 1907.

"The Native College." *Imvo Zabantsundu*, August 10, 1907.

"The Native College." *Imvo Zabantsundu*, January 10, 1908.

"The Native College." *Imvo Zabantsundu*, January 14, 1908.

"The Native College." *Imvo Zabantsundu*, February 11, 1908.

"A Native College." *Imvo Zabantsundu*, June 7, 1910.

"The Native College." *Imvo Zabantsundu*, October 6, 1914.

"Native College Convention." *Imvo Zabantsundu*, February 4, 1913.

"The Native College Movement." *Imvo Zabantsundu*, November 7, 1905.

"The Native College Scheme: Notes in Circulation." *Imvo Zabantsundu*, February 27, 1906.

"Native College Staffing." *Imvo Zabantsundu*, January 26, 1915.

"Native Disruption." *Christian Express*, March 7, 1899.

"Native Education." Editorial. *Imvo Zabantsundu*, July 8, 1885.

"Native Education." *Imvo Zabantsundu*, May 6, 1905.

"Native Higher Education." *Imvo Zabantsundu*, October 10, 1905.

"Native Higher Education, the Need for an Advance." *Imvo Zabantsundu*, October 10, 1905.

"Native Male Voice Choir." *Imvo Zabantsundu*, August 1, 1916.

"The Native Mind—II." *Christian Express*, December 1, 1908.

"Natives and Independence. At a Debating Society." *Imvo Extra*, May 1, 1898.

"The Natives and Their Missionaries." *Christian Express*, February 1, 1908.

"Natives and White Women." *Transvaal Leader*, June 16, 1911.

"A Native South African in America." *Imvo Zabantsundu*, September 2, 1913.

"Native Students." Editorial. *Imvo Zabantsundu*, January 12, 1885.

"Native Traveller" [pseud.]. "Native Travelling." *Imvo Zabantsundu*, October 15, 1912.

"The Negroes and the Native." *Imvo Zabantsundu*, December 4, 1899.

"Negro Immigration." *Imvo Zabantsundu*, December 4, 1899.

"Notes on the AME Church." *Christian Express*, July 2, 1900.

"Ntete" [pseud.]. "The Rev. E. J. Mqoboli's Criticism of the Rev. E. Makiwane's Appreciation." *Imvo Zabantsundu*, November 7, 1911.

"Old Liberia Is not the place for me." *African Methodist Episcopal Church Review*, October, 1916.

"Order of Ethiopia." *Imvo Zabantsundu*, June 13, 1911.

"The Order of Ethiopia of the Church of the Province of South Africa." *Christian Express*, December 1, 1909.

Orpen, J. M. "Glimpse into the Mythology of the Maluti Bushmen." *Cape Monthly Magazine*, IX (1874), 1–10.

"Our Negro Visitor." *Imvo Extra*, April 20, 1898.

"Our Returned African Student." *Southern Workman*, January, 1891, p. 137.

Parks, H. B. "Kaffir University." *Voice of Missions*, March, 1899.
————. "Redemption of Africa, the American Negro's Burden." *Voice of Missions*, September, 1899.
"Pastoral Letter from the General Assembly to the Ministers, Deacons and Members of the Free Church of Scotland in the Synod of Kaffraria." *Christian Express*, February 1, 1899.
Peregrino, F. Z. S. "A Journalist's Tribute to Bishop Coppin." *Christian Recorder*, January 16, 1901.
————. "Light Ahead, the Blackman's Redemption." *Imvo Zabantsundu*, December 5, 1911.
————. "Native National Congress, What It Is." *Imvo Zabantsundu*, March 26, 1912.
————. "Our South African Work and Its Hero [Bishop Coppin]." *Christian Recorder*, May 7, 1901.
"Prof[essor] Kerr's Inaugural." *Imvo Zabantsundu*, March 21, 1916.
"The Proposed Native College: Opinions of the Press." *Imvo Zabantsundu*, November 28, 1905.
"Proposed Native College, a Mission to the Transvaal: Mr. J. Tengo Jabavu Interviewed." *Imvo Zabantsundu*, December 28, 1905.
"The Queenstown College." *Voice of Missions*, March 15, 1899.
"Race and Religion." *Imvo Extra*, May 11, 1898.
Ralston, Richard. "American Episodes in the Making of an African Leader: A Case Study of Alfred B. Xuma." *International Journal of African Historical Studies*, VI (1973), 72–93.
Ranger, T. O. "The Early History of Independency in Southern Rhodesia." In *Religion in Africa: Proceedings of a Seminar Held in the Centre of African Studies* (University of Edinburgh, 1964), 52–74.
————. "The 'Ethiopian' Episode in Barotseland, 1900–1905." *Rhodes-Livingstone Journal*, XXXVII (June, 1965), 26–41.
Redkey, Edwin S. "The Flowering of Black Nationalism: Henry McNeal Turner and Marcus Garvey." In *Key Issues in the Afro-American Experience*, Vol. II, *Since 1865*, edited by Nathan I. Huggins *et al.* New York, 1971.
"Report on University Senior School Leaving Certificate." *Imvo Zabantsundu*, April 19, 1910.
"Resolutions of the Pretoria District of the AME Church." *Christian Express*, July 2, 1900.
"Resolutions on Death of Bishop Henry McNeal Turner, D.D.,

from the Baltimore A.M.E. Preachers' Meeting." *Voice of Missions*, July, 1915.

"Rev. P. J. Mzimba in Scotland." *Imvo Zabantsundu*, October 25, 1893.

Rideout, Conrad A. "African Kings Won to the Gospel." *Voice of Missions*, April 1, 1903.

————. "An Interesting Letter from Con. Rideout." *Voice of Missions*, May 1, 1902.

Rideout, Pamela. "A Letter from Miss P. M. Rideout of South Africa." *Voice of Missions*, March 1, 1900.

Ross, Brownlee J. "Mr. Makiwane's Appreciation." *Imvo Zabantsundu*, October 31, 1911.

Saunders, C. C. "Tile and the Thembu Church: Politics and Independency on the Cape Eastern Frontier in the Late Nineteenth Century." *Journal of African History*, XI (1970), 553–70.

Scarborough, W. S. "Wilberforce University: Its Origin and Growth." *Voice of Missions*, May, 1909.

"Schism in Kafraria." *Free Church of Scotland Monthly*, November, 1898.

"Schism in the Native Church." *Christian Express*, June 1, 1906.

Severance, Claude M. "Why Protestant Christian Negroes of America Should be Most Interested in the Evangelization of Africa." *Voice of Missions*, February, 1907.

"Shall Africa be Mahommedan or Christian?" *Voice of Missions*, September, 1910.

Shepperson, George. "The Afro-American Contribution to African Studies." *Journal of American Studies*, VIII (December, 1974), 249–68.

————. "Ethiopianism: Past and Present." In *Christianity in Tropical Africa*, edited by C. G. Baeta (London, 1968), 249–68.

————. "Ethiopianism and African Nationalism." *Phylon*, XIV (Spring, 1953), 9–18.

————. "Introduction."In *The African Diaspora: Interpretive Essays*, edited by Martin L. Kilson and Robert I. Rotberg (Cambridge, Mass., 1976), 1–10.

Shorter, G. I. "Women's Mite Missionary Society." *Voice of Missions*, August, 1914.

Sishuba, I. G., and H. R. Ngcayiya. "Kind Words." *Voice of Missions*, November, 1904.

Smith, Charles Spencer. "Bishop Smith at Cape Town." *Voice of Missions*, November, 1904.

———. "Bishop Smith's Response." *Voice of Missions*, October, 1904.

———. "The Relation of the British Government to the Negroes of South Africa." *Voice of Missions*, September, 1906.

Smith, S. Henderson. "Manhood Essential to the Negro's Elevation." *Christian Recorder*, October 5, 1893.

Smyth, J. H. "The African in Africa and the African in America." In *Africa and the American Negro*, edited by J. W. E. Bowen (Atlanta, 1895), 69, 83.

Soga, Tiyo. "Lecture by the Reverend T. Soga." *Cape Argus*, June 7, 1866.

"South Africa. Unrest." *Free Church of Scotland Monthly*, June, 1899, p. 130.

"A South African Abroad." *Imvo Zabantsundu*, November 18, 1913.

"South African Christianity." *Voice of Missions*, December, 1898.

"The South African College." *Voice of Missions*, October 1, 1901.

"The S[outh] A[frican] Native College." *Imvo Zabantsundu*, November 24, 1914.

"The South African Native College." *Imvo Zabantsundu*, January 4, 1916.

"S[outh] A[frican] Native College." *Imvo Zabantsundu*, December 5, 1916.

"S[outh] A[frican] Native College. The Opening of Classes. The Principal's Inaugural, Brilliant Address." *Imvo Zabantsundu*, March 7, 1916.

"S[outh] A[frica] Native College: Press Opinions." *Imvo Zabantsundu*, February 29, 1916.

"South African Native College Opening Ceremony . . . An Historic Event." *Imvo Zabantsundu*, February 15, 1916.

"South Africa's Black Peril." London *Daily Telegraph*, June 6, 1911.

"Special Meeting Held at Rondebosch." *Christian Express*, March 1, 1900.

Stewart, James. "The Lovedale Industrial Mission: . . . A Work Kindred to Hampton's in South Africa." *Southern Workman*, January, 1894, pp. 13–15.

"Subsequent Proceedings in the A.M.E. Church." *Christian Express*, March 1, 1900.

"A Sympathiser" [pseud.]. "Rev. E. Makiwane's Appreciation of the Late P. J. Mzimba." *Imvo Zabantsundu*, October 3, 1911.

Tanner, C. M. "South African Notes." *Voice of Missions*, April 1, 1903.

Tantsi, H. N. "The Wilberforce Lillian Derrick Institute." *Voice of Missions*, September, 1910.

"Tembuland Troublers," *Cape Mercury*, March 16, 1893.

"£10,000 for the College." Editorial. *Imvo Zabantsundu*, February 6, 1907.

"A Thembu Meeting." Grahamstown *Journal*, February 28, 1884.

Tipton, C. Robert. "The Fisk Jubilee Singers." *Tennessee Historical Quarterly*, XXIV (Spring, 1970).

Tule, John. "Letter from South Africa." *Voice of Missions*, March, 1896.

Turner, Henry McNeal. "Bishop H. M. Turner, His Lecture on 'Whence Came the Negro?' " *Voice of Missions*, May, 1894.

———. "Bishop H. M. Turner's Tribute to his Colleague." *Voice of Missions*, October, 1904.

———. "Bishop L. J. Coppin D.D., Departs for South Africa." *Voice of Missions*, February 1, 1901.

———. "Bishop Turner and Africa." *Imvo Extra*, April 20, 1898.

———. "Bishop Turner Attacks Baptists." *Voice of Missions*, July 1, 1898.

———. "Bishop Turner on Africa." *New York Age*, February 20, 1892.

———. "Bishop Turner Renders His Report." *Voice of Missions*, June 1, 1898.

———. "Bishop Turner Sees Presi[dent] Paul Kruger." *Voice of Missions*, June 1, 1898.

———. "Bishop Turner's Views. He Will Visit Dutch and British South Africa." *Imvo Extra*, April 20, 1898.

———. "Enroute to Africa." *Voice of Missions*, May, 1893.

———. "My Trip to South Africa." *African Methodist Episcopal Church Review*, April, 1899, pp. 809–13.

———. "Speech of Bishop H. M. Turner Before the National Council of Coloured Men Which Met in Cincinnati, Ohio, November 28, 1893." *Voice of Missions*, December, 1893.

———. "The Turner Convention." *African Methodist Episcopal Zion Quarterly Review*, IV (January, 1894), 181–82.

————. "Vicar Bishop Dwane of South Africa Visits This Country by Special Orders." *Voice of Missions*, December, 1898.

"Two South African Natives Created Barristers-at-Law." *Imvo Zabantsundu*, July 12, 1910.

"Ukhama." *Imvo Zabantsundu*, December 27, 1895.

"The University College." *Imvo Zabantsundu*, January 4, 1916.

van Blunk, Mrs. J. M. S. "Letter from Bulawayo." *Voice of Missions*, March 1, 1900.

van Oordt, J. F. "An Open Letter to the Rev. E. Jacottet." *Christian Express*, June 1, 1908.

Waring, E. J. "The Term Afro-American." *New York Age*, January 2, 1892.

Washington, Booker T. "Booker and South Africa." *Imvo Zabantsundu*, June 24, 1906.

————. "The Educational and Industrial Emancipation of Negro—II." *Christian Express*, August 1, 1908.

————. "The Educational and Industrial Emancipation of Negro—III." *Christian Express*, September 1, 1908.

————. "The Mission Work of the Negro Church" *African Methodist Episcopal Church Review*, XXXII (January, 1916), 186–89.

————. "What Should Education Accomplish?" *Voice of Missions*, July, 1905.

White, A. E. "African Emigration." *Voice of Missions*, December 1, 1899.

"White Women in Danger." London *Daily Express*, June 30, 1911.

Wilcox, W. C. "The Booker Washington of South Africa." *Oberlin Alumni Magazine*, March, 1927.

————. "John L. Dube, the Booker Washington of the Zulus." *Missionary Review of the World*, December, 1909, pp. 917–19.

"Will a Reformation in Africa be Necessary?" *Christian Express*, November 1, 1899.

Willoughby, W. C. "Historic Gathering at Tiger Kloof." *LMS Chronicle*, January, 1905, pp. 312–13.

————. "Notes on the Initiation Ceremonies of the Becwana." *Journal of the Royal Anthropological Institute*, XXXIX (1909), 228–31.

Williams, Howard. "The Native Messiah." *Christian Express*, October 1, 1909.

Williams, Sylvester. "Colour and Politics: Address by Advocate Williams." *South African News*, June 10, 1904.

"A Word from Africa." *Lincoln University Herald*, February, 1909.

Xaba, J. G. "South African Letter." *Voice of Missions*, December, 1895.

Xiniwe, Paul. "Affairs of the African Choir." *Imvo Zabantsundu*, March 17, 1892.

Yako, W. "A Native College." *Imvo Zabantsundu*, June 7, 1910.

Index

Adams College, 26
Adriaanse, Rev., 79, 80
African evangelists, 13, 14, 15, 18, 19
African Methodist Episcopal (AME)
  church, in southern Africa, 39, 52,
  53, 54, 55, 73, 88, 100, 111, 164, 166,
  167; Mokone and, 56, 57, 78, 79, 147,
  148–49; ministers ordained in, 62;
  Kruger on, 63; growth of, 66, 69; and
  Dwane, 76; early station of, 84–85;
  legal status of, 87; and seceders, 93;
  formal Cape government recognition
  of, 98; and Brander, 105; politiciza-
  tion of, 107, 110; and South African
  Missionary Conference, 108; and
  native college, 127; in Southern Rhodesia, 150, 151, 153, 154, 162. See also
  Ethiopian Church of South Africa;
  Fourteenth District
African Methodist Episcopal church
  (1796), in U.S.: founding of, 2–4; and
  evangelism, 3; missionaries of, 45;
  on emigration, 48; Wilberforce and,
  50; legal status of, 88; General Con-
  ference of (1900), 89
African National Congress (ANC; 1912),
  159, 168
African nationalism, 25
African Native Baptist Church, 158
African press, 26
African Reformation, Ethiopianism as,
  73
Africans: as spokesmen, 28; as
  students, 26, 138
Afrikaner Bond, 101
Afrikaners' ambivalence, 9
Afro-American missionary efforts in
  Africa, 45; U.S. opposition to, 46

Allen, Richard, 3, 56
Allenites, 3
Amagqunukwebe tribe, 20
American Board of Commissioners for
  Foreign Missions (ABCFM; 1810), 12
American universities: African criti-
  cism of, 123, 124, 125; campaign
  against, 135; support for, 136
American Zulu Mission, 19, 22, 26, 40,
  58, 91, 140, 158
Atlanta *Evening Journal*, 61
Attaway, Rev. A. Henry, 90, 91, 98, 147,
  148; before SANAC, 107–108

Back-to-Africa movement, 5
Baptist Missionary Society (U.S.), 11
Barotseland, 146
Barotseland National School, 149
Bathoen (Tswana chief), 66, 95, 96, 97,
  121; and clash with Mothowagae,
  144–45
Baviaans Kloof, 10
Bethel Church (Philadelphia), 3
Bethel Institute, 98–99, 105, 119, 165
Bethel mission station, 10
Black Baptists. *See* National Baptist
  Convention
Black consciousness, 34
"Black giant," 111, 159
Black nationalism, 102
"Black peril," 111, 118, 159, 160
Black revolution, 101
Blijde Vooruitzichts Fontein (Fountain
  of Glad Prospect), 11
Bloemfontein *Post*, 123
Blythswood mission school, 26
Bokwe, John Knox, 29, 30
Bongiwe, Titus M., 36

Botswana, 12, 15, 17, 26, 27, 33, 66, 73; prophets in, 94, 95
Brander, Rev. Jacobus, 105, 167
Bridewealth, 27
Bridgman, Rev. Frederick, 158
British South Africa Company, 147, 148, 149
Broadbent, Rev. Samuel, 17
Brown, Rev. John, 27
Bulawayo (Rhodesia), 84

Calvinism, and Afrikaners, 9
Campbell, Rev. John, 14
Cape Argus, 32, 63, 68, 72
Cape Mercury, 23
Cape Times, 24, 124–25
Carey, William, 11
Chalmers, Rev. John A., 16
Chartered company. See British South Africa Company
Chatsworth Institute, 165
Cheeseman, J. James, 48
Chidembo, Isaiah Charles, 153
Christian Express, 27, 39, 49, 58, 100; on Ethiopianism, 64; on missionaries, 69; on Mzimba, 72; on curriculum in native schools, 122; on American education, 125; on Booker T. Washington, 132
Christianity, opposition to, 8, 9, 13
Chubb, Rev. Theophilus, 20
Church of Moses (Ibandla lika Mosi), 92
Church of the Nazarites (Isonto Lama Nazaretha), 158
Climate, in southern Africa, 54, 88
Coillard, Rev. Francis, 146, 147
Coker, Rev. Daniel, 3
Coppin, Bishop L. J., 89, 98, 107–108
Councill, Professor W. H., 54–55
Crummell, Alexander, 45
Cuffe, Paul, 5
Cushites (Blind Johannies), 93

Dalindyebo (Thembu chief), 21, 23–24
Dean, Captain Harry, 5, 82
Delagoa Bay Railroad, 37, 38
Derrick, Bishop William B., 49
De Zuid Afrikaan, 32

Dhlamini, Reuben, 44
Dibebe (Mbukushu headman), 27
Dikkop, Paul, 14
Discrimination, 20, 70, 76, 159, 160, 162
Douglass, Frederick, 45, 47, 51, 59
Dube, Charles, 142
Dube, Rev. James, 140
Dube, Rev. John L., 40, 140–43, 161, 162, 168
Du Bois, W. E. B., 2
Dutch Reformed church, 8, 9, 84, 92, 104
Dwane, Mcebuka, 20
Dwane, Rev. James Mata, 20, 44, 56, 107, 129, 157, 158, 167; as delegate to AME church meeting, 55; as bishop of Fourteenth District, 63; criticism of, 66; breaks with Wesleyans, 73; to U.S., 73; missionary societies named for, 74; fails in fund raising, 76; breaks with AME church, 76, 88–89; joins Anglicans, 80

Education Gazette (Cape Colony), 134
Edwards, Jonathan, 11
Edwards, Rev. W., 10
Ekuphakameni (Zululand), 158
Emancipation, in U.S., 34, 60
Emigration: Afro-American societies and, 45; Bishop Turner on, 59–61; schemes in U.S., 85–87
Ethiopian Catholic Church in Zion (1893), 2, 44, 52, 53, 55; affiliates with AME church, 56–57; criticism of, 58; race and religion in, 64; growth of, 66, 69; Mzimba and, 70; need for leaders in, 164; and dependence on U.S., 167
Ethiopian Church of South Africa, 2, 57
Ethiopianism: defined, 1–2; rise of, 14, 17, 19, 22; Cape Times on, 24; Imvo as prelude to, 28; criticism of, 64; debate on, 65; responses to, 66; at Lovedale, 71; as Reformation, 73; spread of, 96; and African nationalism, 101; white definition of, 102–103; and racism, 106; SANAC conclusions on, 111; in Mashonaland and Rhodesia, 153; and Zulus, 158. See also

Order of Ethiopia (1800)
Evangelism: as AME goal, 3; early, 8
Expatriate Afro-Americans, 36, 37

First Ethiopian Church, 153–54
Fitzpatrick, Rev. I. N., 87, 88, 89
Foreign missionaries, 13, 53
Fort Beaufort *Advocate*, 123, 125–26
Fort Hare University College (1916), 119, 131, 134, 143, 162, 168. *See also* South African interstate native college
Fourteenth District of AME church (1896): formation of, 56, 57; Dwane and, 63, 78, 88, 89; growth of, 75, 165; reorganization of, 87; Coppin and, 98; Brander and, 105; criticism of, 106
Free Church of Scotland, 15, 16, 18; mission schools and newspapers of, 26; jubilee of, 40; Mzimba and, 70, 72, 92; and Ethiopianism, at Lovedale, 71; paternalism in, 72; schism in, 92; land for native college, 131; and merger with United Presbyterian church, 155

Gabashane, Rev. Marcus, 57
General Conference of AME church (1900), 89
Glasgow Missionary Society stations, 11
Goduka, Rev. Jonas, 23, 81
Goode, Rev. James, 95, 96
Govan, Rev., 15
Gow, Rev. Francis, 78, 81, 87, 89

Healdtown mission school, 26, 28
Henderson, Rev. John, 15
Hermannsburg Missionary Society, 26
High schools, need for, 134, 135
Holbrook, Rev., 19
Hottentot legislation of 1809, p. 13
Hottentot tribe, 14. *See also* Khoikhoi
Hulett, Sir James Liege, 103
Hunter, Rev. D. A., 106

Ibandla Lase Tiyopia (Order of Ethiopia), 80
Ibandla lika Mosi (Church of Moses), 92

Impeye, Alfred, 4
Imvo Zabantsundu, 28, 29; on education, 30, 31, 33, 123, 134; on African society and politics, 31, 32, 33, 34; on Virginia Jubilee Singers, 36; on Methodists, 41; on U.S., 49, 64; on Douglass, 51; on race and religion, 64, 65, 66, 82; on Rideout and Dean, 82; on Morris, 82; on black university, 123, 127–28; on blacks to U.S., 124, 137; on Booker T. Washington, 131–32; on Mzimba, 156, 160; on discrimination, 160
Inhlangakazi (mountain in Zululand), 158
Innes, Rose, 33
Isigidimo SamaXosa (Xhosa-language newspaper), 26
Islam, 166
Isonto Lama Nazaretha (Church of the Nazarites), 158

Jackson, Rev. R. A., 4, 81, 85
Jacottet, Rev. Edward, 108, 109, 110
Javabu, Davidson Don, 124, 134, 137–38
Javabu, John Tengo, 23, 28–29; on Afro-Americans, 34; on Turner and Ethiopianism, 64; on education, 120, 124, 126; and native college, 128, 129, 130
Jones, Most Rev. W. W., 80

Kaffir Express, 27
Kaffir University, 75, 123
Kaffrarian Watchman, 36
Kama, Monte, 4
Kanyane, Rev., 44
Kanye mission station, 95, 96–97
Kawa, Peter, 119–20, 123
Kgama (Tswana chief), 28, 55, 94, 99–100, 161
Khoikhoi tribe, 7, 8, 10, 11; and Hottentot legislation of 1809, p. 13
Khumalo, Johannes (Zulu chief), 103
Kicherer, Rev. J. J., 11
Kilner, Rev. John, 18–19
Kilnerton mission school, 26, 42
King Edward Bangwaketse Mission Church, 97
Kok, Rev. J. M., 10

Koranta ea Becoana (Mafeking), 26, 105
Kruger, Paul, 63, 64, 65
Kuhnel, Johann Christian, 10
Kuze, Rev. P. S., 77, 78

Lamplough, Rev. Robert, 20
Legal Free Church of Scotland, 155–56
Legong, Sencho, 145, 146
Lerothodi (Lesotho chief), 99
Leselinyana La Lesotho (Sotho-
   language newspaper), 26
Leshega, William Mathebule, 158
Letsholathebe (Tswana chief), 27
Lewanika, King Lebusi, 99, 146, 147,
   148
Leyds, Dr. J. W., 37, 38
Liberia, 45, 47, 48, 60, 61, 62
Lillian Derrick Institute, 140, 165
Livingstone, David, 15, 17
Lloyd, Rev. Edwin, 28, 96
Locke, Alain, 133
London Missionary Society (LMS), 9,
   10, 14, 15, 17, 18, 121, 161; early stations
   of, 11; and civil rights, 13; periodicals
   of, 26; and politics, 40; at Kanye, 66,
   73, 95, 96, 97; and Tiger Kloof indus-
   trial school (1905), 120; and native
   college, 129
Louw, Rev. A. A., 104
Lovedale convention (1905), 128–29
Lovedale mission school (1841), 11, 18,
   123; Mzimba and, 32, 40, 70–71;
   Ethiopianism at, 71, 96, 155; Baptists
   at, 81
Loveless, Rev. J. H., 152
Lutheran Moravian Protest Society
   (United Brethren Society), 8, 10
Luti, J. B., 65, 160
Lynching, 159, 160

Mabote, Rev. S. J., 85
McAdoo, Orpheus Myron, 34, 35, 36
McAdoo Minstrels. *See* Virginia Jubi-
   lee Singers
McClure, Rev. J. J., 103
MacKenzie, Rev. John, 40
Magqibesa, Abraham, 44, 78
Mahlangeni, Dr. M. Robert, 156

Mahoko a Becwana (LMS periodical),
   26, 27, 28
Makanda, Rev. William, 43
Makgatho, Rev. Micah, 100, 104, 150,
   154
Makiwane, Rev. Elijah, 31, 32–33, 71
Mangena, Alfred, 136
Manye, Charlotte, 39, 49, 50, 51, 52, 55,
   140
Manye, Kate, 52
Marabastad, 42, 43
Marrianhill mission school, 26
Marsveld, Hendrik, 10
Mashaloba, Rev. William G., 78
Matebeleland, 100, 150
Maxeke, Rev. Marshall M., 140
Mazwi, Rev. J. S., 156
Mbele, Moses, 92
Messiahs. *See* Prophets
Methodists, 151–52
Missionaries, foreign: as ivory traders,
   10; welcomed by natives, 12; and pol-
   icy weaknesses, 18, 19; and politics,
   83
Missionary Department of AME
   church, 53, 54, 57, 74, 87
Mission schools, 26; debate on curricu-
   lum in, 29–30
Mission stations, early, 8–12
Moffat, Rev. John Smith, 121
Moffat, Rev. Robert, 10, 15, 17, 68
Moffat mission school, 26
Mogodi, Khukwi, 27
Mokaedi oa Bechuana (LMS periodi-
   cal), 26
Mokolapa, W. J., 146–49
Mokone, Rev. Mangena Maake, 2, 42,
   89, 104, 164; and Wesleyans, 42–43;
   and Ethiopian church, 43–44; and
   AME church, 52, 54, 55, 57, 77, 78, 79.
   See also Ethiopian Church of South
   Africa
Mokotedi, 15, 68
Molehabangwe (Tlhaping chief), 10
Molekudi ua Bechuana (LMS periodi-
   cal), 26
Moller, the widow, 9
Montshiwa, D. G., 136
Montshiwa (Rolong chief), 27

Morija mission school, 26
Morris, Rev. Charles S., 4, 81–82, 92–93
Moshupa Tsela (missionary periodical), 26
Moshweshwe, George T. (Tswana chief), 103, 161
Mothibi (Botswana chief), 12
Mothowagae, 95–97, 144–45. *See also* King Edward Bangwaketse Mission Church
Mphela, Joshua, 44
Msikinya, Rev. D., 98, 129
Mzimba, Rev. Pambani Jeremiah: on politics, 32; and secession, 69–71, 107; and own church, 71; and Free Church of Scotland, 72; growth of his church, 92; and students to U.S., 124, 126, 136; and consolidation, 155, 156; death of, 156; and Ethiopianism, 169. *See also* Presbyterian Church of South Africa

National Baptist Convention, 4, 81, 92, 158
Native Affairs Department, 151, 153
Native college movement, 119, 127. *See also* South African interstate native college
Ncube, Rev. M. C., 84
New York Age, 62, 82
Ngangelizwe (Thembu chief), 20, 21
Ngcayiya, Rev. Henry R., 77, 162
Ngidi, Rev. Mbiyana, 22, 23, 58, 91
Nkomo, Simbini Mamba, 139
Noodsberg, Natal, 22, 23
Northern Rhodesia, 149
Nyuswa, Rev. Sungusa, 91

Order of Ethiopia (Ibandla Lase Tiyopia; 1800), 80, 157
Ordinance 50 of 1828, p. 13
Original Church of the White Bird (Shiri Chena; 1915), 151, 152, 168. *See also* Zvimba, Matthew Chigaga

Pan-Africanism, 59
Pan-regionalism, 25
Paris Evangelical Missionary Society (PEMS), 11, 26, 146

Parks, Bishop H. B., 75
Paternalism, 70, 72
Payne Theological Seminary, 50, 140
Peregrino, F. Z. S., 105
Philip, John, 13
Plaatje, Solomon, 105
Polygamy, 27, 163
Port Elizabeth *Telegraph*, 32
Prejudice, 36, 126
Presbyterian Church of South Africa, 71, 72, 92, 135–36, 139, 155, 156, 165, 168. *See also* Mzimba, Rev. Pambani Jeremiah
Prophets, 94, 145, 163

Qunta, Amos, 65, 70

Racism: early missionaries', 8, 12, 13; and Soga, 16; of American Zulu Mission, 22; McAdoo on, 36; and Afro-Americans, 37; and Mokone, 42–43; Turner on, in U.S., 60, 69; in South Africa, 70; *Christian Express* on, 72; Attaway on, 91; Morris on, 93; and AME church, 104
Radebe, M. S., 104
Read, Rev. James, 13, 17
Reconstruction (U.S.), 34
Rhenish Missionary Society, 11
Rhodes, Cecil John, 28, 41, 42, 55
Rhodesia, 28, 55, 100–101, 153
Rideout, Conrad A. A., 82, 99, 100, 146
Rideout, Pamela, 86–87
Riebeeck, Jan van, 7
Rolong tribe, 17, 27, 42, 66
Ross, John, 37, 38
Rotterdam Missionary Society, 11
Rubenstein, Ruben, 153
Rubusana, Walter, 81

St. George's Church (Philadelphia), 3
San tribe, 7, 8, 11
Schmidt, Rev. George, 8, 10
Schreiner, W. P., 88, 129
Schwinn, Daniel, 10
Secession, 20, 66, 69, 91, 95, 105, 109; and Afro-Americans, 67; and Dwane, 76–80, 88; effects on Fourteenth Dis-

trict, 89; in Barotseland, 146; in Rhodesia, 154
Secessionists, 1, 18, 25, 39, 81, 163; Ngidi as, 22; and AME church, 76–80; Dwane as, 76; Mothowagae as, 95; at Kanye, 97; in Barotseland, 146; in Zululand, 158; Mokone as, 164
Sechele (Botswana chief), 17, 18
Sects, appearance of, 91, 94
Seile (LMS evangelist), 73
Seme, Pixley Ka Isaka, 136
Serrurier, Rev. J. P., 10
Shaw, William, 20
Shembe, Isaiah, 158
Shibe, Simungu B., 91, 92
Sibiya, Rev. John, 92
Sierra Leone, 45, 48, 49
Sihlali, Rev. S. P., 129
Slavery, in U.S., 91
Smith, Bishop Charles Spencer, 110, 127, 166
Smith, Dr. Judson, 19
Soga, Tiyo, 15–16
South African Conference of the AME church, 87. See also Fourteenth District
South African Congregational Magazine, 66, 67
South African interstate native college, 127, 128, 167; fund raising for, 129–30; land for, 131; curriculum and entrance qualifications for, 131, 134; planning for, 128–29; support for, 129. See also Fort Hare University College
South African Missionary Conference (1904), 108–109, 129
South African Native Affairs Commission (SANAC; 1903–1905), 4, 76, 84, 169; and Ethiopianism, 102–103, 155; Makgotho and, 104; Bishop Smith and, 110, 127; conclusions of, 110–11; on higher education, 118–19; Kawa and, 120; Stewart and, 125
South African Native Congress (SANC; 1912), 159, 162. See also African National Congress
South African Society for Promoting the Extension of Christ's Kingdom (1799), 9
South African Spectator, 105
Southern Rhodesia, 150, 152
Southern Workman (U.S.), 37
Spying, on Ethiopians, 152, 153
Stewart, Rev. James, 18, 29, 58, 155; and Mzimba, 71; before SANAC, 102, 107, 125; on higher education, 122, 125; on native college, 128, 129
Stewart, T. McCants, 46

Tanner, Rev. C. M., 100
Tantsi, Rev. H. N., 140
Tantsi, Rev. J. Y., 140
Tantsi, Rev. Jantye Z., 44, 76, 77, 78, 104
Taylor, Herbert, 100–101
Thembuland, 20, 21, 23
Thompson, Jantye, 44
Thompson, R. Wardlaw, 73, 96
Tiger Kloof school, 120
Tile, Nehemiah, 20–22, 23, 24, 53
Tribal chiefs: on missionaries, 17; declining power of, 103; and Ethiopianism, 103
Tswana tribe, 8, 10, 15, 17, 26, 27, 28, 40, 55; as migrant workers and students, 96; and opposition to white rule, 161
Tule, John, 53–54, 55
Turner, Bishop Henry McNeal, 4, 46, 50, 51, 52, 56, 72, 83, 87, 165; on emigration, 47–49, 59, 61, 90; on Tule's appeal, 54; early life and education of, 59–61; American criticism of, 61, 62; and Ethiopianism, 62; in South Africa, 62–64, 68; responds to criticism, 69; and Dwane, 73
Tuskegee Institute (Alabama), 32, 131, 132

Uhlanga Church (National Church), 92
Union of South Africa, 161, 162
Unitas Fratrum. See Lutheran Moravian Protest Society
United Free Church of Scotland, 155–56

University Senior School Leaving Certificate Examination, 135

Van der Kemp, Dr. John, 9, 10
Van Ness, W. W., Jr., 37
Virginia Concert Company. *See* Virginia Jubilee Singers
Virginia Jubilee Singers, 34–35, 36, 37, 39, 59
Voice of Missions (AME periodical), 48, 52, 78, 81, 84, 100, 127; and Turner, 59; on Dwane, 74; on Bethel Institute, 99

Walton, Rev. Avon, 151
Washington, Booker T., 32, 131–34
Watkins, Rev. Owen, 41, 42, 43
Weavind, Rev. George, 42, 43, 44, 57, 58
Wesleyan Methodist Missionary Society, 11, 41
White, Dr. A. E., 86
White, Rev. John, 40
White fears, 101, 111, 150, 159
Wilberforce University (Ohio), 49, 50, 59, 75, 140

Wilcox, Rev. W. C., 140, 141, 143
Williams, Charles, 38, 39
Williams, George Washington, 32, 61
Williams, Rev. Howard, 145
Women's Mite Missionary Society, 51, 74

Xaba, Rev. Jacobus Gilead, 44, 52, 53, 55
Xhosa tribe, 7, 15
Xiniwe, Eleanor, 39
Xiniwe, Paul, 39, 40

Yako, W., 136

Zondi, Johannes, 93
Zonnebloem mission school, 26
Zulu Christian Industrial School, 141, 142
Zulu Congregational Church, 91
Zulu Mbiyana Congregational Church, 22
Zulu tribe, 158
Zvimba, Chief Chigaga, 151, 152
Zvimba, Matthew Chigaga, 151–53, 155, 168